MAR 0 2 2003

Quasi-Democracy?

David K. Stewart and Keith Archer

Quasi-Democracy?
Parties and Leadership Selection
in Alberta

UBCPress · Vancouver · Toronto

Printed in Canada on acid-free paper ∞

ISBN 0-7748-0790-3

Canadian Cataloguing in Publication Data

Stewart, David Kenney, 1962-
  Quasi-democracy?

  Includes bibliographical references and index.
  ISBN 0-7748-790-3

  1. Political conventions – Alberta. 2. Political parties – Alberta. 3. Alberta – Politics and government – 1971- I. Archer, Keith, 1955- II. Title.

JL339.A45S73 2000   324.27123'015   C00-910498-4

This book has been published with the help of a grant from the Humanities and Social Sciences Federation of Canada, using funds provided by the Social Sciences and Humanities Research Council of Canada.

UBC Press acknowledges the financial support of the Government of Canada through the Book Publishing Industry Development Program (BPIDP) for our publishing activities.
Canadä

We also gratefully acknowledge the support of the Canada Council for the Arts for our publishing program, as well as the support of the British Columbia Arts Council.

Set in Stone by Artegraphica Design Co. Ltd.
Printed and bound in Canada by Friesens
Copy editor: Valerie Adams
Proofreader: Stacy Belden
Indexer: Christine Jacobs

UBC Press
University of British Columbia
2029 West Mall, Vancouver, BC V6T 1Z2
(604) 822-5959
Fax: (604) 822-6083
E-mail: info@ubcpress.ubc.ca
www.ubcpress.ubc.ca

To
Brenda O'Neill, and Rachel and Aidan Stewart

Lisa Hurst, and Justin, Caitlin, Ben, Will,
and Isaiah Archer

Contents

Tables

Preface

This book focuses on political parties and leadership selection in Alberta. It is based primarily on mail surveys administered to voters in the 1992 Progressive Conservative, the 1994 NDP, and the 1994 Liberal leadership elections. Leadership selection events provide rare opportunities for observing the internal workings of parties and the people who "stand between the politicians and the electorate." For many years almost every party in Canada chose its leader in a delegate convention dominated by individuals chosen by local constituency associations. These conventions have recently come under intense criticism, and many parties have moved to a form of universal balloting, which allows all party members to vote directly for their leader. This shift represents a major change in the way parties will operate, and raises important questions concerning party democracy and representation.

Each of the parties examined here used a different method of leadership selection. Alberta's governing Conservative Party used a primary system that allowed all members to vote in their own constituency and that was widely credited with helping to maintain the party in office. The opposition Liberal Party allowed members to vote by phone from their own homes, while the NDP maintained the traditional delegate convention. The data collected from voters in each of these elections offers a unique opportunity to directly compare different methods of leadership selection.

The richness of our data also enables us to present a comparison of the parties that have dominated Alberta's politics for the last quarter century. We use the data to examine the factors that influence leadership choice, to develop an attitudinal profile of each party, and to examine party "activists" in terms of their socio-demographic background and their experiences in both provincial and federal politics.

During the period covered by our study, Alberta has been very much in the forefront of Canadian politics, providing a base for the federal Reform Party and garnering national attention for the manner in which its government eliminated the provincial deficit. It is our hope that this analysis of parties and leadership selection in Alberta will interest and enlighten those interested in the politics of a province sometimes termed the "Quebec of English Canada." We can certainly attest that researching and writing this book has both entertained and enlightened us.

We wish to thank the more than 1,500 Albertans who took time from their busy lives to complete and return surveys that contained many detailed, and sometimes personal, questions. And, in an era when participation in political parties is sometimes denigrated as well as thankless, we wish to thank them for taking the time to choose those who lead Alberta's parties. We hope our respondents recognize themselves, their experiences, and their priorities in the pages that follow.

The project would not have been possible without the financial support of the University of Alberta, the University of Calgary, and SSHRC. The project began with grants from the University of Alberta's Central Research Fund and support from that university's Faculty of Arts "Support for the Advancement of Scholarship" fund. Funding from the University of Calgary came from the University Research Grants Committee and from the Faculty of Social Sciences. In addition, SSHRC supported this project through the standard research grants awards.

We are very grateful to Alberta's parties for their cooperation and their support of this project. In particular, we wish to thank Bob Dawson, Ted Carruthers, Dave Williams, Rob Van Wellingham, and Lyle Bleich for their efforts on our behalf. None of them asked us to modify our focus or questions in any way, and all are believers in the value of academic research.

Colleagues at both the University of Alberta and the University of Calgary provided helpful comments and advice on this project. Special thanks are owed to Jim Lightbody, Linda Trimble, Allan Tupper, and Ian Urquhart. Ian Stewart of Acadia and Ken Carty from UBC also provided valuable input, as did those who reviewed the manuscript for UBC Press and the Aid to Scholarly Publication Programme. We also owe a great debt of gratitude to Emily Andrew of UBC Press for her helpful comments and encouragement.

Numerous graduate students provided research assistance. Among these students were Brenda Belikrinovich, Harold Jansen, Rob Groves, Pat Daley, and Len Wilson at the University of Alberta; and Mebs Kanji, Jennifer Stewart, Mark Pickup, and Mitch Gray at the University of Calgary.

During the period that he researched and wrote this book, Archer held administrative positions at the University of Calgary, first in the Dean's office in the Faculty of Social Sciences, and then in the Office of the Vice-President (Research). Both offices provided encouragement and support for maintaining an active research program alongside the administrative needs and responsibilities of the office. Much thanks are given to Stephen Randall, Dean of Social Sciences, and Len Bruton, Vice-President (Research), for recognition of the demands involved and the active facilitation of research and scholarship.

Special acknowledgment and thanks is owed our families. Brenda O'Neill made a significant and material contribution to the completion of this book. The project began with a very limited budget and would not have been possible without her unpaid assistance. While in labour with her first child, she helped prepare the Conservative questionnaire and, a few weeks later, spent untold hours affixing labels and stuffing envelopes. Lisa Hurst had a much less direct involvement in the research for the book, but was heavily involved in creating an environment that makes the research and writing of books possible. We extend our deep gratitude to Brenda and Lisa, and to our children: Rachel and Aidan Stewart; and Justin, Caitlin, Ben, Will, and Isaiah Archer, to whom the book is dedicated.

Quasi-Democracy?

1

Party Democracy in Alberta

Political parties occupy an important place in democratic politics, as they, among other things, provide a link between citizens and the state. It is through parties that citizens have opportunities to affect the composition of governmental elites. In the words of the Royal Commission on Electoral Reform and Party Financing, "Political parties give voters meaningful choices, both in the direct election of their individual Member of Parliament and in the indirect election of a government" (Volume 1: 207). Parties perform a crucial pre-selection function for the political system, since in most liberal democracies, attaining party office is a necessary and occasionally sufficient condition for obtaining government office.

The internal activities of political parties are thus of interest to those concerned with the health of democracy. As Michael Gallagher explains, "the way in which political parties select their candidates may be used as an acid test of how democratically they conduct their internal affairs" (1988: 1). This issue is of more than just academic significance. Citizens in elections are largely restricted to choosing from among the candidates that parties deign to put before them. This point was demonstrated vividly by Boss Tweed (former Democratic Party boss in New York), who suggested: "I don't care who does the electing, just so I can do the nominating" (as quoted in Courtney 1995: 127).

Possession of the ability to choose their party's standard-bearer in a general election is one of the most jealously guarded prerogatives of local party activists in Canada (see Carty 1991). However, the influence local candidates have on election outcomes is not clear, and the role of back-bench representatives in legislatures is not one to which substantial power inheres. Much of the power and influence in Canada stems directly from the party leader. This is a well-documented phenomenon with deep roots in Canadian history. Hugh Clokie, writing in 1945, noted that "the dominant position of the party leader in Canadian politics has often been commented on by foreign observers. It is far greater than in Great Britain, where the allegiance to party principles or programs competes with loyalty as a bond of partisanship. It is also far greater than in the US, where party candidates are nominated locally without any obligation to support the national leader of the party. In Canada, more than anywhere else, it is possible to define a party as being a body of supporters following a given leader" (1945: 91).

Selecting party leaders is therefore one of the most important functions performed by parties, and as Courtney (1973) has shown, the mechanisms that parties utilize to choose leaders carry consequences in terms of who will be selected. In recent years, the selection of leaders in Canada has undergone a shift. For most of the twentieth century, Canadian parties chose leaders in conventions representing both the party elite and delegates elected by the various groupings that comprised the party. This system has recently been challenged as insufficiently democratic, and a number of provincial parties have used, for the first time, a system of universal balloting to choose their leaders. In such a system, every member of the party is eligible to vote directly for the party's leader. The aim of such elections is to move beyond conventions and improve the state of party democracy.

This book examines alternative methods of leadership selection to better understand the implications for democratic governance. The purpose is to identify and assess the various claims for representativeness advanced by proponents for direct and indirect methods of leadership selection. Data drawn from detailed analyses of three leadership selection events in Alberta in the 1990s provides the empirical backdrop for this assessment.

Direct and Indirect Leadership Selection: Alternative Perspectives

As the Royal Commission on Electoral Reform and Party Financing summarizes, "Advocates of direct election argue this approach is more democratic because it limits the influence of the party establishment over the selection of leaders and gives more influence to rank-and-file members. Direct election of party leaders may also reduce the opportunities for abuse of membership rules. It is seen as a credible mechanism for rebuilding public confidence in the leadership selection process" (Volume 1: 280). Criticism of conventions on the basis of an alleged democratic deficit is not new; Duverger noted in his seminal study of parties that "indirect election is a way of banishing democracy while pretending to apply it" (1978 [1954]: 140).

The shift to a more universal system for choosing leaders has attracted considerable criticism. Courtney, for instance, ominously concluded a mammoth study of leadership selection in Canada by writing "the alleged benefits of universal voting may in the long run be more ephemeral than its proponents claim. The switch could ultimately prove problematic for the health of local political organizations and the larger political community in Canada" (1995: 293).

Courtney's point about the negative impact of universal balloting on political parties and the wider political community captures well the generally negative tone of academic assessments of universal ballots. Critics have argued that this leadership selection method will change the nature of leadership campaigns and weaken parties by placing the power to choose leaders in the hands of uninformed voters who may possess only a limited party background.

The move away from caucus selection to conventions in the early part of the twentieth century clearly diminished the role of parliamentarians in the process (Courtney 1973). Leaders were less likely to possess an extensive parliamentary background, and parliamentarians could not determine who would become their leader. Some maintain that the universal ballot will exacerbate this trend. Preyra (1995), for instance, argues that party outsiders will become even more competitive than they were with conventions in part because parties will lose the valuable counsel of party elites in making leadership choices. This point is echoed by Courtney who argues that "a direct universal vote would reduce even further the role that MPs and provincial legislators play in the selection of their leader" (1995: 251). Parliamentarians and other party officials will have no more voice than someone who purchased his or her party membership only minutes before the deadline for registering.

The implication of this change is that it is no longer possible to describe leadership selection as the deliberative choice of a group well-grounded in the party. As Perlin explains, conventions that have been celebrated "as a deliberative body in which the opinions of the party elite can be heard and in which participants have close contact with representatives of every element of the party, [are] better equipped than a mass based election to make informed and wise judgements about the competence of leadership candidates" (1991a: 66).

The consequence of rejecting conventions and allowing ordinary members to vote directly for the leader might be the election of less capable leaders. As Courtney warns, "because the votes of all members are counted equally, parties both forfeit and fail to reward the wisdom, experience and political savvy of their most established and dedicated activists" (1995: 245).

Conventions not only provided a forum for well-informed party activists to deliberate, they also offered a privileged role for constituencies. Most delegates represented constituency associations, and viable candidates needed a presence at the constituency level throughout the country or province. In many universal ballots this will no longer be necessary. Preyra (1994; 1995) suggests that candidates will be able to downplay constituency-level activities because the constituency will no longer be the basis of representation. Presumably, this will lessen the importance of constituency organizations and make potential activists less likely to pursue activities at this level.

The change in the nature of leadership campaigns is also seen as a problem with universal ballots. Critics argue compellingly that universal ballots will cost more, candidates will make more use of the media in trying to reach voters, and face-to-face campaigning will become less important. The cost of conducting a leadership campaign grew dramatically throughout the convention period (see Courtney 1995; Carty 1994). In recent federal conventions, prominent potential candidates have refused to run because they could not raise the required level of funding (Perlin 1991b). It is unlikely that costs would be reduced by a universal ballot, which would require candidates to reach voters throughout the country or province. Moreover, the increased number of voters involved in a universal ballot would make it difficult for candidates to meet voters in a face-to-face fashion. Candidates would be forced to conduct general election-style media campaigns, and voters would become dependent on the media for much of their information. Leadership campaigns with a universal ballot would therefore be accompanied by a substantial growth in the role of money and the media.

Acknowledged in the above critique is the fact that universal ballots will involve a greater number of people and that ordinary party members will not have their preferences mediated by delegates or decisions made for them by the party elite. The direct preferences of a much larger group of party members will determine the party's leadership.

It is likely that the universal ballot electorate will not only be substantially larger than that of a leadership convention, but that those who vote in a universal ballot will present a different demographic profile. The costs involved in attending a leadership convention ensured that most Canadians were unable to participate. This meant that delegates to leadership conventions were predominantly affluent, university-educated males. As well, those under thirty made up a disproportionate share of the convention electorate. Since there are no registration fees and there is no need to travel some distance to a central location, universal ballots should be much more accessible to less-affluent voters as well as to those who might be older or physically challenged. Women were not proportionately represented at conventions, in part because of their relative absence from ex-officio positions (Brodie 1988; Perlin 1991a). Without special representation for the party elite, the leadership selection process should increase the proportion of women in the electorate. Since previous research on women in politics has demonstrated gender gaps in voting and attitudes, the possibility of women comprising a greater proportion of the electorate has profound implications for parties.

Parties deliberately manipulated the convention electorate. In the Liberal and Conservative parties, each constituency was represented equally whether it had ten members or ten thousand. As well, each constituency was required to have a certain percentage of women and youth as part of its delegation. This manipulation worked better for youth than it did for women who never achieved equality at a federal leadership convention (see Courtney 1995). Universal ballots remove barriers to participation, but they simultaneously eliminate the representational guarantees provided by conventions. No longer will constituencies be guaranteed an equal voice in the leadership choice, nor will women and youth be guaranteed representation.

The absence of equal regional representation means, as Courtney explains, that "systems of pure universal suffrage do not ensure equitable regional representation. The potential exists for one or more regions to dominate the selection of leader" (1995: 245). It is not clear whether that is an advantage or disadvantage of universal balloting. Admittedly, the regional guarantees afforded by Liberal and Conservative conventions provided a convention electorate that was regionally representative. Given the importance of regional issues in Canadian politics, equitable representation of the regions was probably beneficial. However, it must be acknowledged that regional representation constructed an electorate that was not representative of the party membership, since "it is an incontestable fact that members and active supporters of any party are more concentrated in some regions, provinces and language groups than others" (Courtney 1995: 281). Regional representation may assist parties in performing a brokerage role, but it clearly diminishes the role of members who come from areas where the party is disproportionately strong. Individual equality is sacrificed for regional equity.

The absence of a certain level of guaranteed representation for women and youth is controversial. Preyra, in his reflection on the 1992 Nova Scotia Liberal tele-vote, reflects this controversy. While that universal ballot left it "to the invisible hand of the marketplace to resolve questions of equity, representativeness, or responsiveness to the needs of differently abled social interests ... senior citizens, people with financial or physical disabilities, parents with young children, geographically isolated constituencies ... who were effectively disenfranchised because they were often unable to attend or get selected as delegates were suddenly empowered" (1994: 5-7). Similarly, Perlin indicated that the representation of women and youth (and the more affluent) would be dramatically affected by the universal ballot. In his words, "the people choosing leaders will no longer be predominantly from higher status groups, women are likely to have a more equitable role and the representation of young people is likely to be reduced" (1991a: 87). The reduced role for youth is likely positive since "interviews with student activists who participated in the 1983 and 1984 conventions and data from the surveys of delegates to those conventions, indicate that young party members see politics primarily as a means to personal ends and that they take little opportunity to involve themselves in discussions regarding public policy" (1991b: 201).

As discussed previously, scholarly opinion is less positive about the impact of the composition of the universal ballot electorate with respect to party background. Despite a dramatic increase in contests for delegate spaces (see Hanson 1992; Carty 1988a), convention delegates were generally well grounded in their party. As Courtney explains, "the vast majority of those who served as delegates to political leadership conventions overwhelmingly have had several years of experience in the party" (1995: 287). This is unlikely to be the case with universal ballots.

The ability of voters in universal ballots to select themselves, and the need for competitive candidates to recruit new voters, virtually ensures that many will have only a limited background in the party. As well, since many of the voters may be inspired by, or recruited by, a particular candidate, they "could prove to be short lived in their enthusiasm for the party" (Malcolmson 1992: 24).

This point brings us almost full circle in the discussion of universal balloting. A large electorate with limited background in the party will not have the opportunity for interaction with candidates and "would be far less likely to be as informed as the party members who are usually convention delegates" (Malcolmson 1992: 25). Moreover, this electorate will be more dependent on the media for information. Thus, the changed political background of voters has implications for the quality of decision making, the nature of the campaign, and the profile of the party.

In general, then, comparisons of conventions with universal ballots find the latter wanting. However, William Cross (1996) provides a more positive assessment of universal ballots. In his discussion of the twelve universal ballots held between 1985 and 1995, he found that the parties using this mechanism experienced "a significant increase in membership" (303) and that "the experience thus far with direct election does not appear to indicate a significant increase in the cost of running for provincial party leadership" (307). Similarly, Stewart, in an earlier discussion of universal balloting, argued that in "evaluating the universal ballot it is important to avoid comparing it to an idealized convention model" (1997: 127). The invasion of delegate selection meetings by candidates and their organizations has made it virtually impossible for activists on the wrong slate to become delegates (Schumacher 1993: 8), and this trench warfare "has also devalued the deliberative nature of conventions" (Stewart 1997: 128; see also Carty 1994). Moreover, in recent conventions, delegates have become increasingly dependent on the media for information and have focused on choosing a leader based on assessments of "electablility" (Perlin 1991b). It seems appropriate to conclude, therefore, that many of the "deficiencies" of universal ballots are also associated with recent manifestations of conventions.

The Trend to Direct Election

Regardless of the merits or demerits of universal ballots, it appears that universal ballots are becoming the new norm for the selection of party leaders in Canada. As Perlin acknowledges, "there is good reason to expect that direct election of leaders will be widely adopted. Once one party uses this method, its more democratic aura will put pressure on other parties to use it as well" (1991a: 86). All of the parties represented in the federal House of Commons have put in place some sort of universal ballot for selecting their next leader, and, at the provincial level, most Canadians are governed by someone chosen through a universal ballot process. There is, however, a wide variation in the kinds of universal ballots that have been used to date. Some provide for a form of mediation, some allow for restrictions on who is eligible to vote, and "there is no consensus across or within the parties on what this new institution should look like" (Carty and Blake 1999: 221).

Analysis of universal ballots in operation is crucial to understanding the impact of this evolution on parties and politics in Canada and in forging a consensus on what mechanisms work best, particularly given the centrality of leaders in election campaigns and legislatures. As well, in the light of the Canadian reality we think it best to parallel the ideas of Gallagher: "The way in which political parties select their [leaders] may be used as an acid test of how democratically they conduct their internal affairs" (1988: 1).

Leadership Selection in Alberta

We pursue this analysis by examining universal balloting in the context of Alberta politics. Between 5 December 1992 and 14 November 1994, the three major parties in Alberta all chose new leaders, and each of these parties utilized a different selection method. The governing Progressive Conservatives used an open primary system in which all party members could vote directly for the leader by attending a polling station in their riding. The official opposition Liberal Party used a tele-vote in which each member who purchased a personal identification number (PIN) by a specific deadline could make their leadership choice over the telephone. Aside from the use of technology, this system in many ways resembles a closed primary.[1] And the smallest party, the New Democratic Party (NDP), used a traditional convention that we are able to use as a control in our study. We present case studies of each of these processes in the hope that they will further our understanding of the implications of different mechanisms of leadership selection and the state of internal democracy in Alberta's political parties. Given the centrality of leaders to politics in Canada, our study should also provide further insight into the major parties in Alberta. Carty notes that leadership elections provide a window into parties (1988a: 84). We shall use this window to examine each of these parties with respect to the characteristics and views of their "activists." The views of these activists will enable us to assess the degree to which each party reflects Alberta's political culture and to enhance our understanding of the nature of politics in Alberta.

Outline of the Argument

The book is structured in the following manner. We provide a brief overview of party politics and political culture in Alberta and describe each of the leadership selection methods as well as our data-collection method. We then present a case study of the Alberta Conservative Party. This analysis focuses on two areas. First, we examine the degree to which the Conservative leadership election involved voters who were not members of the federal Conservative Party. In this context, we focus both on voters who supported the federal Reform Party and those who were not members of any federal party, and contrast these individuals with those who were members of both the provincial and federal Conservatives. Next, material is presented that describes the participants and analyzes voting by looking at socio-demographic characteristics, attitudes, and factors peculiar to the 1992 race as well as information on the degree of attitudinal consensus among voters.

We then present similar material on the Liberal and NDP leadership elections. As we noted above, one of the more positive predictions for universal ballots was its potential for involving more women. We therefore examine each of the parties and processes in order to assess the degree to which the representation increased and how the increased presence of women in the electorate relates to participation and political opinions. We look at the degree to which women and men in each process differed with respect to voting choice, demographic characteristics, and attitudes, and probe for gender differences that cross party lines. The presence of such differences will provide further insight into the implications of using a leadership selection process that enfranchises a larger (and more representative) proportion of women. We present conclusions regarding the relation of party and leadership selection process to this issue. We conclude our analysis by explicitly comparing the three leadership election systems and the three parties and by presenting our overall assessments of the processes and their implications for leaders and parties both in Alberta and more generally. Before moving to our examination of the leadership elections, we will provide a context for this analysis by considering party politics and the political culture in Alberta.

Party Politics in Alberta

Although the political science literature on provincial politics in Canada is generally limited, in relative terms, much has been written about party politics in Canada's fourth-largest province. Party politics in Alberta seem different from those in neighbouring provinces. For instance, throughout Alberta's history as a province, only three changes of government have occurred. In 1921, the United Farmers of Alberta (UFA) defeated the Liberals, who had governed the province since its creation in 1905. In turn, the UFA lost every seat it held in the legislature in 1935 as the Social Credit party, aided by the Great Depression, swept into office under the leadership of the controversial William "Bible Bill" Aberhart. Following Aberhart's death, Ernest Manning assumed the leadership and led both the party and the province until 1968. His successor, Harry Strom, promptly led the party to defeat in the 1971 election. The 1971 election brought into office the Progressive Conservative Party under the leadership of Peter Lougheed. Lougheed served as premier until 1985, when he was replaced by Don Getty. Getty's decision to resign in 1992 ushered in the leadership election that provides the point of departure for this study.

Alberta's electoral history demonstrates a provincial tendency to keep governments in office for long periods of time. In the broader Canadian context, Alberta is notable but not exceptional on this measure. Electoral politics in Alberta appear more distinctive with respect to the paucity of seats won by opposition parties. Indeed, a party history of Alberta that focuses on electoral success needs to devote very little space to chronicling opposition parties. Their history chronicles the struggle for survival rather than for victory.

Throughout virtually all of the Social Credit's tenure in office, as well as the Lougheed Conservative era, opposition parties comprised only a corporal's guard in the legislature. Much has been written about this phenomenon. Perhaps the most famous study was C.B. Macpherson's *Democracy in Alberta*. Macpherson claimed that Alberta possessed a "quasi-party system" based on two characteristics: "One was [their relatively] homogeneous class composition, the other was their quasi-colonial status. The former seemed to make a party system unnecessary, the latter led to a positive aversion to party. The absence of any serious opposition of class interests within the province meant that alternate parties were not needed either to express or to moderate a perennial conflict of interests. There was apparently, therefore, no positive basis for an alternate party system" (1962: 21). More recently, Gurston Dacks has presented a similar analysis outlining what he calls an Alberta consensus based on "the alienation Albertans have felt towards national political institutions ... and the inclination of Albertans to relate to provincial politics in terms of the interest they share in a single dominant commodity" (1986: 187).

Macpherson's analysis has been challenged in recent years on a number of fronts. Some suggest that while his observations may have once been true of Alberta, the province has changed. Dacks makes the point that the decline in natural resource revenue in the province in the late 1980s carries with it a "loss of confidence in one or two commodities which integrated Alberta society for so many decades" (1986: 192). Albertans therefore might well begin to support other parties, ushering in an era of stronger opposi- tions and more competitive politics. A more direct assault by Edward Bell (1993) suggests that Macpherson was in fact inaccurate in his description of the class composition of Alberta and that the province was never as homo- geneous as he implied. Finally, critics have suggested that Alberta's unique- ness in terms of weak oppositions is created by the electoral system as much as by the class structure and political culture. As Peter McCormick explains, Albertans "scatter opposition votes in such a fashion that each opposition party suffers heavily from the punitive effects of the single member plural- ity system ... Some 80% of the anti-government vote seems able to wander without much hesitation from one party to another" (1980: 91, 95).

From each of these perspectives, an appreciation of a partisan diversity greater than generally attributed to Alberta politics is gained, along with a sense that the province's unique patterns of small oppositions are not in- evitable. Indeed, the period of 1986 to 1993 was marked by ever-increasing opposition representation in the legislature, as the number of opposition MLAs increased from four in 1982 to twenty-two in 1986, twenty-four in 1989, and thirty-two in 1993 (see Table 1.1). The size of the opposition in Alberta was thus coming more and more to resemble opposition sizes in the rest of the country.

One of the reasons offered for the change in opposition size is germane to this study: leadership. Archer has suggested that the pattern of Conserva- tive dominance from 1971 to 1985 was based to a significant degree on Lougheed, and when he was no longer the Conservative leader, many ques- tioned "their continuing support for the party" (1992: 124-5). This empha- sis on leadership recurs in Alberta politics. The Conservative victory in 1971 is partially credited to leadership. As Archer suggests, "this change occurred for several reasons. Most important was the effect of leadership ... Positive

Table 1.1

Alberta election results, 1979-97: Seats and vote percentage*

	PC		Liberal		NDP		Other		Total seats
1979	74	(57%)	–	(6%)	1	(16%)	4	(21%)	79
1982	75	(63%)	–	(2%)	2	(19%)	2	(16%)	79
1986	61	(51%)	4	(12%)	16	(29%)	2	(8%)	83
1989	59	(44%)	8	(29%)	16	(26%)	–	(1%)	83
1993	51	(44%)	32	(40%)	–	(11%)	–	(5%)	83
1997	63	(51%)	18	(33%)	2	(9%)	–	(7%)	83

* Vote percentages are shown in parentheses.

attitudes towards Lougheed far outstripped those for any other party leader" (1992: 117). Similarly, the massive Social Credit victory in 1935 must be attributed at least in part to the charisma of Aberhart and his ability to inspire faith on the part of ordinary Albertans. Subsequently, Ernest Manning became so widely respected in Alberta that the Conservatives under Lougheed were very reluctant to attack him, and some have questioned whether the Conservative breakthrough would have been possible had Manning held on to the reins of the Social Credit party. Finally, much of the Conservative misfortune from 1985 to 1993 has been laid at the feet of Don Getty, who in the words of *Edmonton Journal* columnist Mark Lisac, "had come to symbolize ineffectiveness" (1995: 30).

The importance of leadership is also indicated by Les Pal who speaks of the "strategic intervention of such leaders as Aberhart, Manning and Lougheed, who reshaped the political culture to meet new circumstances" (1992: 3-4). More recently, the perpetuation of the Conservative Party in power in 1993 is laid largely at the feet of Ralph Klein, the party's current leader, whose "personal popularity had much to do with the Tories' election victory" (Tupper and Taras 1994: 68). Alberta politics has been dominated by a few strong leaders to a degree that exceeds even the federal experience. Given the appropriate set of circumstances, leaders seem able to transform the fortunes of the province's political parties. This ability is facilitated by Alberta's political culture.

Alberta's Political Culture: Alienated, Conservative, and Populist

Identification of the three key elements in Alberta's political culture is uncontroversial. The province's political culture can be described as alienated, conservative, and populist. We will briefly discuss each of these features.

Provincial party politics is not carried out in a vacuum. Relations with the federal government and the province's political culture help establish the framework in which party politics takes place. Indeed, Alberta's political culture has in part been shaped by the province's relationship with the federal government. Perhaps the most obvious manifestation of Alberta political culture is alienation from the federal government. As Gibbins notes, "distrust of the federal government has been a prominent feature of western alienation, and a sense of powerlessness vis-à-vis that same government has been a constant source of antagonism and concern" (1979: 144). Certainly few would dispute that Albertans feel they are not treated fairly by the federal government, and, with the exception of the Mulroney era, the majority of Albertan MPs have consistently sat on the opposition benches. The litany of issues that fuel the perceptions of alienation includes the delay in granting provincial control over natural resources, transportation policy, tariff policy, low levels of transfer payments, disallowance, and energy policy (including the controversial National Energy Program implemented by the Trudeau government in 1980). It is important to note that this alienation is of a particular kind. As Gibbins explains, "western alienation in Alberta is not symptomatic of political disengagement or apathy. To the contrary, it has been the source of a good deal of political energy." Furthermore, "western alienation is also central to the political culture which both shapes and reflects political behaviour in the province" (Gibbins 1992: 71; 70-1).

Another key element in the Alberta political culture is its relative "conservatism."[2] Gibbins describes this as "a strong belief in the spirit if not necessarily the practice of free enterprise, a concomitant belief in the desirability if not the actuality of small fiscally conservative governments, a tolerance if not affection for one party governments" (1979: 143). With respect to electoral politics, this conservatism was reflected in Alberta's consistent election of Conservative MPs to the federal House of Commons in an era when the Liberals were consistently forming federal governments. In 1993 and 1997, the election of mainly Reform MPs again symbolizes this "conservative" streak.

At the provincial level, only the Social Credit and Conservative parties have been able to form governments since 1935. Indeed, Alberta is the only western province in which neither the NDP nor its CCF predecessor have ever formed a government. In 1971 when the Conservatives ended the Socred hold on power, the Conservative Party succeeded by neutralizing ideology and focusing on "safe change," that is, a change of faces but not policies (Elton and Goddard 1979: 52). In the early 1990s when the Liberals began to threaten the Conservative hold on power, it was a result of Liberal Party actions to position itself in a similar manner. Their emphasis was on the fiscal and managerial incompetence of the government, and, in the 1993 election, the Liberal leader travelled the province with a "debt clock" and promised "brutal" cuts in spending if his party was elected (Stewart 1995).

Finally, the Conservative victory in 1993 followed an election campaign in which they promised (and subsequently delivered) "massive cuts" in provincial spending. In 1993, more than four in five Albertans supported parties promising radical changes in government spending of a neo-liberal variety. The introduction and implementation of these changes, while met with some criticism, was largely supported by Albertans. As Archer and Gibbins note, "most Albertans are neo-conservatives who find themselves in agreement with the broad outlines of the Klein government" (1997: 470). In 1997, the Klein government was re-elected with an increased majority in the legislature and a majority of the popular vote. The Liberal Party, as we shall see in Chapter 4, made a conscious decision to present a more left-wing focus. Following this repositioning, the party saw its seat total cut almost in half and its share of the popular vote fall by almost seven percentage points.

In short, the four-year record of a government described as engaged in the "large-scale social reengineering of a province's political culture to conform with the demands of moral conservatism and the neo-liberal agenda of the global corporations" (Harrison and Laxer 1995: 3) was overwhelmingly endorsed by the Albertan electorate. Given this evidence, the description of Alberta's political culture as "conservative" is unlikely to generate much controversy.

The final element of Alberta's political culture that we wish to highlight is populism. A populist element has extensive roots in Alberta's history. Macpherson refers to a general aversion for parties (1962: 21) and this is manifested in the UFA's advocacy of direct democracy and relaxing the bonds of party discipline. Additionally, Social Credit launched attacks on many elites of the day. A desire for the wider involvement of ordinary citizens in politics and a distrust of experts have been recurring themes in Alberta's public opinion. It is no accident that Reform, a party that celebrates the "Common Sense of the Common People" and advocates the introduction of recall, initiative, and the wider use of referenda, has had its greatest success in Alberta. And the current premier's success owes partially to his populist image. As Gillian Steward explains, "the image of Ralph Klein as 'ordinary' is deeply embedded in the minds of Albertans, and is one of his greatest assets. Almost everyone refers to him as Ralph rather than Klein, or The Premier. He revels in the role of the ordinary man who has managed to capture one of the highest political offices in the land" (Steward 1995: 23). Tupper and Taras explain that in 1993 "the Conservative campaign was based almost entirely on packaging his folksy charm and everyman image and in presenting the Conservatives as 'Ralph's Team.' The strategy was to deflect attention away from the legacy of the Getty government and make the election into a personality contest" (1994: 68). This desire for the election to turn on personality again points out the importance of leadership in Alberta. We now briefly outline the campaigns that preceded our leadership elections.

The Leadership Contests

Despite the propinquity of the leadership selections studied in this book, the three parties chose leaders in rather different circumstances. However, a characteristic all of the parties shared was that they chose their leader in a period of some turmoil. The Alberta Conservatives were the first to choose a new leader in December 1992. That party, which had governed Alberta for more than twenty years, seemed in desperate shape. It trailed in the polls, and some pundits were suggesting that the Tory dynasty was over. The selection of Ralph Klein and the leadership election itself have been credited with the change in fortune for the party (Schumacher 1993: 8). In 1985, when Don Getty was chosen as leader, the Conservatives used a traditional convention. This particular convention was marred by negative publicity and criticism. Indeed, one analysis of that election suggested that "Don Getty ... never fully recovered from the damage done by the leadership contest. Alberta Tories may provide important lessons to all Canadian parties on how not to select leaders" (Archer and Hunziker 1992: 81). The party was determined not to repeat this experience and decided to organize an election in which every party member could vote directly for the premier. Using a universal balloting system that permitted all members who were able to visit a polling station to cast a vote, the race attracted a record nine candidates and was extended to a second ballot a week later. Even more importantly, the party's membership soared as more than 80,000 Albertans cast a ballot on one of the two weeks of the balloting. Building on the momentum of his leadership race, Klein went on to score a victory in the June 1993 provincial election.

The first casualty of the Klein victory was the New Democratic Party. It went from the official opposition to virtual annihilation as it was unable to elect anyone to the legislature in 1993. The party's leader resigned and a traditional leadership convention was scheduled for February 1994. The leadership election attracted only one major candidate, former federal MP Ross Harvey, and three candidates who had never held public office. The race and convention attracted little in the way of public or media attention, and in virtual obscurity a surprisingly large convention of more than 400 gave Harvey an easy victory.

The Liberal Party chose their new leader in the context of disappointment. The party expected to win the 1993 election, and their failure to do so spelled the end for Laurence Decore as leader. Despite leading the party to a sixty-year high in terms of the popular vote and forming the largest opposition the legislature had seen in decades, Decore stepped down. In a decision apparently much regretted, the party used a tele-vote to choose Decore's successor. In order to participate in the tele-vote, party members had to pay a ten-dollar registration fee one week before the vote. A PIN was sent to each person registered, and on voting day, individuals with access to a touch-tone phone could dial in and, after entering a valid PIN, cast an electronic vote. The tele-vote proved less attractive to Albertans than the Tory direct vote; only 19,030 people registered to vote and just over 11,000 voted on the first ballot. Unlike the Conservatives, the Liberals used an immediate re-vote with the trailing candidates removed. The number of people voting on the second ballot declined to 9,065.

Five candidates, including four sitting MLAs, sought the Liberal leadership, and it became clear that the selling of PINs would be crucial for winning. In moves reminiscent of the 1985 PC leadership convention (see Archer and Hunziker 1992), some of the candidates were rumoured to be engaging in "dirty tricks" and mobilizing ethnic communities in their support. In the end, Sine Chadi, the candidate who had sold the most registrations, did not win, but apparently only because a significant number of the proxy votes he submitted were not voted. This, combined with a number of technical problems, led to the process being described as a "fiasco" (Martin 1994: D1), the runner-up threatening to sue, the party being forced to hold an inquiry, and the winner, Edmonton MLA Grant Mitchell, leaving with a somewhat dubious prize. It is apparent that the three leadership elections were each different from one another as well as interesting in other ways. Before further examining these contests in detail, it remains for us to outline the manner in which we obtained our data.

Data Collection Method

Our analysis of the three parties and the three leadership elections is based largely on surveys administered to samples of the participants in each of the leadership election processes shortly after the voting concluded. Data on the Conservative election were obtained from a survey of voters who participated in the second, run-off election in December 1992, between the two front-runners, Ralph Klein and Nancy Betkowski. Using lists provided by the party, second-ballot voters were identified and surveys were sent to 2,728 of the 78,251 voters (see Table 1.2). A systematic sample stratified by constituency was drawn from party lists. Beginning with the fourth name on each constituency list, surveys were sent to every twenty-seventh second-ballot voter. Due to list problems, two constituencies were not surveyed. Nine hundred forty-three usable responses were obtained, and these respondents proved quite representative both in terms of reported vote and region of residence. In addition to the survey data, voting results supplied by the party provided the actual vote totals for each riding on both ballots. This data will be presented along with the survey data in an effort to illustrate the geographic nature of candidate support coalitions.

Unfortunately, a survey based on second-ballot voters cannot provide an accurate depiction of first-ballot voters. This was demonstrated by the fact that more respondents claimed to have voted for the eventual winner Ralph Klein than for runner-up Nancy Betkowski, although Betkowski actually had a one-vote lead after the first ballot. As well, more than three-quarters

Table 1.2

Survey return rates

	Number of voters	Voters surveyed	Responses	Response rate
1992 PC	78,251	2,728	943	35%
1994 NDP	422	422	220	52%
1994 Liberal	11,004	2,500	586	23%

of the respondents who indicated they had voted on the first ballot claimed to have voted for Klein or Betkowski, while the overall support for those candidates was around 63%. Consequently, support for the minor candidates is underestimated.[3] These results suggest that many of those who voted for the minor candidates on the first ballot (particularly those who voted for the third- and fourth-place finishers) did not make the effort to turn out to vote again. It is thus impossible to claim that the respondents provide an accurate sample of the first-ballot voters. Nonetheless, since no other avenue for examining first-ballot behaviour exists, the chapters on the Conservatives will also explore the first-ballot results, albeit more tentatively.

A randomly distributed survey was used to collect data on participants in the 1994 Alberta Liberal tele-vote. Surveys were sent to 2,500 of the 19,030 people who registered for the Liberal tele-vote, and almost 600 replies were received. The replies proved unrepresentative with respect to reported vote, as the proportion of respondents who admitted to voting for the runner-up, Sine Chadi, was substantially smaller than the actual proportion of the vote he received. We were not surprised by the relatively low number of responses received from Chadi supporters. The Liberal Party's registration forms allowed registrants to indicate that they would prefer that their names not be released to academics for a survey.[4] The Chadi campaign advised their voters to respond in this manner. Moreover, as Chapter 4 will reveal, many of Chadi's supporters had difficulty in communicating in English, and some of the people whose names were registered by the Chadi camp professed ignorance of their voting eligibility. "Partisans" of this nature are unlikely to respond to mail surveys.

Although the paucity of responses from Chadi voters is disappointing, we remain confident in the importance of the data set. Those Chadi supporters who did respond provide a fascinating portrait of the kind of voters who can be enfranchised with a tele-vote. And we are confident in the representativeness of respondents from the other candidates. When we eliminate Chadi voters from consideration, the reported votes of respondents is closer to the actual proportion of the vote those candidates received.

We received the highest response rate from the survey of NDP delegates. Given the relatively small number of people who attended the February 1994 NDP convention, we were able to send surveys to each of the 422 delegates. Two hundred and twenty responded, and an analysis of reported votes indicates that the respondents are representative of the convention at large.

Initial Conclusions

The three data sets provide the only comparative data on party activists in Alberta. The richness of these data allows us to draw conclusions about the parties, partisans, and leadership elections that would not otherwise have been possible. Analysis of the three parties and their leadership elections reveals a surprising degree of diversity in the opinions expressed by party activists. Alberta, despite a tradition of one-party dominance, possesses active parties with activists whose beliefs resemble partisan differences found elsewhere in the country (see Archer and Whitehorn 1996: 154). Moreover, in each party women and men hold divergent political views, suggesting that the involvement of more women in political parties has implications far beyond simple mathematical equality.

The opinions of the activists suggest one reason why the Conservatives have dominated politics in Alberta for such an extended period. The views of their activists are consistently the most "conservative" and "populist," and thus tap into a very important part of the province's political culture. As well, the Conservative voters resemble the broader Alberta electorate much more closely than the participants in the Liberal and NDP leadership elections. The Conservative Party's dominance of Alberta politics is certainly not accidental.

Earlier in this chapter we discussed some of the issues involved in allowing ordinary members a greater voice in the selection of party leaders. Perlin succinctly summarized the question for debate as follows: "Is it better to follow the prescriptions of the elite theory of democracy and leave the choice of party leaders to an informed elite who will make 'more competent' judgements, or is it better to continue the process of democratization that has led the parties along the path of a progressive broadening of participation in this critical decision?" (1988: 313). The case studies we present on Alberta leave us uniquely positioned to comment on the different methods of choosing leaders.

Our examination of leadership elections includes the NDP convention, and we find that there was much to recommend that mechanism. For instance, voters were more informed about the candidates and had increased opportunities to interact with them. As well, the convention delegates were much more deeply rooted in the party than were Liberal and Conservative voters. The NDP convention went smoothly and efficiently, but as Chapter 5 indicates, that convention was not typical of most leadership conventions and, even at that atypical gathering, most of the delegates wanted to see a more inclusive form of leadership selection. We accept their judgment and weigh the relative merits of the Conservative Party's open primary and the Liberal tele-vote. In this competition, as in the province more generally, the Conservatives win easily.

In a recent discussion of universal ballots, Carty and Blake note "a trend towards the 'enhanced democratization' of parties which involves them giving members a greater say in parties" (1999: 211). The universal ballots in Alberta undoubtedly gave party members a greater voice and involved more people in the selection of leaders thereby contributing to the "democratization" of the parties involved. Nonetheless, as Michels (1962) demonstrated

in his work on parties, it is difficult to describe any party as fully democratic. For virtually all political parties, the best description they could wish
for their internal activities is "quasi-democratic."

Our analysis of the Liberal tele-vote suggests that "quasi-democratic" is
actually a somewhat flattering description. Many voters did not know if
they had voted, the majority of votes for one candidate arrived in the trunk
of the car, controversy surrounded decisions about which votes counted,
and the outcome was threatened by lawsuits. As we demonstrate in Chapter
4, the Liberals' problems were partially self-inflicted. However, our examination of universal balloting indicates that tele-voting is much more susceptible to abuse than voting by paper ballot.

With tele-voting, control over many aspects of the process is ceded by the
party to outside experts – a loss of control that carries risks for parties. As
well, the use of this technology has yet to evolve to a stage where parties
can expect flawless execution. And even if the technology works perfectly,
other concerns remain. In an earlier examination of tele-voting, Carty found
that "the principal reservation televoters are left with is a concern that the
technology cannot guarantee that only properly qualified electors cast ballots. As this is a version of the problem of equality (allowing only one vote
per elector), and thus the integrity of the democratic process, it is not an
insignificant issue" (1996: 20). This is an understatement. The inability to
ensure "one person one vote" or to be certain that the vote is cast by the
registered voter should lead parties to reconsider the alleged benefits of voting by phone.

This is not to say that the paper ballot utilized by the Conservative Party
provides a perfect example of democracy in practice. As Cross pointed out,
"direct election processes come with their own shortcomings" (1996: 314),
and this was certainly true of the 1992 PC election. Membership in the
Conservative Party possessed little cachet – it was simply a ticket required
to vote for the premier and no ongoing commitment to the party or its
"ideals" was required of the ticket holder. Indeed, many such tickets were
purchased after the first ballot was over and thus many voters may have
had little familiarity with the discussions that transpired during the three-
month campaign. For most democratic theorists, democracy implies more
than just the number of people voting. Ideally, there should be an engaged
nature to the participation. It would be erroneous to describe the Conservative voters as "engaged." As mentioned above, many members joined only
after the first ballot, and only a small minority of voters attended all candidate forums or candidate meetings. This is not to say that they missed much
in terms of policy debate since, as with many conventions, there was little
discussion of political issues.

That the Conservative election must also be described as "quasi-democratic"
is not an indictment of universal balloting. Few would describe the actual

operation of leadership conventions as democratic, and the development of universal ballots was driven in part by the problems associated with conventions (MacIvor 1994). With the packing of delegate selection meetings and the courting of ethnic blocs, conventions were far from textbook examples of "democracy." At recent federal conventions, policy debate has been limited, and delegates seem to have focused on choosing leaders for their "electability" (see Perlin 1991b; Carty 1994; Stewart 1997). Regardless of whether leaders are chosen in conventions or universal ballots, intraparty democracy is an ideal that has not been realized.

The Conservative universal ballot constituted an advance with respect to "descriptive representation." While Tory voters did not provide a miniature replica of the wider Alberta electorate; women, the elderly, and those without university degrees were more equitably represented than they had been at leadership conventions. As critics predicted, Conservative voters possessed only a limited party background. However, fears that their uninformed decisions would weaken the party were not borne out. To the contrary, the Conservative election energized the party, and although it was expected to lose the ensuing election, it secured another majority government in 1993.

Although we conclude that from an ideal perspective there were a number of shortcomings in the process, it has more to recommend it than the tele-vote utilized by the Liberals. The tele-vote was such a disaster that the Liberals abandoned it when they chose a new leader in 1998. Despite their disappointing 1994 experience with universal balloting, the party did not revert to a convention process. Instead, they utilized a paper ballot that was in many ways similar to that used by the Tories in 1992. The Liberal choice provides strong evidence in support for our contention that the universal ballot adopted by parties should be one that involves physical attendance at the polls and the presence of scrutineers for each candidate. Those who believe that "the citizen's role in politics should be limited to participation in periodic elections to choose among elites seeking office through the mechanism of competitive party politics" (Perlin 1991b: 197) will never be satisfied with universal ballots. However, while "it now appears that universal voting, in one form or another is going to be adopted by most Canadian parties, it is not clear whether traditional paper ballots cast in public polling places or televoting from home will be the method of choice" (Carty 1996: 18). Careful examination of the actual use of these universal ballots will help to identify the measures that might diminish the significance of "quasi" as a prefix for intra-party democracy.

2
The "United Right"?
Lessons from the 1992 PC
Leadership Election

In 1985, the governing Progressive Conservative Party of Alberta was forced to select a replacement for retiring premier Peter Lougheed. The party that Lougheed had led into the legislature in 1967, and into power in 1971, had become a dynasty. It had governed the province for fourteen years, held seventy-five of the seventy-nine seats in the legislature, and averaged more than 55% of the vote over the three most recent elections. Unfortunately for the party, the leadership transfer did not go smoothly. As noted in the introductory chapter, Archer and Hunziker's analysis of the 1985 convention process that anointed Don Getty as Lougheed's successor suggests that "Alberta Tories may provide important lessons for all Canadian parties on how not to select leaders" (1992: 81).

Academics were not alone in negatively evaluating the 1985 experience. Many Tories were dissatisfied with the entire leadership convention process. Two internal committees were struck to review the selection process, and in 1991, on the basis of their reports and recommendations, the party made two substantive changes to its constitution. The first called for a direct vote by all members to choose the next leader of the party. Thus, in 1992, when Don Getty decided to step down, the Conservatives were ready to attempt a new method of choosing their leader: an all-member vote, or universal ballot. The second change, while not directly related to the issue of leadership selection, helped determine eligibility for participation in this universal ballot. Traditionally, Alberta Tories were closely linked with the federal Tories and provincial members were expected to be, at the very least, supporters of the federal party. In 1991, though, with the federal Tories unpopular in Alberta (as well as in much of the rest of the country) and federal Reformers deciding whether their movement should enter the arena of provincial politics, Alberta's Tories voted to reduce their ties with the federal cousins. In particular, they removed from their constitution references to promoting the "interests and principles" of the federal PCs and the requirement that provincial members "work" for federal PC candidates (Laghi 1991: A1).

The 1992 leadership selection process, in which Ralph Klein overcame a one-vote deficit on the first ballot to defeat Nancy Betkowski handily on the second, thus constituted a major break with the past. Not only did every member of the party have the opportunity to vote directly for their favourite candidate, but it was possible that these voters would possess no ties to the federal PC Party. In fact, under the rules established for participation, it was quite possible that voters would not even possess previous ties to the provincial PC Party.

This chapter examines the 1992 PC leadership selection process in three ways. First, we note some of the crucial rules governing the leadership selection process and relate some campaign "highlights." Second, it assesses the degree to which universal ballot participants differ from delegates to leadership conventions. Third, it focuses on the federal connections of the participants in order to compare members of the federal Progressive Conservatives, members of the Reform Party, and federal independents – those who are not members of any federal party.

The analysis begins by examining voters in terms of their political background and involvement in the selection process. One criticism of universal ballots stresses doubts regarding the ability of voters "to make informed and wise judgements about the competence of leadership candidates" (Perlin 1991a: 66). This criticism assumes that voters in a universal ballot will have neither the background nor the opportunity to make personal assessments of the candidates and will therefore rely more on the media. An attempt is made to assess the validity of such contentions in the Alberta context. Following this, levels of party involvement are discussed in reference to the federal connections noted above. Next, a discussion of demographics is presented. Conventions have been criticized for the non-representative nature of delegates to such gatherings. Using past convention data, a contrast is drawn with participants in the universal ballot in an attempt to determine if, in fact, different sorts of people are involved in a universal ballot. Demographic comparisons are also made in reference to federal partisanship. Flanagan (1992) noted that the Reform Party had been attacked by other parties and the media on the grounds that its membership was "grossly atypical of Canadian society." He maintained that this was probably also true of other parties, but that comparable data did not exist. This work allows that question to be addressed in a limited way by comparing Reformers with members of the federal Conservatives, federal independents, and the general Albertan population.[1]

This comparison is pursued through an analysis of attitudes. The chapter notes the level of disagreement among second-ballot voters and then looks specifically for differences in attitudes among federal Tories, Reformers, and independents. This charts the beliefs of Reformers, making possible an evaluation of Preston Manning's claim that Reform is a populist party (1992:

104), while also assessing his contention that the party is "not right wing" (Dobbin 1992: 138). It should also highlight some of the difficulties and possibilities involved in efforts to "unite the right." Finally, candidate preference is examined to determine whether the federal partisan dimension had an impact on voting.

The PC Universal Ballot

At the outset of this chapter, it is important to recall some of the details of the 1992 leadership contest. In 1985, when Klein's predecessor Don Getty was elected leader, the Conservatives utilized a traditional leadership convention that involved heavy competition among the candidates at delegate selection meetings across the province. The negative publicity surrounding these gatherings, and the bad feelings developed among party activists, helped prompt the party to change its constitution and allow all members to directly vote for the leader when the position again became vacant (see Schumacher 1993: 8). The rules adopted for this selection process were minimal. In order to participate one needed only to be a Canadian citizen, sixteen years of age or older, and have lived in Alberta for the preceding six months. And, of course, one also had to purchase a five-dollar Conservative membership for 1992. There were no deadlines or cut-off points for obtaining a membership. Indeed, memberships were available at the polls on the day of each of the ballots.[2] As with traditional leadership conventions, an absolute majority was necessary for victory. If no candidate secured a victory on the first ballot, a second ballot would be held a week later with the choice limited to the three leading vote recipients. To avoid a third ballot, a preferential ballot would be used the second week.

The "premier primary" was a huge success. In a round table on leadership selection, Conservative MLA Stan Schumacher maintained that "the adoption of a direct election format has had a dramatic and rejuvenating effect on the PC party ... [and] created genuine excitement and prominent media coverage" (1993: 8). The process involved thousands of Albertans, with more than 52,000 voting on the first ballot and more than 78,000 people turning out for the second vote. The race attracted three times as many candidates as the 1985 convention, but generated nowhere near the same amount of negative media and public attention.[3] Six members of the Getty cabinet sought the leadership, as did one former member of Peter Lougheed's cabinet and two individuals who had never before sought elected office as Tories.[4] The campaign was neither exciting nor riven with intense policy debates.[5] The highlights were the all-candidate forums held in regional centres across Alberta. Given the large number of candidates, the two- to three-hour forums, with opening and closing remarks by each candidate, allowed for limited policy debate. Klein, the environment minister, was perceived as the front runner, a status engendered or enhanced by endorsements from a majority of the Tory caucus.

The first-ballot results took most observers by surprise. Confounding expectations, Health Minister Nancy Betkowski, on the basis of overwhelming support in her home town of Edmonton, finished one vote ahead of Klein. Betkowski's lead somewhat underestimated the strength of Klein's candidacy, as he ran first in forty-five of the eighty-three constituencies. The two front-runners were well ahead of the other seven candidates, who, in total, attracted less than 40% of the vote and carried just fourteen ridings. The gap between the two front-runners and the other candidates was also surprising in light of claims made by third-place finisher Rick Orman's campaign that they had sold more than 15,000 memberships (Braid 1992b: B6). If this number was accurate, barely half of those who acquired these memberships turned out to vote for Orman. The gap between Orman and the front-runners was sufficiently large to induce Orman to forgo his right to contest the second ballot. While rules required the inclusion of Orman's name on the ballot, he, in fact, did not campaign and urged his supporters to support Betkowski. Orman was joined in his support of Betkowski by five of the other six candidates, contributing to the impression that Betkowski was headed for a relatively easy second-ballot victory.[6] One of the other candidates, Culture Minister Doug Main, went so far as to claim that Ralph had "zero growth potential" (Helm 1992a: A5). This turned out be a rather erroneous assessment.[7] Despite their joint service in Don Getty's cabinet, the two finalists had divergent political careers. Betkowski possessed an extensive Tory pedigree. She had served as an executive assistant to Lou Hyndman, one of the five PC MLAs who entered the Alberta legislature with Peter Lougheed in 1967. Hyndman had served as both provincial treasurer and as intergovernmental affairs minister and Betkowski had assisted him in both portfolios. When Hyndman retired from politics, Betkowski won the nomination in his Edmonton Glenora constituency and replaced him in the legislature. She went on to serve loyally in Don Getty's cabinets as minister of education and subsequently as health minister. Moreover, she was a prominent member of Getty's inner circle, serving in his inner cabinet as a member of both the Treasury Board and the Priorities, Finance and Co-ordination committee (PFC). In spite of these credentials, she was supported by only one other member of caucus.

Klein's Conservative credentials were of more recent vintage. A former broadcast journalist, Klein served nine years as a popular mayor of Calgary and for most of that time was reputed to be a Liberal. Indeed, there was a movement at one time to draft Klein as Liberal leader. Klein was recruited as a PC candidate in 1989 by Don Getty and following his victory immediately joined the cabinet as environment minister, a portfolio he held throughout the second Getty administration. Klein was well liked by Tory back-benchers and was endorsed by the majority of these legislators in the leadership election. However, his popularity did not extend to Getty's cabinet, as Klein was backed by only a minority of the group that worked most closely with him. Indeed, the PFC was notable in its lack of support for Klein. Of the eleven members of this inner cabinet, only three supported Klein in his quest for the leadership.

The direct confrontation between Klein and Betkowski was not marked by policy debate.[8] Betkowksi and Klein both continued to present themselves as the agents of change, but the major sources of attention were the endorsements of Betkowski by the other candidates, her confident refusal to debate Klein on TV (an attempt to deny him the extra publicity such an encounter would provide), and suggestions from Klein's caucus supporters that Betkowski could not win an election for the party. Some even suggested that Betkowski's gender would hinder her ability to serve as an effective premier. As Lloydminster MLA Doug Cherry put it, "You know women, they get moody." Mr. Cherry later attempted to calm those outraged by his comments by claiming he was only joking. However, this attempt was somewhat undercut by his choice of words. As he explained "you know what the female race is like. Some days aren't as good for them as others – same as men" (as quoted in Laghi 1992: A7).

Klein and his supporters went to great lengths to portray Klein as the new candidate, while depicting Betkowski as part of the old Tory team. In Klein's words, "I've only been there three and a half years. Nancy has been around since the beginning ... She is really the Tory establishment" (as quoted in Panzeri 1992: A7). In addition to this allegation, Klein also emphasized the notion that supporters of opposition parties were trying to get Betkowski elected. As he put it, "I don't know if the Liberals are voting for Nancy because they like her. I think the Liberals who are voting for her think that I'm going to be Laurence Decore's worst nightmare" (Panzeri 1992: A7).[9] When the second-ballot results were finally announced on 5 December, Klein once more surprised most observers by defeating Betkowski handily, garnering almost 60% of the total vote. Some observers felt that Betkowski's campaign might have grown complacent after the first-ballot lead and the endorsements, while Klein supporters were jolted out of their complacency as a result of their first-ballot setback (Aikenhead and Crockatt 1992: A1; Geddes 1992: A1).[10]

Political Background

One of the supposed advantages of the universal ballot is the direct voice it gives ordinary party members in the choice of their leader. As Courtney notes, "the universal ballot is favored over conventions because it is more accessible to the general population" (1995: 241). But this has concomitant

Table 2.1

Political background of PC voters by federal membership

	1985 (%) $N = 325$	1992 (%) $N = 943$	Federal independent (%) $N = 606$	Federal PC (%) $N = 188$	Federal Reform (%) $N = 124$
Party member < one year*	14	55	65	24	46
Joined party just to vote*	NA	55	65	22	55
Joined after first ballot*	NA	18	23	4	20
Joined party pre-1985*	46*	29	19	61	35
Held party office*	59	5	3	11	7
Plan provincial PC vote*	NA	74	62	76	56
Plan federal PC vote*	NA	57	49	79	4
PC voter 1989 Alberta*	NA	79	75	91	85
PC worker 1989 Alberta*	80*†	18	11	39	19
Work next time*	NA	26	20	49	21
Referendum "Yes" vote*	NA	50	52	70	11

Notes: For pre-1985 membership, the 1985 figure relates to members since 1975.
Census figures are from 1991 unless 1986 is specifically noted.
*   1985 figures based on different questions.
†   Differences among the three federal groups produced X^2 values significant at the .05 level.

costs, since rank-and-file members, virtually by definition, are less likely than delegates to possess an extensive record of party involvement and service. The degree to which this actually proved to be the case in Alberta's 1992 vote is somewhat staggering. A substantial proportion of the voters who made the ultimate choice of leader had very little background in the party and only a marginal involvement in the campaign. This raises questions as to the ability of these participants to make a careful, well-informed decision regarding party leadership.

In 1985, the Conservative leader was selected by delegates well grounded in the Tory party. Eighty-six percent of them had been members of the party for at least a year, 80% had worked on a provincial campaign, and 59% of them had held some sort of party office (Hunziker 1986: 86, 88, 89, 92). Moreover, most of the delegates (75%) were officially members of the federal Conservative Party. Voters in the 1992 universal ballot did not possess this kind of pedigree (see Table 2.1).[11] Only 5% of the 1992 voters ever held an office in the provincial party, and fully 55% of them joined the party for the first time the year of the vote. More significantly, a majority of the participants (55%) admitted to joining the party just to vote for the new leader! Not surprisingly then, former Tory workers were a distinct minority; only 18% of the voters claimed to have worked for the party in the 1989 election. Obviously, the leadership decision was not made by long-term rank-and-file members of the provincial party. Courtney's fear that with a universal ballot "parties both forfeit and fail to reward the wisdom, experience and political savvy of their most established and dedicated activists" (1995: 246) appears to be well founded.

Ties to the federal Conservatives were less common than in 1985. The seven years separating the two events saw significant changes in Alberta politics: the Reform Party was launched, it elected an MP in a by-election, and, in an unprecedented province-wide vote in 1989, it elected a Senator. All this took place in a climate in which the federal Tories grew increasingly unpopular and often trailed Reform in provincial polls. Tory dominance at the federal level in Alberta was no longer axiomatic. In this new environment, as one might expect, card-carrying members of the federal Tories constituted a minority in the selection process. Only 35% of the second-ballot voters in 1992 professed to be members of a federal political party, and of that group, only 57% were Tories. Fully 38% of the voters who held a federal party membership belonged to the Reform Party. Another 5% were members of other federal parties, particularly the Liberal Party.[12] Participants in the selection process can thus be easily grouped into three categories on the basis of membership in federal parties: federal independents (65%), federal Tories (21%), and federal Reformers (14%).

The ability to make such distinctions highlights the significant changes wrought by the new selection process. The relatively high proportion of Reformers who participated in the selection of a provincial Tory leader becomes even more striking when one notes the number of Reform members in Alberta. Flanagan reports that on 8 April 1992 there were 45,488 Reform Party members in Alberta (1992). Using the 78,251 second-ballot voter total as a base, it appears that roughly one-quarter of Reform's 1992 Alberta membership voted in the provincial Tory leadership race. This suggests that the decision of the provincial PC Party to lessen its ties with the federal party was an astute strategic move that kept open a provincial home for thousands of Reformers.[13]

Not only did the 1992 voters possess very shallow roots in the Conservative Party, few of them indicated that they wished to be involved more heavily. Only 26% of the voters said that they planned to work for the party in the next election and a full quarter did not even expect to vote Conservative provincially. Leadership voters' lack of commitment to the party was even wider with respect to federal politics: just 57% said they would vote PC in the next federal election. The support level for Reform went far beyond its card-carrying members: 27% of the provincial Tory voters planned to support Reform federally. The federal Liberal Party also seemed attractive to a number of provincial Tories, 12% of whom were ready to vote Liberal federally. Even the federal New Democrats could look forward to support from almost 2% of these voters.

A potential danger of the universal ballot is that the party will be swamped by supporters of other parties who have somewhat mischievous intentions.[14] In the 1998 federal PC universal ballot, Joe Clark described David Orchard and many of his supporters as "tourists" in the Conservative Party. Clark was implying that many of these people had not been supporters of the party and had no long-term interest in it. In spite of some media coverage of such "tourists" in 1992, it appears that the leadership was determined by people with at least some interest in the Conservative Party. Seventy-nine percent of the second-ballot voters supported the party in the 1989 provincial election and, since a further 7% did not vote, this meant that only 14% of the participants actually voted for another political party in the previous election. Of course, the significance of this figure is a matter of interpretation, for while the 14% constitute only a minority, it is still a rather healthy proportion, and one that could certainly make a difference in a tight race.

In terms of past voting behaviour, it is also intriguing to note the reported votes of the Conservative leadership election participants in the 1992 Constitutional Referendum. The Conservative leadership campaign and the constitutional referendum campaign overlapped for a period of almost six weeks. Provincially, Conservative MLAs campaigned enthusiastically for a "Yes" vote, but were unable to convince most Albertans of the necessity for such a vote: 60.3% of Albertan voters voted "No." The MLAs were rather more successful in convincing those who would participate in the selection process. Of those leadership voters who voted in the referendum, 49.7% voted "Yes," a number well above the actual provincial vote. This provides an indication that participants in the universal ballot were not completely representative of the average Albertan voter.

The distinctions among independents, Reformers, and federal Tories provide insight into the issues of future and past party involvement. The cross-level Tories possessed stronger roots in the provincial party and were more committed to future Conservative activities. Sixty-one percent of the federal Tory members joined the provincial party for the first time before 1985. Reformers also possessed some background in the provincial party, with 36% reporting pre-1985 original memberships. In contrast, less than a fifth of the independents possessed such extensive ties. Indeed, more than 20% of the independents joined the party for the first time after the first ballot. Not all Reformers were former provincial Tories, since 20% joined only in time for the second vote.[15] Only 4% of the federal Tories could be placed in this "arriviste" category. Federal Tories were also unlikely to admit joining the provincial party just to vote for the new leader, with only 22% of them admitting such a motivation. A majority of Reformers (55%), however, made such an assertion, as did almost two-thirds (65%) of the independents.

The contrast between federal Tories and the others was also evident with respect to past and potential future work for the provincial party. Thirty-nine percent of the federal Tories worked for the provincial party in 1989, and half of them planned to work again in the next provincial election. Independents possessed the least work experience – only 11% worked in 1989 – and showed little inclination to change their inactivity, with only 19% planning to work in the next election. Reformers again fell between the other two groups, albeit much closer to the independents, with 19% reporting past work experience and 22% planning future work. It is perhaps significant to note that the proportion of independents who said they would work in the next election was almost double the proportion that worked in the past. There was no such huge growth among Reformers, perhaps betraying the federal emphasis of these partisans.

Obviously, participation in a universal ballot does not transform all voters into party workers. However, if all those who said they would work for the party in the next election carried through, then the universal ballot may have provided the party with thousands of new campaign workers. Although conventions have been praised as "an effective mechanism for the recruitment of new activists for the party" (Perlin 1991a: 66), it seems unlikely that they were followed by such a huge influx of new workers. Particularly noteworthy in this context is the large number of independents ready for future provincial election work.

Federal partisanship was strongly associated with 1992 Constitutional Referendum voting, and it becomes apparent that the small majority for the "No" side among leadership voters was due to the presence of federal Reformers. Two-thirds of the federal Tories followed the cues of their federal and provincial party leaders and voted "Yes," while 52% of the independents also supported the "Yes" side. In contrast, 89% of the Reformers cast a "No" ballot. Similarly, patterns of federal partisanship are significant in identifying the non-Conservative voters from 1989. Three-quarters of the "other" party voters were federal independents, 11% were Reformers, and another 8% were members of either the federal Liberals or New Democrats. Less than 5% of the federal Tories voted for another provincial party, suggesting a rather strong degree of brand loyalty. The gap between Reformers and the others with respect to referendum voting begins to suggest that the presence of so many Reformers in the provincial PC Party must have an impact on the overall image of the party. The failure of the majority of provincial Tories to support their party's position on the Charlottetown Accord appears largely due to the behaviour of those provincial Tories who had another leader to follow – Preston Manning. This provides direct evidence that the movement toward universal balloting will alter the composition of leadership electorates.

Involvement in the Process
The previous section demonstrated that the move to a universal ballot

definitely broadened the 1992 leadership voting roster beyond long-term PC members, a situation that is not universally welcomed. Critics have also raised fears about the way in which universal-ballot participants will participate in the election. As well, fears are expressed that the universal ballot is likely to be marked by diminished personal contact. That is, voters will not have the same level of opportunity to meet candidates, or to evaluate them personally, that delegates to conventions possess (see, for instance, Malcolmson 1992: 24). All-member votes, then, may be more likely to resemble general elections, with voters dependent on the media for information and the quality of decision making correspondingly reduced (Courtney 1995: 287). Malcolmson warns that individuals who join the party to participate in the leadership election "could prove to be short-lived in their enthusiasm for the party and they would be far less likely to be as informed as the party members who are usually convention delegates" (1992: 25).

As we saw earlier, all leadership voters were not transformed into party workers, although it appears that thousands may indeed have undergone such a transformation. The Alberta Conservative leadership election also provides evidence of the diminished personal contact and lower levels of information available to the participants. Hunziker has shown that most of the delegates to the 1985 Alberta PC convention met personally with at least one of the candidates and that almost three-fifths of them met the eventual winner (1986: 116). Indeed, most of the delegates heard from the candidates at one of the leadership forums where it was also possible to observe some interchange among the candidates. Moreover, all of the delegates possessed the opportunity to observe the candidates on the Saturday of the convention, as the candidates attended a series of issue forums and answered questions from the floor (Gibbins and Hunziker 1986: 5).

As Table 2.2 shows, the majority of 1992 leadership voters did not have the same level of involvement with the candidates. Only 20% of the voters attended one of the five regional all-candidate forums, and just 30% were able to meet even one of the candidates personally during the campaign. Only 26% attended a candidate-sponsored campaign event. It is obvious that the opportunity to meet candidates or to hear the candidates in a joint appearance at a forum was seized by only a minority of the voters. Although only one-fifth of the voters actually attended an all-candidate forum, 83% of the voters professed themselves satisfied with the forums. It may be that more voters were exposed to media coverage of these events. One respondent said that he did not need to attend a forum because he could see what he needed to on television.

Only a minority of voters experienced direct contact with a candidate's organization. The Klein and Betkowski organizations proved most efficient, and even they approached less than half of the voters. In contrast, more than half of the 1985 delegates reported contact with workers for the weakest

Table 2.2

Involvement in 1992 PC election by federal membership

	1985 (%) N = 325	1992 (%) N = 943	Federal independent (%) N = 606	Federal PC (%) N = 188	Federal Reform (%) N = 124
Met a candidate (during all-candidate meeting)	59	30	25	51	26
Attended forum	60	20	16	33	24
Worked for candidate*	NA	20	15	37	20
Attended event*	NA	26	20	44	26
Phoned campaign office	NA	24	23	30	21
Persuaded others*	NA	65	62	72	64
Saw TV ads	NA	78	80	75	73
Saw print ads	NA	87	86	91	84
Heard candidate on radio	NA	74	73	75	71
Saw TV coverage of first ballot	NA	75	75	75	71

* Differences among the three federal groups produced values of X^2 significant at the .05 level.

candidate (Hunziker 1986: 116). 1992 voters also had the less onerous option of phoning candidate offices for information – at least half the candidates had 1-800 numbers available – but again, only a minority (24%) exercised even this option. The lack of direct contact with the candidates did not seem to bother the voters. Almost all of them (93%) felt that the universal ballot was an improvement over conventions and that they had enough information available to them to make an informed choice (91%). Indeed, 65% of the voters admit to attempting to persuade others to support the same candidate they did.

While only a minority of voters experienced direct contact with the candidates or their organizations, most claimed some familiarity with the various campaigns (see Table 2.2). Eighty-seven percent read candidate newspaper advertisements, 77% saw one of the candidates' television commercials, 74% heard candidates speak on the radio, and 61% said they had seen other forms of candidate advertising as well. An amazing 75% watched coverage of the first-ballot voting results on local cable television, which provided them with an opportunity to hear brief speeches from the three candidates who would appear on the second ballot.

As expected, voters were very dependent on the media for information about the candidates and campaign. Voters were asked to rate a number of potential sources of information as either "very important," "somewhat important," or "not important" in terms of providing them with the information they needed to make their voting decision. Television coverage received the highest "very important" ranking, with 51% choosing that option.

Newspaper coverage was cited as "very important" by 48%, and candidate speeches by 49%.[16] By way of contrast, 25% rated candidate literature as "very important," only 23% gave that rating to conversations with workers, and just 13% ranked candidate events that highly.

The partisan dimension allows for a deeper analysis of the level of campaign involvement. One would expect the cross-level Tories to have been most heavily involved in the campaign and least dependent on the media for information, while the independents would be anticipated to have been least involved and most dependent on the media. There is some indication that this was the case (see Table 2.2). Federal Conservatives were most likely to attend an all-candidates meeting (one-third of them did so) or to work for a candidate (37%). They were also much more likely to attend a candidate's campaign event (44% did so) and were more likely than not to meet a candidate during the campaign (51%). In each case, the Reformers were more active than the independents.

A scale was constructed to illustrate these levels of involvement. A voter who attended no candidate events, nor any of the leadership forums, and who did not meet a candidate, nor phone a candidate's office, rated a "0" on the scale, while a voter who did all of those things received a "5." The mean involvement score for Tories was 1.94, for Reformers 1.20, and for independents only .98 (see Table 2.3). Only 11% of the voters received either a four or five on this scale, but of that group, fully 40% were federal Tories. Moreover, while 53% of the independents and 48% of the Reformers scored a zero on the involvement scale, only 29% of the Tories were that uninvolved. However, more than half of the federal Tories scored two or lower, indicating that while the level of involvement does correlate with partisanship in the expected manner, the real story is the absolute low level of involvement for all three groups.

Federal partisanship was even less relevant in assessing exposure to candidate advertising. There were no significant differences among the three federal groups in terms of the candidate advertising they experienced; candidate messages reached similar proportions of the Tories, Reformers, and independents. Federal partisanship was also unhelpful in analyzing the sources of information. Admittedly, it was only among independents that a majority rated newspaper and television coverage as "very important," but

Table 2.3

Mean participation level of PC voters by federal membership

Overall N = 943	Independent N = 606	Federal PC N = 188	Reform N = 124
1.2	.98	1.94	1.2

Note: Differences of means are significant at better than the .05 level.

the group differences were not statistically significant. The only significant differences were found with respect to the importance of candidate events as sources of information, and that relates mainly to the greater unwilling-ness of cross-level Tories to say such events were "not important."[17]

Demographics

The starting points for a demographic examination of participants in lead-ership selection processes must be gender and age. Perlin (1991a), MacIvor (1994), and Courtney (1995) have noted that parties adopted affirmative action rules in order to ensure the participation of a specified proportion of women and youth in conventions. As Courtney states, "systems of univer-sal ballots do not allow for the affirmative action quotas that the parties

Table 2.4

Socio-demographic characteristics of PC voters by federal membership

	1985 (%) N = 325	1992 (%) N = 943	1991 (%) census	Federal independent (%) N = 606	Federal PC (%) N = 188	Federal Reform (%) N = 124
Women*	30	47	50	51	40	35
Mean age*	43	48.5	NA	46.4	51.9	52.8
Age > 65*	6	14	NA	12	20	17
Age < 25*	16	5	19	6	5	3
University degree	46	35	14	33	41	34
Not finished high school	6	13	36	13	10	13
Income > $50,000	44	55	45	57	63	61
Income < $20,000	NA	7	15	9	4	4
Prof. occupation*	10	10	NA	14	11	12
Self-employed*	21	27	NA	21	36	44
Farmer*	10	10	7 (1986)	8	11	15
Alberta born	65	55	56 (1986)	55	52	63
Residency > 15 years*	NA	87	NA	85	91	94
British origin*	NA	42	43 (1986)	41	49	39
Canadian ethnicity*	NA	19	4	18	17	26
Catholic*	NA	18	26	20	15	13
No religion*	NA	17	19	18	13	18
Anglican or United*	NA	26	25	24	38	20
Regular church* attendance	NA	28	NA	25	31	36

Note: Census figures are from 1991 unless 1986 figures are specifically noted.
* Differences among the three federal groups produced values of X^2 significant at the .05 level.

have developed to ensure that youth and women are adequately represented at their conventions" (1995: 245). Gender and age also provide a useful place to start examining Reformers, since that party is supposedly most attractive to men and older people more broadly. Flanagan (1992) argues that in reality Reform's membership is no more male or elderly than other parties. The data presented here bring some empirical evidence to bear on these questions.

It is immediately clear that the universal ballot involves a larger proportion of women than did the old convention process. Thirty percent of the delegates to the 1985 Alberta PC Convention were women (Hunziker 1986: 66), while women accounted for 47% of the second-ballot voters in 1992. The universal ballot brought about a substantial increase in female participation (see Table 2.4). Upon further analysis, we find that there is a surprising discrepancy between the proportion of women found among the federal independents and those found within the two federal parties. While only 36% of the federal Reformers and 40% of the federal Tories were female, slightly more than half (51%) of the federal independents were women. Thus, there seems to be some merit to Flanagan's contention that Reform has received somewhat unfair characterizations as overwhelmingly male, since it appears that federal Tory members were also more likely to be male.

The changes accompanying the universal ballot are also demonstrated by an examination of the age of participants. Conventions attracted more young delegates. In 1985, the mean delegate age was forty-three and 16% of the delegates were under twenty-five, while only 6% were over sixty-five (Hunziker 1986: 66). In 1992, the mean age was an older 48.5 and the proportion of participants over sixty-five had more than doubled to 14%. Only 5% of the voters were under twenty-five.

Noteworthy age differences were evident among the three federal groups. While the mean age for Reformers was slightly higher than that for Tories, and none of the Reform respondents were under twenty-one, there were actually more Tories over the age of sixty-five (20% versus 17%). As with gender, the divergence between federal independents and members proved more arresting. The mean age of independents was more than five years lower than that for either of the federal parties.

Our review of age and gender illuminates the changes wrought by the universal ballot. It involved significantly more women and a noticeably older group of voters. With regard to federal partisanship, it is interesting to note the similarity between federal Reformers and Tories, and the corresponding difference between those participants and independents. The proportion of female voting members from the two partisan groups was no higher than that found at federal conventions in 1983 and 1984 (see Perlin 1991a: 61). Yet, among independents, women outnumbered men. In opening up the process to those with less political involvement, the universal ballot in Alberta served to mitigate the gender gap in participation. This process also involved more older people, and although this was more pronounced among federal members than among independents, even within the latter group the proportion over sixty-five was double that of the 1985 convention. Conventions tended to overrepresent youth at the expense of the elderly, but the Alberta universal ballot did the reverse. The universal ballot produced an electorate that in terms of gender resembles the overall electorate much more closely than did the previous delegate convention. It also appears that the resemblance was enhanced by the openness of the process to those not interested enough to be members of federal parties.

The status of participants provides another important contrast with conventions. Study after study has found convention delegates to be relatively affluent and highly educated individuals from high-status occupations (see Perlin 1991a: 61). One of the reasons offered for this elite tint to conventions is the high cost of attending such gatherings. Attendance and registration costs often totalled in the thousands of dollars, effectively excluding many citizens as potential delegates. Since the costs of participation in a universal ballot are substantially lower, one would expect voters to more closely resemble the general population, and this is found to be the case with respect to education. In 1985, 46% of the delegates (in itself a rather low total) held at least one university degree and only 6% had not finished high school (Hunziker 1986: 69). The 1992 participants were both less likely to hold university degrees (only 35% did) and to have finished high school (13% did not). Since only 14% of Albertans held university degrees at this time, this portion of the population was substantially overrepresented. Those who did not finish high school were correspondingly underrepresented, as they constituted 36% of the population, but just 13% of the leadership electorate.

The 1992 voters appear about as affluent as the 1985 delegates. In 1985, 44% of the delegates reported family incomes in excess of $50,000 (Archer and Hunziker 1992: 91). In 1992, after seven years of inflation and pay raises, 55% of the voters had similarly high family incomes. Universal-ballot voters appear relatively affluent when contrasted with the general population, only 45% of whom possessed incomes above the $50,000 level. As well, while the 1991 census revealed that 15% of Albertans had family incomes below $20,000, only 7% of the 1992 voters exhibited an equally low financial status.

Participants in the 1992 leadership selection do not seem substantially different from the 1985 delegates with regard to occupation either. Educators, lawyers, doctors, and other professionals made up roughly the same proportion of both electorates, and so did farmers, ranchers, and homemakers. The most prominent difference is in the proportions of students and retired people. In 1985, students accounted for 10% of the delegate total, and only 6% were retired (Hunziker 1986: 72). The order was reversed in 1992 and the deviation magnified: 18% retired and 3% students.

Status differences among the three federal groups were structured differently from those relating to age and gender. The federal Tories appeared better educated and more affluent than other participants, but differences on these dimensions were not statistically significant. Differences in occupation were a bit more interesting. Of particular interest were those individuals claiming to be self-employed. Forty-three percent of the Reformers claimed to be self-employed, as did 36% of the Tories. In contrast, only 21% of independents fell into that category. Business occupations revealed the same pattern, encompassing one-third of the Tories and Reformers but only 12% of the independents.

A relatively high proportion of independents reported lower-status occupations. Sixteen percent of the independents cited occupations in which they could be classified as clerical workers, tradespeople, manual labourers, or hourly employed, while only 6% of the Tories and 9% of Reformers possessed such occupations. While this seems to suggest that federal party members had somewhat higher-status jobs, the case is not that clear. For instance, lawyers, doctors, and educators accounted for 14% of the independents, but only 11% of Tories and 12% of Reformers. As well, while independents were least likely to be farmers or ranchers (8%), more than 10% of the Tories and 15% of Reformers claimed such a background.[18]

Overall, the voters still seem to be quite well educated and affluent, although the proportions are not as high as one finds at conventions. In general, participation in the universal ballot is still a middle-class endeavour, albeit one that involves more people and provides more opportunities for slightly lower-status individuals to become involved. Nevertheless, the process was scarcely inundated with unemployed Albertans or those living in poverty.

Distinctions based on ethnicity, religion, and region have long animated Canadian politics, and an assessment of the Tory voters on this dimension is critical to understanding the new electorate. It proved difficult to compare the 1992 voters and the Albertan population because a large proportion of the Tory voters (19%) claimed "Canadian" as their ethnic origin. Nonetheless, the ethnic origins reported by the primary participants mirrored the rank order of the 1991 census. Those of British origin accounted for the largest proportion of the electorate, followed by German, Ukrainian, and French. Forty-two percent admitted British origin, German was claimed by 12%, Ukrainian by another 7%, and French by 3%. Aboriginal peoples accounted for 1%, while 4% claimed a non-European background. With so many claiming only Canadian ancestry, direct comparisons with the general population are of limited utility. However, it is interesting to note that in the 1991 census only 4% of Albertans claimed Canadian as their ethnic origin. Leadership voters were considerably more likely to make such an assertion.

Ethnic origin is quite revealing in reference to federal partisanship. Federal Tories were most likely to claim British ancestry, with almost half of them (49%) making such claims. Only 41% of independents and 39% of Reformers described their ancestry as British. More than a quarter of Reformers claimed their origin as "Canadian," while the corresponding figures for Tories and independents were each less than a fifth. Also revealing is that while 4% of the participants claimed a non-European origin, none of the Reformers indicated such a background.

The Conservative primary voters were drawn disproportionately from Protestant denominations and, therefore, as in most of the country, Catholics are not proportionately represented in Alberta's Conservative party. While Catholics make up more than a quarter of the provincial population, only 18% of the leadership voters were Catholic.[19] The number of voters claiming no religious affiliation (17%) was only slightly under the population level of 19%. Religious affiliation again helped to distinguish voters on the basis of federal ties. Independent voters were most likely to claim a Catholic affiliation, while Reform contained the smallest Catholic proportion. Federal Tories were most likely to belong to the larger Protestant denominations, with 38% naming either the Anglican or United churches as their religious affiliation. In contrast, only 24% of the independents and just 20% of the Reformers belonged to either of these denominations. Obviously then, the smaller Protestant groups were well represented in the ranks of Reformers and independents. Almost a third of Reformers and 28% of the independents identified themselves with those sects. Just 20% of federal Tories did so. Those claiming no religious affiliation were most numerous among Reformers and least common among the federal Tories. Finally, as the discussion of ethnicity hinted, those claiming a non-Christian affiliation were particularly scarce in Reform ranks: 1%. Non-Christians accounted for 3% of the independent total and 4% of Tories.

Figures on church attendance further identify differences among the three federal groups and again suggest a body of voters that does not accurately depict overall provincial demographics. In spite of the large number of Reformers who claimed no religious affiliation, as a group, Reformers appeared more religious than the Tories and far more zealous than independents. Reformers were much more likely to attend church almost every week than were other voters (37%, compared to 31% of the Tories and 25% of independents). Actually, what appears most striking is the difference between federal partisans and independents. The independents were least likely to regularly attend church. More than half of them (52%) attended services a couple of times each year or less. The corresponding figure for Reformers was 36%, and for Tories, 37%. Indeed, 28% of the independents said they never went to church, compared to 20% of Reformers and 18% of the Tories. The federal partisans, then, were more likely to be regular churchgoers. Forty-six percent of the Tories attended church at least once a month, as did 50% of Reformers. This level of attendance appears to set them well apart from most citizens (see Bibby 1987: 89).

Before moving to the attitudinal comparisons, it is important to examine residency questions. In the past, provincial Conservative conventions resembled federal conventions in providing for equal representation of each constituency. Given the nature of boundary drawing in Alberta, this ensured an overrepresentation of rural areas and an underrepresentation of Calgary and Edmonton. With no such provisions in effect for the universal ballot, it was impossible to predict whether voters would be distributed evenly throughout the province or would overrepresent areas of Tory strength. One of the fears of opponents of the universal ballot is that it would not provide the celebrated proportional regional representation produced by the convention system (Courtney 1995: 286).

Justification for such fears cannot be found in the 1992 Alberta universal-ballot experience (see Table 2.5). The regional background of voters in 1992 closely resembles that of the 1985 delegates.[20] Voters represented all areas of the province in similar proportions to the representation provided by delegates. The size of the home community reported by participants also showed only a small change, albeit one that favoured urban areas. In 1985, 61% of the delegates came from communities with more than 10,000 residents (Hunziker 1986: 67), while in 1992, 66% of the participants resided in such communities. Given the strength of the Conservative Party in the more rural parts of the province and its weakness in Edmonton, it seems clear that the universal ballot did not wildly overrepresent areas of Conservative strength at the cost of representation from other areas.

Table 2.5

Region and community size by federal membership

	1985 (%) $N = 325$	1992 (%) $N = 943$	Federal independent (%) $N = 606$	Federal PC (%) $N = 188$	Federal Reform (%) $N = 124$
Calgary or Edmonton area*	54	57	58	59	45
Southern Alberta*	15	12	10	12	23
Hometown > 500,000*	NA	44	45	49	32
Hometown, 10,000-499,999*	NA	22	21	20	28
Hometown < 10,000*	39	34	33	31	40

* Differences among the three federal groups produced values of X^2 significant at the .05 level.

Differences in regional concentrations among the three federal groups were again quite instructive. Reformers were least likely to be found in the Calgary or Edmonton areas, with only 45% of them claiming such a residence. In contrast, almost three-fifths (59%) of independents and Tories resided in the two major centres. Southern Alberta seemed to be the centre for Reformers; 23% of them said they resided there. Indeed, in that part of the province, Reformers actually outnumbered the federal Tories. Reformers were also proportionately more likely to come from central Alberta than were other voters. The heart of Reform seems to be in southern and central Alberta, where the proportion of their members exceeds the overall proportion of voters. McCormick's description of Reform voting strength rising as one moves from north to south (1991: 345) also captures the pattern of Reform membership as revealed by the PC universal ballot.

The pattern with respect to community size was not as marked. Reformers were not found predominantly in rural Alberta, although they were less likely than other participants to live in the two largest urban areas. Only a third of them were from the Edmonton or Calgary areas, while more than 45% of Tories and independents lived in those cities. Reformers were most common in the towns and small cities of Alberta.[21] Federal Tories and independents provided almost mirror images in terms of region and community size. Both were more reflective of the general population than were Reformers. Differences among the federal groups on this dimension were not, however, statistically significant.

Although the primary voters resembled 1985 delegates with respect to region and community size, the 1992 voters were less rooted in the province than the delegates. Almost two-thirds of the delegates were born in Alberta (Hunziker 1986: 68), but nearly half (46%) of the 1992 voters were born outside the province. Here again the voters provided a more accurate representation of the general population, 56% of whom were not born in Alberta. Voters who were Reform members were most rooted in the province, while federal Tories were most likely to have migrated to Alberta at some point.

Attitudes
While it was possible to compare delegates and voters in terms of demographics, it is largely impossible to make such comparisons with respect to attitudes. Accordingly, this section focuses on the similarities and dissimilarities among the three federal groups. Before making such assessments, it is important to note the degree of attitudinal division among the voters.[22] As Table 2.6 makes clear, considerable disagreement existed.[23] Very few of the attitudinal questions showed high levels of consensus. Indeed, the use of a consensus index indicates the mean consensus score to be only 15.8, while the median was 13.5.[24] Moreover, on twenty-two of the twenty-seven

attitudinal questions, the score did not reach the midpoint on the scale, coming in below twenty-five. Put another way, on only five of the questions did the proportion of voters taking the same position reach 70%. Substantial disagreements existed among the 1992 voters.

Table 2.6 also indicates the populism and conservatism of leadership voters. In general, they believed in the wisdom of the grassroots and opposed government regulation and activity. Populist positions provide a practical starting point for federal comparisons. McCormick's description of Reform highlighted the importance of populism (1991: 350), and Manning described Reform as a populist party (1992: 104) These data provide an opportunity to contrast Reformers with federal Tories, as well as independents, on this dimension, and the contrast is striking. Reformers were, in fact, more populist than other participants.

Populist beliefs were common among leadership voters: 91% agreed that "we need a government that gets the job done without red tape," 69% thought most problems could be solved if they were brought back to the grass roots, 63% trusted the "simple, down-to-earth thinking of ordinary people rather than the theories of experts and intellectuals," and 48% wanted referendums held on all constitutional amendments.

To simplify analysis of voter attitudes, a number of attitudinal indices were constructed.[25] A populism index was created by summing "populist" responses on the four variables discussed above. Despite the generally high levels of populism, Reformers were substantially more populist than other participants. The mean populism score (out of 4) for Reformers was 3.18, while for Tories it was 2.45, and for independents, 2.58. Thus, while populism flourished among all voters, Reformers provided the most fertile soil. Two-thirds of the Reformers offered populist responses to three of the four questions. Fewer than half of the Tories or independents displayed this level of populism. Manning's description of Reform as a populist party is well-supported by the attitudes of Reformers who participated in the leadership election.

Differences among the three groups were also evident with respect to "individualism." Reformers have been characterized by some as "Tories in a hurry," as citizens who glorify the individual and are relatively hostile to government action. They are often considered to be true believers, as it were, that the government that governs best, governs least. Some might characterize them as "business liberals."[26] There appears to be much truth to such characterizations, as the attitudinal responses given by these Reformers weaken Manning's attempt to eschew a "right wing" label for his party.

Scales measuring collective versus individual responsibility and general attitudes toward government reveal the more individualistic and anti-government opinions held by Reform members. Reformers were more individualistic than the Tories and considerably more individualistic than

Table 2.6

Federal membership of primary voters by issue position

	Total (%) N = 943	Consensus index	Independent (%) N = 606	PC (%) N = 188	Reform (%) N = 124
Don't spend tax dollars on the sick	7	43	8	5	9
Need government to get things done without red tape	91	41	95	94	97
Rely on selves not government*	84	34	80	87	94
Quebec separation inevitable*	19	31	19	18	40
Reduce government even if services cut*	80	30	81	87	96
Abortion decisions between women and their doctors*	75	25	80	82	61
Better to elect people who espouse strong Christian values*	30	21	33	35	60
Unions essential part of democracy*	31	19	38	33	21
Grass roots can solve problems*	69	19	74	73	91
Charlottetown Accord was a good deal*	32	18	38	59	6
Community should support seniors*	33	17	42	29	27
Rural MLAs can't serve as many people	34	17	36	42	42
Government should work to improve the status of women*	36	14	41	37	11
Many welfare programs unnecessary*	64	14	68	73	83
Give Alberta companies preference for provincial contracts	37	13	41	36	33
Trust down-to-earth thinking*	63	13	66	64	88
Provinces should have more power	40	10	49	42	48
Foreign ownership threatens independence*	41	9	52	38	36
Negotiate Native provincial land claims*	58	8	70	69	57

Most unemployed people could find jobs*	43	7	44	46	59
Government should ensure living standard*	44	7	53	41	27
Social programs should remain universal*	44	6	54	50	21
Regulations stifle personal drive*	45	5	41	39	73
Ensure independent Canada even if it means lower living standard	55	5	61	68	55
What politicians do on their own time is their own business	52	2	56	57	53
Referendums on all constitutional changes*	48	2	53	44	72
FTA has been good for Alberta	48	2	60	83	78

Notes: The percentages for total in agreement exclude those who had no opinion or disagreed. For the federal groups, the percentage in agreement is based only on those who agreed or disagreed.

* Attitudinal differences among the three federal groups produced values of X^2 significant at the .05 level.

independents, receiving a mean score of 1.87, compared to 1.61 for Tories, and just 1.38 for independents.[27] With respect to views toward government action, Reformers again occupied the polar position of opposing government activities, with the independents at the other extreme. Reformers scored .38 on a scale we call "Pro-Welfare" and .47 on a "Pro-Government" scale.[28] The corresponding mean scores for independents were .93 and 1.01. The Tories were in the middle, but closer to the independents than to Reform.

A few examples of responses to specific questions provide a more graphic illustration of this pattern. Seventy-three percent of Reformers selected a position maintaining that government regulation stifles personal drive, while about 60% of independents and Tories adopted the alternate position that without regulations some people will take advantage of the rest of us. As well, while only 27% of Reformers agreed that government should ensure everyone has a decent standard of living, 41% of the Tories and 53% of independents took that position.

Reformers' distaste for government-run programs could also be seen in their responses to questions about the value of universal social programs, the possible unnecessary nature of many welfare programs, and the possibility of reducing government even if cuts in services result. Reformers were more likely than either Conservatives or independents to oppose universal social programs, to believe that a lot of welfare programs were unnecessary, and to favour reduced government even if services were cut. On each of these questions, the independents were least likely to agree with the Reformers. The question of universality particularly highlighted the position of Reformers. Seventy-nine percent of them opposed universality, as opposed to 50% of the Tories and 46% of the independents. Independents were more supportive of government activity than either Tories or Reformers.

Economic nationalism was also stronger among independents than among Tories or Reformers. Independents were least likely to agree that the Free Trade Agreement was good for Alberta, and a majority of them agreed that Canadian independence was threatened by foreign ownership. Less than 40% of the Tories or Reformers agreed that foreign ownership threatened our independence. A "Continentalism" scale revealed only a small difference between Reformers (1.49) and Tories (1.45), but showed both to be well above the 1.14 average of the independents.[29] In general, then, independents were located to the "left" of the federal Reformers and Tories attitudinally.

A number of other attitudinal questions provide further evidence of how partisan opinion divisions are structured. Independents were most likely to agree to negotiating land claim settlements with natives and to believe that unions form an essential part of Canadian democracy. Reformers were least likely to hold such opinions. Reformers displayed a striking level of disagreement with the other participants with respect to the desirability of electing candidates who espouse strong Christian values. Well over half (60%) of Reformers believed such a factor was positive. In contrast, the vast majority of Tories and independents held the opposite view. Reformers were also least likely to agree that abortions are a matter between a woman and her doctor, but even there, 61% of them agreed. More than 80% of other participants took that position. One attitudinal question shed particular light on the nature of Tory opinions. Almost three-fifths of the federal PCs agreed that the Charlottetown Accord was a good deal for Canada. A solid majority of independents disagreed (62%), as did an overwhelming majority of Reformers (94%).

Examination of the attitudes held by the federal partisans indicates the degree to which the division accounts for the lack of consensus among leadership voters. It also provides evidence of the "right wing" nature of Reform attitudes. If Reform is not a "right wing" party, it nonetheless provides a home for a large number of individuals with "right wing" views. On almost all of the attitudinal questions asked, Reformers were most likely to give what would generally be considered to be the more "conservative," "business liberal," or "right wing" response. Attitudinal differences between Reformers and independents were much wider than the differences between federal Tories and independents. Across the twenty-seven attitudinal variables, the mean difference between the proportion of Reformers and independents agreeing with a specific statement was a striking 16%. For Tories and independents, the gap was a relatively moderate 7%, and even this deviation was inflated by the huge 21% difference between those groups on the quality of the Charlottetown Accord and the even larger 23% division on whether the Free Trade Agreement was beneficial for Alberta. On both of these issues, the willingness of federal Tory members to defend major policy initiatives of the Mulroney era is noteworthy. Additionally, Reformers held opinions closer to those of the independents on these issues. The Tories also occupied a polar position on the populism questions. On virtually all other questions they fell between Reformers and independents, and were much closer to the independents than to the Reformers. Independents shared Reform evaluations of the Charlottetown Accord and held relatively populist positions, but the bulk of their opinions shared more common ground with the Tories.

Voting Preference

The final part of this chapter links it with the next. We scrutinize the most important aspect of a leadership selection process: the selection of a leader. To conclude this chapter's analysis, we ask, "Were differences in federal partisanship related to leadership choice?" The answer is "yes." Federal partisanship was significantly associated with voting on both ballots. On the second ballot it manifested itself in disproportionately high levels of

Table 2.7

Primary vote by federal membership

Second-ballot vote*	Betkowski (%) N = 348	Klein (%) N = 534	
Independents	40	60	
PCs	47	53	
Reformers	30	70	

First-ballot vote*	Betkowski (%) N = 268	Klein (%) N = 296	Other (%) N = 103
Independents	39	42	18
PCs	40	39	22
Reformers	21	39	41

* Differences among the three federal groups produced values of X^2 significant at the .05 level.

support for Betkowski from federal Tories. She attracted support from almost half (47%) of these voters but was able to garner the support of only 40% of the independents and 30% of Reformers (see Table 2.7). Reformers proved to be the staunchest second-ballot backers of Klein. Such was not the case on the first ballot.

Examining first-ballot support for Betkowski, Klein, and the other candidates reveals that the three federal groups had clearly different choices.[30] A plurality of independents supported Klein, a plurality of federal Tories backed Betkowski, and more Reformers voted for the seven minor candidates than for either of the two front-runners (see Table 2.8). On the first ballot, as on the second, Reformers were most reluctant to cast a Betkowski ballot. Another trend that carried over from the first ballot was the relative weak support for Klein among federal Tories. Independents were the second-ballot voters most likely not to have voted the first time.

The relative disdain first-ballot Reform voters had for Betkowski, along with the preference of independents for Klein, helps explain the surprising recovery and resulting victory secured by Klein on the second ballot. Betkowski's strongest support was from federal Tories, who were most likely to have voted on both ballots. Ninety-one percent of the amazing increase in turnout on the second ballot came from Reformers and independents, groups in which support for Betkowski was relatively weak. Unfortunately for her candidacy, her most supportive group proved to have the least between-ballot growth potential.

Reformers' dislike for Betkowski was also evidenced by preference rankings. While Tories gave her a mean preference rank of 2.9, and independents a 3.56 (in each case a score that trailed only Klein), Reformers ranked her at 4.93, which was behind Klein and two other candidates. The behaviour of

Table 2.8

PC election results, 1992

	First ballot	Second ballot
Betkowski	16,393	31,722
Klein	16,392	46,245
Orman	7,649	284
Main	5,053	
Oldring	2,789	
Quantz	1,488	
Nelson	1,250	
McCoy	1,115	
King	587	
Total	52,725	78,251

Reformers and independents in the process appears to have aided the Klein victory. Reformers' involvement also strengthened the support levels for the minor candidates, or at least for those minor candidates further to the right.

Conclusions

Many of the fears and hopes of opponents and supporters of the universal ballot were borne out by the Alberta experience. The leadership decision was made by individuals possessing only a limited background in the party, and these voters were not all transformed into loyal party workers. Voters did not possess the same direct opportunity to personally meet and evaluate the candidates that delegates had in the past and were quite dependent on the media for information about the candidates and the campaign. On the other hand, the universal ballot provided an opportunity for more Albertans to participate in the selection and attracted higher proportions of women and elderly voters than conventions. Those without university degrees were also more proportionately represented. Almost all of the participants liked the experience and wanted the party to use a similar process in the future. Nor was this positive evaluation of the process limited to ordinary voters. Party president Ted Caruthers was both exuberant in his description of the event and excited by the large number of participants who had never before held a Tory membership card (Gunter 1992: 6). Voters were presented with a choice of nine candidates; a wider range of alternatives than that provided by the three-candidate race of 1985. There was little of the negative publicity that marred the 1985 convention, and the week between the two ballots saw stories on the party's choice dominate media attention. It seems unlikely that a convention would have produced more favourable publicity.

The involvement of different federal partisans in the process reveals interesting differences among Albertan federal independents, Reformers, and Progressive Conservatives. The actual participation of Reformers and independents in the process appears to have facilitated the selection of Ralph Klein, while simultaneously providing the party with a more populist image. Attitudinal comparisons reveal Reform members to be significantly further to the right than members of the federal Tories, with independents to the left of both of these partisan groups, but relatively closer to the Tories. The involvement of so many Reformers in the provincial party undoubtedly made it much more hospitable to those holding more right wing views. Independents were more likely to be female and under twenty-five years of age than were the federal partisans and, in general, were more reflective of the characteristics of the general population. Members of federal parties, like delegates to leadership conventions, did not resemble the general population in demographic terms. Reformers appeared more rooted in the province than Tories and revealed a different pattern in terms of religious affiliation. Federal Tories were more involved in the process than other voters, better educated, more affluent, more likely to claim British ancestry, and more likely to belong to a mainline Protestant denomination. In short, they projected a higher status and more traditional profile. While independents appeared more similar to Tories in attitudes, they were closer to Reformers on status measures and shared, to a degree, Reform's populism.

A full understanding of the 1992 leadership election must evaluate it in the light of the party's 1991 constitutional changes. On this measurement, it must be termed a success. The Reform Party decided to remain exclusively federal in orientation, and no new right wing party arose to challenge the provincial Conservatives. Moreover, membership sales accompanying the universal ballot left the party with a 1992 membership total of well over 100,000. The process appeared to function smoothly, and the party, unlike the Alberta Liberals (as well as the Liberals in BC and Nova Scotia), who used a tele-vote in their 1994 leadership selection, received virtually no negative publicity. The continuation of the process into the second week proved beneficial to the party in terms of media attention and in allowing more than 25,000 extra people to have a say in choosing the leader. Six months after he was chosen as Conservative leader, Ralph Klein led the party to an election victory, and the party, for the first time since 1982, actually increased its share of the popular vote. In the next chapter, we will talk more directly about the factors that helped make Klein successful in the leadership election.

3
Electing the Premier

On 15 June 1993, as the Alberta Conservatives celebrated their seventh consecutive majority government, Premier Ralph Klein joyously and somewhat incongruously welcomed them to the "miracle on the prairie." The claim regarding the miraculous nature of the victory was based on the party's low standing in the polls prior to Klein's election as leader in December 1992.[1] This chapter examines the leadership selection process that made Klein premier and prepared the way for the Conservative recovery. As explained in Chapter 2, the Conservatives in 1992 did not use a delegate convention to choose their leader. Instead, for the first time in Western Canada, they made use of a universal ballot, which permitted every party member to vote directly for the leader. We have seen that this event afforded a rare opportunity to examine party members as opposed to convention delegates. In this chapter, we examine one of the most fascinating aspects of the Conservative leadership process by focusing on the choices voters made about who they wished to see lead their party. As Chapter 2 demonstrated, the universal ballot involved a rather different electorate from that involved in the traditional convention process. Therefore, extensive attention is paid to some of the factors likely to be affected by the universal ballot process, and we assess their impact on candidate support coalitions.

The chapter begins by probing for geographic, gender, age, and status divisions among voters in differing candidate support coalitions. Since, as the previous chapter indicated, representation on the basis of these characteristics is quite different in a universal ballot, they are examined in order to determine whether they are related to voting in 1992. The examination of attitudes is also continued from Chapter 2. With respect to attitudes, the emphasis is on noting the opinions of members and determining whether issue positions help distinguish support coalitions. Following this, some of the other unique characteristics of the all-member vote are investigated with respect to their impact on candidate support. In particular, this chapter examines the ties that participants had to the Conservative Party and their level of participation in the campaign, and seeks to determine whether this had any relationship to voting decisions. Since this was the first universal ballot to be decided by a run-off ballot held well after the first vote, we analyze the "transfer" of votes from the first ballot to the second. Finally, a comparison is presented between voters who voted only on the second ballot and those who voted on both ballots.

Geography

The logical starting point for an examination of voting in the 1992 Conservative leadership race is the regional distribution of voters. Chapters 1 and 2 both referred to the fear expressed by critics of the universal ballot that such a process would produce an electorate that might not reflect the province's population distribution. This fear was unrealized in the 1992 Conservative election. This conclusion is not based solely on our survey data nor does our discussion of the association of geography with voting rely exclusively on that source. The Conservative Party released the voting results on a constituency-by-constituency basis. These results indicate that fears about the non-representative nature of members were unfounded, but that a relatively strong "friends and neighbours" effect was at work (see Stewart 1992). That is, the candidates tended to receive their strongest support from the region that contained their home constituency.

This was especially strong for Betkowski. Her candidacy was most popular in Edmonton, where she won a second-ballot majority in fourteen of the seventeen ridings. In contrast, she was able to carry only seven of the ridings outside the capital. Obviously, Betkowski's vote share was also substantially higher in Edmonton than in the rest of the province. She took 61% of the votes cast in the capital city, but could garner only 32% of the Calgary vote and just 34% elsewhere. Betkowski's strongest first-ballot results were also obtained in Edmonton where she won pluralities in eleven of the ridings and had a much higher vote share than she attracted elsewhere in the province.

First-ballot support for other candidates was also regionally based. Culture Minister Doug Main averaged 15% of the vote in Edmonton and won pluralities in two ridings. He was able to average only 2% of the Calgary vote and 11% in the rest of the province. Other candidates benefited from this "friends and neighbours" support. Social Services Minister John Oldring carried both ridings in his home town of Red Deer, and Lloyd Quantz's only victory came in the Olds-Didsbury riding where he lived. Rick Orman was not only able to carry his home riding in Calgary, but he also finished first in two adjacent ones. Orman's level of support in that city was higher than it was elsewhere in the province. Finally, although they were unable to carry any ridings, the two weakest candidates, Elaine McCoy and David King, secured their highest level of support in their own constituencies.

Table 3.1

Geographic distribution of primary vote

	Betkowski	Klein	Other	N
Calgary	32% (34%)	49% (66%)	19%	213 (273)
Edmonton	54% (57%)	24% (42%)	22%	201 (228)
Rest of province	29% (31%)	46% (67%)	25%	308 (376)
Hometown > 500,000	46% (45%)	36% (55%)	19%	312 (386)
Hometown, 10,000-499,999	35% (45%)	36% (55%)	29%	168 (213)
Hometown < 10,000	27% (27%)	52% (73%)	21%	228 (283)
N	268 (348)	296 (534)	163	

Notes: Second-ballot results are in parentheses. Both region and community size produced values of X^2 significant at the .05 level. The actual distribution of second-ballot votes based on the constituency results was as follows: Edmonton: Betkowski 59%, Klein 41%; Calgary: Betkowski 32%, Klein 68%; Rest of province: Betkowski 34%, Klein 66%.

Ralph Klein was not nearly as dependent on support from his home town of Calgary. Indeed, his strongest level of first-ballot support came from outside that city (see Table 3.1). This is not to say that Klein lacked popularity in Calgary. He was well ahead of the other candidates in first-ballot support in that city and on the second he won every riding but one.[2] Klein won impressive second-ballot victories virtually everywhere in the province except Edmonton, where he carried only three of the seventeen ridings. His candidacy was unquestionably weakest in Edmonton.

The constituency results indicate that Klein was clearly the choice of Tories outside of Edmonton. Survey results show that he was particularly popular in the southern part of the province, where he won almost 80% of the vote. If the Alberta Tories had used the system utilized by the federal Tories in 1998 to choose their leader, in which each riding was assigned 100 points to be awarded in proportion to the vote regardless of the number of members, Klein would have had a very comfortable lead on the first ballot.[3] Klein would have received 2,935 points, Betkowski 2,347, and the other candidates would have shared the remaining 3,018.[4]

On first examination, the voter survey indicates that an urban/rural division existed. Betkowski's support was strongest among voters in cities of over 500,000 and weakest in communities of under 1,000. However, as in provincial politics generally in Alberta, a broad urban/rural cleavage was averted by the fact that Calgary shared more in terms of political preferences with the smaller cities and rural areas than it did with Edmonton. Betkowski's Edmonton base was probably not an asset to her campaign. The party had demonstrated in 1989 that they could hold power without Edmonton, since they managed to win only two of its seventeen ridings.

Carrying Edmonton was not essential to their governing coalition. Conservative voters who were concerned with maintaining their support base might not have been attracted to Edmonton's choice. Moreover, Edmontonians did not really come through for Betkowski on the second ballot. The turnout in Edmonton ridings increased by an average of just 124 voters, compared to 524 voters in Calgary, and 280 voters in the rest of the province.

Explanations of the 1992 outcome must take geography seriously. Klein's victory was based on a combination of overwhelming support in the rural parts of Alberta and the city of Calgary. Betkowski's defeat owed in part to her inability to move beyond an Edmonton base on the second ballot, despite the endorsements she received from candidates based in Calgary and central Alberta. Betkowski actually lost some ground on the second ballot, running first in fewer ridings than she had on the initial vote. It is perhaps symbolic that the turnout on the second ballot was lower than on the first in only eight ridings – and Betkowski won six of those ridings. The political almanac of the 1992 Conservative leadership election and the 1989, 1993, and 1997 provincial elections reveal that victory in Alberta politics is possible if one captures two of the three geographic constituencies: Edmonton, Calgary, and the rest of the province. The results suggest that the easiest combination is that of Calgary and "the rest." Success in Edmonton apparently is necessary neither for winning the Conservative leadership nor for winning a provincial election.

Social Characteristics
Leadership conventions in Canada have been marked by a number of divisions based on social characteristics.[5] Two of the more noteworthy characteristics have been gender and age (see Courtney 1995; Archer and Whitehorn 1997; Brodie 1985; Perlin, Sutherland and Desjardins 1988). Both these variables were important in conventions partially because the under-representation of these groups inspired convention rules that specified that a certain proportion of the constituency delegation had to be female, and that another proportion had to be under a certain age. Obviously, a universal ballot can make no such requirements. As we saw in the previous chapter, the switch to a universal ballot in Alberta resulted in a substantially higher proportion of women being involved, while simultaneously dramatically reducing the proportion of youth in the process. In the face of these changes, it is important to assess the relationship of these characteristics with voting choice.

Given the efforts of some Klein supporters to raise gender issues, combined with media stories about women networking to elect Betkowski (see Chapter 6),[6] gender would certainly be expected to play an important role in support coalitions. Women played a significant role in the process, as

Table 3.2

Primary vote by socio-demographic characteristics

	Betkowski (%)		Klein (%)		Other (%)	N	
Men	29	(33)	47	(66)	24	398	(462)
Age > 65	29	(34)	50	(66)	21	107	(121)
Age < 25	33	(37)	43	(63)	23	30	(43)
University degree	50.4	(58)	26	(42)	23	278	(312)
Not finished high school	20	(21)	63	(79)	17	89	(106)
Income > $75,000	49.8	(49)	31	(51)	19	221	(269)
Income < $20,000	20	(30)	58	(70)	22	50	(60)
Professional occupation	48	(57)	35	(43)	18	40	(44)
Business	38	(39)	41	(61)	21	184	(205)
Farmer/rancher	21	(26)	54	(74)	25	67	(76)
Homemaker	46	(46)	22	(54)	32	37	(52)
Educator	48	(56)	28	(44)	23	60	(66)
Administrator	41	(47)	34	(53)	25	44	(51)
Health care	57	(59)	24	(41)	20	51	(59)
Clerical	38	(28)	34	(72)	28	32	(46)
Sales	21	(35)	51	(65)	28	39	(52)
Student	54	(50)	15	(50)	31	13	(18)
Hourly employed	13	(13)	70	(87)	18	40	(60)

Notes: Gender, education, income, and occupation produced values of X^2 significant at the .05 level. Second-ballot results are in parentheses.

they accounted for 47% of the second-ballot voters, and there was a gender gap. Klein's coalition contained proportionately more men than women and significantly fewer women than Betkowski's (see Table 3.2). More than half of the Betkowski voters were women, and she was supported by 45% of women who voted, but by only 35% of the men. If anything, this gap was less substantial than one might have expected from the media coverage. The gender gap actually appears stronger on the first ballot, where Betkowski led Klein by thirteen percentage points among women but trailed him by eighteen points with men. The data indicate that Betkowski and Elaine McCoy were the only candidates to receive more than half of their votes from women. In general, then, the gender gap took the form of higher levels of support for female candidates from female voters. Male voters were considerably less likely than female voters to support Betkowski.

While a gender gap was apparent in 1992, there was little evidence of a generation gap. One might have predicted more of a split on the basis of age. For instance, a *Calgary Herald* story on the possible impact of voters in the sixteen to twenty-four age group suggested that youth preferred Betkowski over Klein on the first ballot (Alberts and Zurowski 1992: A1). The survey results provide no evidence of such a split. On both ballots,

Betkowski and Klein won similar levels of support from those under twenty-five, those between twenty-five and sixty-five, and those over sixty-five.[7]

The universal ballot differs from leadership conventions in terms of its ability to involve citizens of lower status. As Perlin noted, "every study of Liberal and Conservative conventions has found that two-thirds or more of the delegates come from the wealthiest, best educated and highest status occupational groups in the Canadian population" (1991a: 61).[8] The universal ballot, with its substantially lower involvement costs, permits a wider range of citizens to participate and, as the previous chapter revealed, in Alberta in 1992, a relatively lower-status electorate was enfranchised. Most of the voters had not attended university, most of them were not professionals, and most of them had family incomes below $75,000. Thus, measures of social economic status could well have relevance for candidate support patterns.

This proved to be the case. A study of educational attainments indicates a clear difference in the support coalitions. On the first ballot, a majority of the voters who held university degrees supported Betkowski, while a majority of those who did not backed Klein. (Education levels had less impact on the support for minor candidates.) Betkowski's support from better-educated delegates continued on the second ballot. She actually won over 60% of the votes cast by delegates who had some post-graduate education. In contrast, Klein won the support of 79% of the delegates who had not completed high school. The fact that the universal ballot involved fewer individuals with university degrees and more who did not complete high school may have created an electorate more supportive of Klein, and thereby weakened chances for Betkowski.

Support for Betkowski was also higher among more affluent Albertans. On the first ballot, she won a plurality from voters whose family incomes exceeded $75,000, and on the second ballot these affluent Albertans provided her with her highest vote share. Betkowski's support was directly related to income: the higher the family income, the larger her share of the vote. Since the universal ballot, with its low involvement costs, permitted more low income voters to participate, the process probably once again worked in Klein's favour. Level of income, like level of education, had very little impact on the support for minor candidates.[9]

Occupational categories also help to differentiate support for the two major candidates. On the first ballot, Betkowski did best with students and health care workers, and attracted disproportionate support from professionals, educators, homemakers, and administrators. Klein's highest levels of support came from labourers, tradespeople, or others who were hourly employed, salespeople, and farmers or ranchers. A very distinct difference in supporters is apparent. These differences largely persisted on the second ballot. Professionals, health care workers, educators, and students provided at least half of their votes to Betkowski. Those in other occupational categories provided the bulk of their support to Klein, with the hourly employed, farmers or ranchers, and clerical workers proving the most supportive. As with education and income, it seems likely that the tendency of the universal ballot to lower the proportion of students and professionals participating had negative repercussions for Betkowski. Indeed, these data suggest that had the Conservatives used a more traditional party convention format, in which delegates typically have much higher socioeconomic status, Betkowski's prospects would have been enhanced. The universal ballot was not incidental to Klein's victory.

Attitudes toward Policy

The importance of positions on political issues to understanding leadership choices is subject to some debate. In his examination of voting at the 1983 and 1984 federal Conservative and Liberal leadership conventions, Johnston argued that "the decisive factors in both Liberal and Conservative delegates' behaviour seemed to be ideas about policy" (1988: 215). However, in a study of the 1985 Alberta PC leadership convention, Gibbins and Hunziker concluded that "the policy preferences of convention delegates had no significant impact on their voting behaviour" (1986: 14). The impact of attitudes on voting decisions in a universal ballot remains to be demonstrated. Given that the process involves an electorate that is more diverse in terms of status, one might expect that issue differences would be rather substantial.

This section focuses on the similarities and dissimilarities in attitudes held by supporters of the various candidates. Before making such assessments, it is once again useful to note the overall level of attitudinal division among the voters.[10] As we saw in Chapter 2, very few of the attitudinal questions showed high levels of consensus. In fact, on only five of the twenty-seven attitudinal questions did the proportion of voters taking the same position reach 70%. Ample opportunity existed for attitudinal divisions to affect the voting for specific candidates, and, in fact, they did.

At the simplest level, it was possible to identify a number of areas in which a majority of Betkowski supporters were on one side of an issue and a majority of Klein supporters were on the other. Such differences were apparent regarding whether the government should ensure a decent standard of living; whether ordinary people's thinking was more to be trusted than that of experts; whether most unemployed people could find work; whether what politicians do on their own time is their own business; whether social programs should be universal; whether the provinces need more powers; and whether referenda should be held on all constitutional amendments.

The Conservative leadership voters were fairly "populist" and "conservative" in their political views. In general, they appeared to believe in the wisdom of the grassroots, while opposing government regulation and activity. Chapter 2 demonstrated the generous level of populist beliefs among leadership voters. For example, it was noted that 91% of the respondents agreed with the notion that "we need a government that gets the job done without a lot of red tape." As for the level of "conservatism," 84% believed that we should rely on ourselves, not government; 80% felt that government should be reduced even if services were cut; and 64% agreed that a lot of welfare programs are unnecessary. In contrast, only 44% wanted social programs to remain universal, just 36% wanted government to work to improve the status of women, only 33% agreed that the community should support seniors, and a mere 31% believed that unions are an essential part of democracy.

In an effort to simplify the analysis of the impact of issue positions on candidate support, we again utilized indices that were constructed or adapted from previous studies of provincial conventions. These scales attempted to measure levels of populism, tendencies to adopt individualistic as opposed to collectivist positions, opinions on the need for an active government, attitudes toward economic integration with the US (continentalism), and moralistic and feminist perspectives.[11] Except for continentalism, all of these scales revealed significant differences with respect to candidate support on at least one ballot (see Table 3.3).

Populism proved most strongly associated with voting. As Table 3.3 reveals, Klein first-ballot supporters were significantly more populist than other participants. This trend persisted on the second ballot, with Klein voters obtaining a mean populism score of 2.99, while Betkowski supporters scored only a 2.12. To further illustrate this tendency, the bulk of the second-ballot voters (59%) scored a three or a four on the populism scale and over 70% of

Table 3.3

Mean score of PC candidate's supporters on opinion indices

		Betkowski N = 268 (348)	Klein N = 296 (534)	Other N = 163
Populism	(4)*†	2.08 (2.12)	2.91 (2.99)	2.76
Feminism	(2)*†	1.26 (1.18)	1.08 (1.02)	0.75
Moralism	(2)*†	0.72 (0.77)	0.51 (0.61)	1.07
Pro-government	(3)*†	1.09 (1.04)	0.92 (0.88)	0.71
Pro-welfare	(3)*	0.88 (0.86)	0.89 (0.82)	0.61
Individualism	(4)*	1.50 (1.47)	1.46 (1.53)	1.77
Continentalism	(3)	1.28 (1.22)	1.29 (1.29)	1.28

Notes: The number following the name of the scale indicates the number of items.
Second-ballot means are in parentheses.
*   Differences of means for the second ballot are significant at better than the .05 level.
†   Differences of means for the first ballot are significant at better than the .05 level.

them supported Klein. Betkowski enjoyed majority support from the minority of voters who offered two or fewer populist responses.[12] The first-ballot Klein and Betkowski voters displayed a similar difference of opinion, while to a very large degree supporters of the minor candidates shared the populist orientations of the Klein voters.

The overall conservatism of the voters, as measured by the individualism scale, was not as strongly related to voting. There was a significant association on the first ballot, but this appears largely due to the beliefs of the supporters of the minor candidates. With a mean score of 1.77, they were substantially more individualistic than either Klein voters (1.46) or Betkowski supporters (1.50). With the elimination of minor candidates from the second ballot, the individualism scale ceased to be significantly associated with voting.

Similarly, attitudes toward welfare issues and an active government were significant on the first ballot. Again, supporters of the minor candidates were less open to government activities than those who supported either Betkowski or Klein. On the final ballot, only the scale measuring positive attitudes toward government remained significant. Betkowski voters, with a mean score of 1.04, were somewhat more sympathetic to government action than Klein supporters, who scored 0.88.[13]

Voters who supported the minor candidates stood out for their "moralistic" attitudes. A small scale attempting to measure such values was constructed using responses to questions asking whether we should elect people who espouse Christian principles and whether what politicians do on their own time is their own business. A majority of those giving the "moralistic" response in each case backed minor candidates, and their mean score was well above that of Betkowski supporters and double that of Klein voters.[14] This scale continued to differentiate Betkowski and Klein supporters on the second ballot, with Betkowski supporters demonstrating higher scores.

The attitudes of voters toward gender-related issues also revealed differences and confirmed the traditional nature of the beliefs of supporters of the minor candidates. Responses to questions asking whether the government should actively work to improve the status of women and whether abortion was a matter to be decided between a woman and her doctor were summed up in an attempt to assess the impact of more "feminist" beliefs on voting. As one might expect, given the gender gap in voting, Betkowski voters were most likely to give two "feminist" responses. On the first ballot 38% of her voters responded affirmatively in both cases, while only 25% of Klein voters, and just 17% of the supporters of minor candidates gave such responses. The degree to which supporters of the minor candidates were concerned with women's issues is demonstrated by the fact that the plurality of these voters gave negative responses to both questions. "Feminist" responses remained associated with voting on the second ballot. Betkowski's highest level of support came from voters giving two "feminist" responses, while her lowest level of support was from those giving none.

Attitudinal differences clearly affected support coalitions, and the strongest impact was apparent with respect to populism. Klein, as his later election campaigns would indicate, proved to have a very distinct populist appeal. His second-ballot victory was no doubt aided by the fact that most of those who supported minor candidates held populist attitudes. Supporters of the minor candidates appeared to possess the strongest individualist and traditionalist set of values. Without these candidates on the second ballot, the individualist scale ceased to be significantly associated with voting. This indicates that while Betkowski supporters were substantially less populist, and more supportive of feminism, they were not significantly less individualistic or favourable toward welfare. Indeed, Klein voters were actually more supportive of maintaining universal social programs and more likely to believe that government should help individuals if they got some bad breaks. Despite the policy actions subsequently undertaken by the Klein government and Betkowski's defection to the Liberal party, Klein's victory should not be understood as the triumph of the party's right wing.

Party Involvement

The move to choose a leader by a relatively inclusive process enabled individuals with very little past involvement in the Conservative Party to play a role. In this section, an attempt is made to determine whether involvement in the Conservative Party (or lack thereof) is helpful in understanding support coalitions.

Most of the 1992 voters were previously inactive in party affairs. One can recall from Chapter 2 that a mere 5% of the survey respondents were former party office holders with the provincial PCs, and more than half of them originally became PC members in 1992, the year of the leadership vote. In fact, 55% claimed to have sought membership for the sole purpose of casting a leadership ballot. Those who had worked previously for the provincial Progressive Conservatives were a minority group accounting for less than one-fifth of the voters. Party newcomers played a large role in the leadership decision. If Betkowski was, as Klein alleged, the candidate of the party establishment, her candidacy could be assumed to be on very shaky ground given the reduced role of party "insiders." Adding credence to this notion is the fact that among second-ballot voters, only 35% indicated membership in a federal political party, and only 57% of that group were federal Progressive Conservatives. A notable 38% of the voters in possession of federal party memberships were affiliated with the Reform Party.

Despite Klein's allegations that Betkowski was the establishment candidate, she appears to have benefited initially from the rather loose party ties required of voters. On the first ballot, she won pluralities from respondents who claimed not to have been members of the party when Getty resigned or who said they had become members just to vote for the new leader. Even the influx of new, mainly Klein voters on the second ballot only partially overcame this. Sixty-one percent of Betkowski voters claimed to have joined just to vote for the leader, compared to just over half (52%) of Klein voters. Former party workers were more supportive of Klein. On the first ballot, he was 18 percentage points ahead of Betkowski among those who had worked for the party in 1989, but enjoyed a lead of less than one percentage point among non-workers. A similar trend was evident with respect to the reported 1989 votes. On the first ballot, Klein's best showing was with those who had voted PC, while the 7% who had not voted were as likely to support Betkowski as Klein, and the 14% who had voted for another party preferred Betkowski. This pattern continued on the second ballot, with Betkowski enjoying majority support from the voters who had voted for another party in the 1989 election. It is important not to overestimate these tendencies. The vast majority of Betkowski supporters were also Conservative voters in 1989, and her support from other parties' voters accounted for less than a fifth of her total. Nonetheless, this kind of support may have harmed Betkowski. As noted earlier, the Klein forces argued that Liberals were participating because they were afraid of facing Klein in a provincial election. In response to a question on why he had voted the way he had on the second ballot, one Klein voter responded that he wanted to defeat all the Liberals and New Democrats who were trying to elect Betkowski. It is impossible to know how widespread these perceptions were, but it is unlikely that they helped Betkowski in general. In a discussion of the 1992 Nova Scotia Liberal tele-vote, Preyra (1994) noted how easy it would be for supporters of other parties to involve themselves in the process. If anything, the Alberta PC process was more open to infiltration, but contrary to the fears of some Tories, provincial New Democrats and Liberals did not invade the process in order to elect Betkowski. Klein's victory was one of Tories over Tories, not Tories over Liberal and New Democrat partisans. Klein was able to raise fears about an "invasion" to motivate new supporters to come out for the second ballot.

Betkowski's relative lack of support from 1989 provincial PC voters was counteracted to some degree by her support from those voters who were members of the federal PC Party (see Table 3.4). Betkowski was supported by high-profile federal MPs such as Joe Clark, Jim Edwards, and Bobbie Sparrow (Ovenden 1992: A5). This support was likely of some benefit, since on the first ballot she won a plurality from those who were federal Tory members, and on the second ballot these Tories remained her strongest supporters, with 47% backing her. In contrast, she had the second-ballot support of only 40% of the voters who did not belong to a federal party and a mere 30% of the federal Reformers. On the first ballot, the federal

Table 3.4

Vote by PC Party background

	Betkowski (%)		Klein (%)		Other (%)	N	
Held party office	27	(33)	44	(67)	29	41	(42)
Not held office	37	(40)	41	(60)	22	686	(840)
Member before 1992	33	(38)	45	(62)	22	379	(389)
1992 member	41	(41)	36	(59)	23	346	(489)
Joined just to vote	44	(44)	33	(56)	23	352	(487)
Did not join just to vote	30	(34)	48	(66)	22	370	(390)
1989 party worker	28	(36)	46	(64)	26	153	(149)
1989 non-party worker	39	(40)	39	(60)	22	571	(729)
1989 PC voter	34	(37)	43	(63)	23	586	(687)
1989 non-voter	37	(45)	37	(55)	27	41	(64)
1989 non-PC voter	54	(51)	29	(49)	18	91	(121)
Federal PC	40	(46)	39	(53)	22	166	(173)
Federal independent	39	(39)	42	(61)	18	450	(583)
Federal Reformer	21	(29)	39	(70)	41	96	(111)

Notes: Second-ballot results are in parentheses. For the first ballot, federal membership, 1989 vote, 1989 party work, joined just to vote, and date of initial membership all produced values of X^2 to at least the .05 level. For the second ballot, federal membership, 1989 vote, and joined just to vote produced values of X^2 significant to at least the .05 level.

Reformers delivered plurality support to the minor candidates, with only about a fifth of them supporting Betkowski. Obviously, this relative disdain for Betkowski continued on the second ballot and undoubtedly helped Klein secure a comfortable victory. The high level of support for the minor candidates from federal Reformers, combined with our earlier discussion regarding the role of "moralistic" and "individualistic" opinions, helps develop a clearer picture of the section of the provincial party electorate to whom those candidates appealed. It appears that this was not a section with which Betkowski was likely to be popular, regardless of her endorsements from those candidates.

The operation of the universal ballot makes it possible that the only direct involvement voters may have in the leadership selection process is when they cast their ballot. As we showed in Chapter 2, most voters did not meet a single candidate during the campaign, attend any of the regional all-candidate forums, or participate in other campaign events. Less than half of the voters reported being contacted by workers for any of the candidates, and only one in four utilized the toll-free information lines provided by many candidates. This lack of direct contact with the candidates or their campaigns did not trouble the voters as almost all of them (91%) felt they had enough information available for them to make an informed choice. Indeed, almost two-thirds of the voters claimed that they attempted to persuade others to support a particular candidate.

Table 3.5

Vote by participation in 1992 PC election

	Betkowski	Klein	Other	N
Attended forum	35% (45%)	36% (55%)	29 %	173 (173)
Did not attend forum	38% (38%)	42% (62%)	20 %	551 (706)
Attended campaign event	34% (45%)	37% (55%)	29 %	216 (223)
Did not attend campaign event	38% (38%)	42% (62%)	19 %	506 (655)
Met a candidate	33% (44%)	38% (56%)	29 %	257 (264)
Did not meet candidate	39% (38%)	42% (63%)	19 %	465 (613)
Phoned for information	39% (38%)	34% (55%)	28 %	184 (215)
Did not phone	36% (38%)	43% (62%)	21 %	538 (661)
Participation index	1.07 (1.12)	1.02 (0.91)	1.47	

Notes: Second-ballot vote is in parentheses. For the first ballot, all percentages and means are significant to at least the .05 level. For the second ballot, only the participation index produced significant differences between the two candidates.

Given this relative lack of participation in the campaign (see Table 3.5), we attempted to determine whether the voters who participated most extensively differed in their candidate preference from those who did not participate. As it turns out, supporters of the minor candidates appear to have been the most involved in the campaign. They were significantly more likely to have attended an all-candidates meeting or a candidate's campaign event. They were also more likely to have telephoned a candidate's office for information. Finally, they were much more likely to have actually met a candidate during the campaign. Fully 46% of them report such contact, as opposed to about 33% of Klein and Betkowski backers.[15] Nonetheless, the overall level of involvement was quite low. A scale similar to that utilized in Chapter 2 was constructed to aid in the attempt to measure campaign involvement. A voter who attended an all-candidate forum and a campaign event, met a candidate, and phoned a candidate's office would receive a four, while those who did none of these would attain a zero. The mean participation score for all first-ballot voters was 1.14. Minor candidate supporters recorded the highest means, with Betkowski voters just slightly ahead of Klein backers. On the second ballot, both the mean involvement level and the involvement score for Klein voters dropped, while the mean for Betkowski supporters increased slightly. Despite slight differences, the most striking conclusion is the relatively low levels of participation from supporters of all the candidates. Regardless of which candidate they supported, most voters did not involve themselves very heavily in the process. Those who supported Klein were the least involved in the process.[16]

The "Gate Crasher" Phenomenon
One of the more interesting features of the selection process was the ability

of voters to purchase memberships after the first ballot.[17] The rules regulating participation on the second ballot permitted thousands who had not voted the first week to become part of the process on the second, and thousands availed themselves of this opportunity. In assessing the support coalitions of the major candidates, it is essential to understand which voters chose to participate only on the second ballot and the manner in which their votes were distributed. Obviously, Klein beat Betkowski handily on the second ballot, but was this because of the behaviour of new voters or because supporters of the minor candidates refused to follow their "leaders" to Betkowski?

Given the characteristics of minor candidate supporters noted earlier, one might expect that they declined to follow their candidates to Betkowski. Indeed, according to the *Alberta Report* (Gunter 1992: 6), "voters who had supported one of the seven unsuccessful candidates on the first went heavily to Mr. Klein on the second." This is only partially accurate. Rather surprisingly, the survey data suggest that Betkowski was able to secure the majority of votes cast by those voters (53%), indicating that the candidate endorsements may well have had an impact. Nonetheless, it is clear that the minor candidates were not able to deliver the bulk of their support, both because almost half deserted and voted for Klein, and even more importantly, because many of those who supported losing candidates on the first ballot abstained on the second ballot. The reported first-ballot votes of second-ballot voters underestimate the total vote received by the bottom seven candidates. The deviation is strongest for Orman and Main. Similarly, it appears that Betkowski may not have been successful in getting all of her first-ballot voters back to the polls on the second Saturday, since her first-ballot vote is also underestimated. Moreover, Betkowski was unable to hold the support of all of her first-ballot voters: 11% of them (mostly men) backed Klein on the second. Klein voters possessed much greater loyalty, as only 2% of them switched to Betkowski (see Table 3.6).

Table 3.6

Second-ballot vote by first-ballot behaviour

	Second ballot Betkowski (%) $N = 348$	Second ballot Klein (%) $N = 534$	N
First vote for Betkowski	89	11	262
First vote for Klein	2	98	290
First vote for others	53	47	135
Did not vote on first ballot	20	81	185

Notes: Value of X^2 significant at $< .01$. Due to rounding, percentages may not equal 100.

Klein was able to hold on to his first-ballot support and fight Betkowski to a virtual stand-off among supporters of the minor candidates who voted again. This, combined with defections from the Betkowski camp, would likely have been enough to give Klein a narrow victory on the second. These factors, however, do not explain the immense proportions of the Klein victory. The magnitude of his victory appears largely due to the "gate crashers" – those who did not vote on the first ballot. The vast majority of these new voters, more than 80%, opted for Klein over Betkowski.

Betkowski's rejection by these new voters was virtually universal. For instance, despite the gender gap in support discussed earlier, the women "gate crashers" appeared slightly more supportive of Klein than the men who crashed the gates. Indeed, more than 80% of the women who did not vote on the first ballot supported Klein on the second. The political pundits who predicted that a large number of women would take out memberships in order to elect the first female premier in Alberta were completely wrong. The women who entered the process after the first ballot were overwhelmingly opposed to Betkowski. If consideration were limited to those who had voted on the first, Betkowski would have retained her comfortable majority among women. The behaviour of women who voted only on the second ballot mitigated the gender gap.

These new voters add a completely novel dimension to the study of the leadership selection process. Virtually no one had expected that the votes of these new participants would be so heavily skewed. The one-sided behaviour of these new voters makes it important to examine their backgrounds. These gate crashers were not long-time Conservatives who had been unable to vote, for whatever reason, on the first ballot. The vast majority of them were newcomers to provincial Tory party politics. Seventy-eight percent of them said they joined just to choose the new leader, and 75% took out memberships for the first time after the first ballot.

The gate crashers were indistinguishable from other voters on most social demographic variables. For instance, there were no significant differences with regard to ethnicity, place of birth, length of residence in Alberta, religious affiliation, or age. Nor were there significant differences in community size or region. Interestingly, given the gender gap in voting, the majority of those who voted only on the second ballot were women, while the majority of those who voted twice were men. This set of women voters was, as we have seen, obviously very hostile to Betkowski.

There were some distinguishing status characteristics for gate crashers. Those who voted on both ballots were more likely than the gate crashers to hold university degrees or to report careers in business, education, administration, or the professions. A higher proportion of the gate crashers reported their occupations as clerical, sales, or homemaker. The generous rules for late participation thus helped enfranchise an electorate more reflective of the general population.

The new voters differed significantly from the other participants with respect to involvement in the party. Overall, they were less interested in politics, and almost half (48%) became PC members for the first time on the day of the second ballot. Only 20% of them had initially joined the party prior to Getty announcing his retirement. In contrast, 57% of the other voters had initial memberships predating this event. As noted above, 78% of the gate crashers said they joined the party only to vote for the leader, but less than half (49%) of the other voters made such a claim. Fewer of the new voters were members of a federal party, and most of those who were were federal Reformers. Not surprisingly then, two-thirds of them had rejected the Charlottetown Accord, while over half of the other voters supported it. Finally, the second-ballot-only voters were six times less likely to have worked for the party in 1989, and three times less likely to say they would work for the party in the next election.

As one would expect, the new voters were less involved with the campaign. To summarize briefly, they were less likely to say they paid a great deal of attention to media coverage of the campaign and were roughly three times less likely to have met a candidate during the campaign, known a candidate prior to the campaign, attended a candidate event, or attended an all-candidate meeting. They were also more populist in their attitudes than other voters.[18]

Almost three-fifths of those who voted on both ballots felt that it should not be possible to purchase memberships on the day of the balloting. If we assume that this would have disenfranchised the bulk of the gate crashers, the process would have been different. Those who voted only on the second ballot exacerbated the tendency of the universal ballot to involve individuals possessing relatively sparse ties to the party and relatively little involvement in the campaign. A ballot without these voters would also have involved a higher proportion of individuals with high-status jobs and university educations.

Conclusions

It would be inaccurate to wholly attribute Klein's victory to the rules that permitted new voters to join after the first ballot. It appears that Klein would have won even in the absence of such rules. That is not to say that the rules had no impact. As we have seen, not all first-ballot voters returned to the polls a week later, and those who did not were more likely to have backed Betkowski or one of the minor candidates than Klein. If a preferential ballot had been used the first time, it is conceivable that Betkowski might have won the leadership. The intervening week allowed a number of her first-ballot supporters to defect and may have lulled some of her supporters into such a sense of security that they did not bother to vote on the second. The time lag also permitted a number of those who supported the minor candidates to decide they did not really care enough to choose between the two front-runners. Finally, the intervening week and the knowledge that Klein was not a sure winner energized thousands of those who preferred Klein over Betkowski to secure a party membership for the second ballot. If first-ballot Betkowski supporters may have been lulled into a false sense of security by the first-ballot results, it seems that those results simultaneously punctured the false sense of security possessed by Klein supporters.[19] A preferential first ballot would not have permitted such considerations.

The universal ballot utilized by the Conservatives attracted an impressive number of Albertans to the polls. Virtually all of the participants liked the process, although 27% wanted the party to use a convention to select their next leader. The process enabled many Albertans who could certainly not be considered party regulars to have a voice in the selection of their next premier. It also permitted participation by those whose acquaintance with the campaign and the candidates came through the media rather than through personal knowledge or meetings. In this respect, the process appears to resemble an election more than a leadership convention.

It seems clear that the relatively non-restrictive regulations for participating helped push the total number of voters much higher than it might otherwise have been. A number of differences in candidate support coalitions were evident. An examination of the simultaneous impact of variables linked to candidate support (see Table 3.7) indicates the significance of gate crashers. The rule allowing individuals to purchase memberships after the first ballot enabled thousands of new voters to cast a ballot on the final Saturday, and they played a major role in Ralph Klein's victory. All things being equal, these voters were 19% more likely to support Klein. The rule permitting this practice substantially aided Klein's candidacy.

There were many other differences in the support coalitions of the two leading candidates. Betkowski supporters were more likely to be women, more likely to hold university degrees, and far more likely to be from Edmonton. In terms of beliefs, they were less likely to agree with populist statements, were more likely to take pro "feminist" positions, and were also more likely to adopt moralistic positions. Klein's supporters stand out for their populism and relatively low-status socioeconomic positions. The premier's image of being a man of the people appears to have some grounding in reality. The role of populism is revealed in Table 3.7. All things being equal, a voter at the populist extreme was far more likely to support Klein than a voter who rejected all the populist positions. No other variables were associated as strongly with leadership choice.

The popular perception that the minor candidates represented the right wing of the party receives only mixed support. The strongest support for

Table 3.7

Multiple determinants of Conservative leadership choice

	Klein vs. Betkowski (2nd ballot)	Klein vs. Betkowski (1st ballot)	Klein vs. minor candidates	Betkowski vs. minor candidates
Rural	.03	.05	.08	.06
Joined after 1st ballot	.19†	–	–	–
Pro-welfare	.06	.14	.12	.02
Moralism	-.15†	-.18*	-.38†	-.22†
Male	.12†	.18†	.06	-.11*
Populism	.45†	.45†	.20*	-.18*
Rich	-.05	-.08	.02	.10*
Edmonton	-.17†	-.20†	-.08	.15†
Individualism	-.02	-.08	-.08	-.03
Feminism	-.12*	-.15*	.10	.21†
University degree	-.14†	-.11†	-.10*	.01
Pro-government	-.03	-.08	.05	.15
Constant	.40	.41	.56	.62
R-squared	.26	.26	.18	.18

Notes: Table entries are regression coefficients. Dependent variables are dummy variables that scored 1 if vote for candidate listed first and 0 for candidate(s) listed second. The attitudinal and participation variables are continuous variables. The other variables are dummy variables that scored 1 if respondent had characteristic, 0 otherwise. Rural refers to community size less than 10,000. Rich refers to family income over $75,000.
* Statistically significant at .01 level
† Significance at .05 level.

this view is on the questions comprising the "moralism" scale. Klein, and Betkowski to a lesser extent, were supported by those with lower scores on the "moralism" scale. Supporters of the also-rans were much more likely to believe that the province would be better off electing people with strong Christian values and not agreeing that the personal lives of politicians were their own business. To the extent that voters found these issues most pressing, the data suggest that a run-off between Klein and Betkowski left them with nowhere to go. Many of them apparently sat out the second ballot.

Other issues demonstrated significant differences between the supporters of Betkowski and minor candidates more so than between Klein and minor candidates. On demographic characteristics, the only significant item for Klein was education, in which his supporters were less likely to be university-educated. For Betkowski, in contrast, males were less likely to back her and wealthier respondents and those from Edmonton were more likely to support her. The major attitudinal predictor of Klein support, apart from "moralism," was the presence of populist sentiment. For Betkowski, populism had a negative impact, whereas feminism had a positive impact on her support. In view of the above, it is perhaps surprising that Betkowski was able to win a majority of second ballots cast by those who backed candidates who did not make it onto the final ballot. Given that there were more men than women among these voters and that they were more populist than Betkowski first-ballot supporters, it would not have been surprising to see a majority of them opt for Klein. That this did not transpire may indicate that candidate endorsements carried some weight.

The Conservative Party clearly judged the "premier primary" a success. Schumacher provided a glowing endorsement of the event, arguing that "direct election of a leader is the wave of the future and represents a commitment to the ideal of democratization which effectively diminishes the power of the so-called establishment. It is truly the politics of inclusion put into practice" (1993: 9). The party's president, Ted Carruthers, was also enthused about the process, calling it "the greatest exercise in democracy ever seen in our province" (as quoted in Gunter 1992: 6). Thousands of people participated, there was not much negative publicity and, unlike most leadership transfers,[20] it was followed by an election victory. Many of the features of this universal ballot seem to have worked to the advantage of Klein,[21] who was likely better placed to preserve the Tory dynasty than Betkowski. Nonetheless, if, instead of broadening the ballot after the disaster of 1985, the party had decided to narrow the franchise and allow, as some have suggested, only MLAs to vote, the outcome would have been identical, since Klein had the support of more than half of the MLAs. It is somewhat ironic that a result identical to the one involving more than 80,000 Albertans and costing many thousands of dollars could have been obtained simply by letting the Conservative MLAs choose the leader. Whether Klein would have been able to go forward from such a caucus selection to the "miracle on the prairie" is less certain.

4

Electronic Fiasco: The 1994 Liberal Tele-Vote

The selection of provincial party leaders has increasingly shifted away from the traditional method of leadership conventions to a system of universal balloting, which theoretically allows all members to vote for the leader. This institutional evolution responds, to some degree, to citizen dissatisfaction with our existing system of representative democracy. The universal balloting process remains in a formative stage; no two parties have adopted identical sets of rules for the selection of their leaders and, as Courtney indicates, "there has been no widespread consensus on a preferred model of universal balloting" (1995: 231). Nonetheless, in the early experiments, tele-voting has emerged as the most popular manifestation. Between 1990 and 1995, four of the nine parties that utilized a universal ballot opted for this method (Courtney 1995: 237). Tele-voting permits all members in possession of a personal identification number (PIN) and with access to a touch-tone phone to dial a 1-900 (or 1-800) number, enter their code, and then cast a direct vote for the candidate of their choice.[1] Given its ability to combine technology with an extension of voting rights, tele-voting seems to capture the spirit of the times. Casting votes over the telephone has not been completely successful, however, and it carries inherent dangers with respect to the kind of competition it facilitates.[2] The emergence of tele-voting as the most popular type of universal ballot makes it important to analyze the way the system works in different settings. This chapter presents a case study of the 1994 Alberta Liberal tele-vote with the aims of advancing comprehension of the effects of tele-voting and providing a window into the provincial party utilizing it. This analysis of the Liberal tele-vote is based partially on a survey of those who registered for the tele-vote and partially on interviews with Liberal Party officials and leadership candidates. It attempts to describe and analyze what took place and examines the support coalitions of the various candidates.

The 1994 Liberal experiment with tele-voting as a means of choosing a leader had serious problems. An independent review of the process conducted by Saskatchewan lawyer Timothy Stodalka recommended that the party abandon tele-voting and utilize mini-conventions to choose the next leader.[3] The media evaluation of the process was scathing. One example of this media reaction comes from *Calgary Herald* columnist Don Martin, who described the Liberal election as a "debacle, fiasco, computerized catastrophe, electoral boondoggle, or as one MLA called it, 'an electronic Holocaust' – add them all up and you've almost got a dictionary ready definition of this Dial-A-Leader horror show" (1994: D1). Martin's graphic description was consistent with other media commentary, and its reference to electronics and "dial-a-leader" might lead one to conclude that the Alberta Liberal election was just another example of the difficulties inherent in tele-voting, another manifestation of the problems that initially beset the Nova Scotia Liberals in 1992, when they were forced to cancel their first attempt at tele-voting. (The *Halifax Chronicle Herald*, in its first edition following that abortive attempt to tele-vote [8 June 1992: C1], included stories headlined "Reach Out and Punch Someone," "Liberals Suffer Universal Suffrage," and an editorial entitled "Look Ma Bell, No Leader." The editorial concluded that "Canadian democracy, after all, has survived pretty well on secret ballots cast and counted by hand. And following events Saturday, the Liberal party could do with a little tried and true.") However, the Alberta Liberal "debacle" stemmed from more than difficulties with telephones, and its problems were not all associated with technological breakdowns. Media coverage prior to the voting difficulties was also critical. Before any votes were cast, *Edmonton Journal* columnist Mark Lisac suggested that "the real loser today will be the party itself – done in by its organizational weaknesses and by the apathy ... of Alberta voters" (1994: A8).

The Alberta Liberal tele-vote revealed the penetrability of the universal ballot as a mechanism for choosing leaders. A well-financed candidate who possessed only limited connections in the party, and who was supported by just one MLA, came very close to victory.[4] Indeed, controversy surrounded the question of whether, in fact, he had won, since the counting of proxy votes became crucial to the outcome. A victory by this candidate might have thrown the Liberal party into chaos. Martin suggested that "two things would happen very quickly. The Klein government would find itself swamped with Liberal defections and enough Liberals would declare themselves independent to form the official opposition" (1994: B4). Considering the above information, the Liberal leadership election provides a fascinating opportunity to examine the tele-vote in operation.

The 1994 Liberal Tele-Vote
In August 1994, the Liberal Party and Maritime Telephone and Telegraph (MT&T) announced the tele-vote with much fanfare and confidence. Two weeks after a shaky start in Nova Scotia, in which a vote had to be cancelled,

MT&T oversaw a successful vote and then went on to hold another successful tele-vote for the BC Liberals in 1993. Surveys of participants in these
votes revealed general satisfaction, with 61% of the BC participants preferring their tele-vote to conventions or paper balloting (Blake and Carty 1994:
16), and more than 90% of the Nova Scotian voters indicating their belief
that the tele-vote was the best method for choosing future leaders (Stewart,
Adamson, and Beaton 1994: 154). The Alberta Liberal Party examined the
earlier tele-votes and produced a fourteen-page document outlining the Rules
of Procedure. The process initially seemed likely to be successful, with a
mechanism that was now "tried and true." Of course, assessments of the
1994 Liberal leadership election must take into consideration the competitive position of the party. Although it held official opposition status, as did
its Nova Scotian and British Columbian counterparts, it seemed least likely
of the three groups to win an upcoming provincial election. Individuals
who participated in the Alberta Liberal leadership selection process were
almost certainly choosing an opposition leader rather than someone who
was just an election away from the premier's office. Thus, the Liberal Party
was not choosing its new leader in the most advantageous of circumstances.
In years prior, the party had expended much effort positioning itself as a
safe change in "one party dominant Alberta" (Archer 1992) and, after a
strong showing in the 1989 election, seemed poised for victory. Unfortunately
for the Liberals, the governing Conservatives replaced their unpopular premier with the more populist Ralph Klein and resurrected Conservative hopes
(see Stewart 1995). In the election of 1993, the Conservatives managed to
retain power, edging the Liberals by a margin of four percentage points.
Many Liberal candidates had expected victory and could not be consoled
with their popular vote and official opposition status. Among the dis-
consolate was leader Laurence Decore, who made clear his reluctance to
continue in an opposition role.

As we have seen in previous chapters, the leadership selection process
utilized by the Conservatives in 1992 was given partial credit for their re-
surgence. The party experimented with a universal ballot permitting members to vote directly for the premier. Polling stations were set up in each
constituency, and the process essentially enabled all Albertans who wished
to vote for their premier to do so. The Conservatives experienced a phenomenal growth in party membership, and on the second ballot an impressive 75% of the membership turned out to vote.[5] The Liberal tele-vote proved
less inspirational.

Albertans were not energized by the opportunity to vote by telephone.
Previous universal ballots were generally associated with a growth in party
membership (Blake and Carty 1994), but this proved not to be the case for
the Alberta Liberals. As one party official confessed, "there was not a huge
increase in membership."[6] At the beginning of the campaign, the party had

approximately 50,000 members, and at the end of the process membership had climbed to only around 60,000.[7] In contrast, the membership of the BC Liberal Party grew by 265% over the course of their leadership event. This, despite the fact that the BC contest was one-sided (see Blake and Carty 1994).

Five candidates sought the Alberta Liberal leadership. The early favourite and eventual winner, Grant Mitchell, a veteran MLA from Edmonton, was first elected to the legislature in 1986. He had challenged Decore for the leadership in 1989 and launched his campaign for Liberal leader in 1994 shortly after the position was declared open. Three other sitting MLAs, all with less experience, challenged him. Sine Chadi, an Edmonton business-man, and Adam Germain, a Fort McMurray lawyer, were elected to the leg-islature in 1993 and so possessed only eleven months of legislative experience. Gary Dickson of Calgary was marginally more experienced, having entered the legislature after a by-election in 1992. The final candidate, Tom Sindlinger, was a former Tory MLA who had been thrown out of the caucus by Lougheed and had been uninvolved in politics for some time.

The election took three ballots to decide, and the counts were delayed by technological difficulties that threatened to derail the process. After the first ballot, Mitchell led Chadi 4,799 to 3,772. Germain was a distant third with 1,663, Dickson a discouraging fourth at 706, and Sindlinger trailed with only 64 votes. Sindlinger was removed from the ballot, and Dickson attempted to throw his support to Germain. The second vote utilized a prefer-ential ballot. On the first count, Mitchell was some 600 votes ahead of Chadi, with Germain a distant third. Most of Germain's supporters preferred Mitchell to Chadi, who had become a figure of controversy in the cam-paign, and the distribution of these voters left Mitchell almost 1,200 votes ahead of Chadi (see Table 4.1). Mitchell's victory remained in dispute for some time, as rumours that telephone lines were temporarily inoperational in part of the province led Germain to file an appeal, and a failure to count all the proxies submitted by the Chadi camp left that candidate contem-plating a law suit.[8] Considerable debate ensued over whether or not many of Chadi's proxy votes were allowable under the Rules of Procedure.

The total votes cast on the first ballot left the Alberta Liberals as record holders in the tele-voting category, since fewer than 7,000 votes were re-corded in Nova Scotia and BC, and only 3,300 Saskatchewan Tories voted in their contest a week after the Liberal contest (Courtney 1995: 359). Less impressive was the failure of the candidates on the second ballot to record as many votes as they had on the first, and this between-ballot leakage only partially illustrates the paucity of Liberal interest in the process. Although the Alberta Liberals achieved the highest tele-vote total vote count, the Al-berta Liberal tele-vote holds the dubious distinction of having exhibited the lowest-ever membership turnout in a system of universal balloting (see

Table 4.1

Alberta Liberal leadership election results

	First ballot	Second ballot	Third ballot
Chadi	3,772	3,587	3,794
Dickson	706		
Germain	1,663	1,357	
Mitchell	4,799	4,121	4,934
Sindlinger	64		
Votes cast	11,004	9,065	8,728
Registered voters	19,030		
Party members	56,000*		

Note: The remaining figures are those released by the party.
* This estimate of the number of party members comes from Courtney (1995:359).

Courtney 1995: 359). Barely a third of the party's membership registered to vote (19,030), and of this number only 58% voted on the first ballot. Previous tele-votes produced much larger proportionate turnouts of the registered voters. In BC, 85% of those registered cast a ballot, and in Nova Scotia the turnout was 94%. The Alberta tele-vote has to be considered somewhat disappointing in terms of its impact on the growth of the party and the level of interest shown by those who were eligible to vote.[9]

The Alberta Liberal experiment also failed to catch the positive attention of the media. Most of the campaign drifted by with only occasional coverage. The province-wide coverage was essentially limited to candidate profiles and discussions of the all-candidate forums.[10] The week prior to the vote ended the media's disinterest in the process, but the attention the party gained was scarcely what it had hoped for. In the week preceding the vote, the *Edmonton Journal* and *Calgary Herald* together published twenty articles on the Liberal event, but these articles were almost uniformly negative, with headlines such as "Liberals Hit Snag over Forms," "Dirty Tricks Charged," "Grit Execs Hit for 'Gestapo' Tactics," and "Liberals Heading for Vote Disaster." The coverage of the actual vote and outcome was equally negative, with Alberta residents opening their Sunday papers to see "A Mess from Start to Finish," "Hi-tech Dream Turns to Nightmare," and "A Tele-nightmare." It would have been difficult to arrange more negative coverage.

In short, the process used by the Liberals failed to generate significant membership growth, produced an extremely low voter turnout, and was accompanied by media coverage that in the print media, at least, was extremely negative. Historically, parties in Canada have looked to leadership races to generate enthusiasm and excitement for and within the party. The Liberal tele-vote accomplished none of these things, and the Liberal election looks even worse when juxtaposed with the successful universal ballot used by their Conservative competitors in 1992. There are, however, a number of reasons why the Liberals should not have expected the same kind of membership growth, voter turnout, and positive media coverage that the Tories received. The Conservatives were in power when they chose their leader, and data from American state primaries suggest that turnout is higher for parties that have recently won higher vote shares (Jewell 1984: 192). Albertans who cast votes in the Tory election had the first opportunity in their lives to vote directly for the next premier. The Liberal election did not afford the same opportunity.

Choosing to use a tele-vote may also have discouraged participation. The Liberals in BC, despite enjoying a competitive advantage over the Social Credit party, attracted only 6,540 voters in their tele-vote, while 14,833 turned up at polling stations to vote for the leader of the dying Social Credit Party (Courtney 1995: 359). As well, American research indicates that turnout is lower in closed primaries, those in which there is an advance deadline for voter registration. Turnout is higher in open primaries, where voters can register at the polls (Jewell 1984: 189). The Conservative race in Alberta permitted the purchase of a membership at the polls on voting day, and their turnout benefited from this, since almost a third of the electorate purchased their memberships in this manner. The tele-vote precludes this sort of involvement, as the distribution of PINs requires an earlier cut-off point. A tele-vote, particularly one held by a party in opposition, might thus be expected to generate less enthusiasm and citizen participation.

The Liberal leadership election was obviously not cause for celebration within the party. Any election leaving in its wake questions about legitimacy, concerns that votes were not counted, and threats of legal action requires investigation. We attempt to describe and assess the reasons for such a result and conclude that campaign strategies, the Rules of Procedure, and technological difficulties all contributed to the disappointing outcome.

The Electorate and the Campaign

In universal ballots in general, and tele-voting in particular, it is of crucial importance to determine the composition of the electorate. This is of more significance in tele-votes because the technology requires the use of PINs, which must be distributed before election day. (Indeed, MacIvor, in a discussion of tele-voting, claimed that the "constitution of the Alberta Liberal party was incompatible with the technology of tele-voting" [1996/97: 15] because it did not leave enough time for PIN distribution.) There are thus two stages to the leadership contest. The first involves the registration of as many people as possible, and the second involves turning out as many votes as possible from those who are registered.[11] Both stages proved highly problematic for the Liberals.

Table 4.2

Registrations and proxies submitted by Liberal candidates

Candidate	Number of registrations	Proxies submitted	Proxies submitted on time
Chadi	8,449	3,567	1,407
Dickson	179	0	0
Germain	1,385	23	23
Mitchell	7,756	807	545
Sindlinger	12	0	0

Source: Data provided by chief electoral officer.

When the tele-voting process was launched in the summer of 1994, MT&T appeared quite optimistic about the kind of competition that would accompany tele-voting. As their press release explained, "using this technology changes the way candidates communicate with voters. Campaigning focuses on presenting ideas to a wide range of individuals, instead of on winning delegates and backroom deals" ("Tele-Voting" 1994). The actual campaign quickly made a mockery of MT&T's contention that the campaign would focus on presenting ideas. It became apparent that selling registrations was critical to the viability of candidates. One of the candidates immediately grasped the essence of securing victory, and as he put it, "all it takes is signing up people."[12] Indeed, that realization pushes the tele-vote to its logical conclusion, as an event that does not focus primarily on debate and persuasion but rather on affecting the composition of the electorate.

The competition over registrations divided the candidates into two tiers: the two front-runners (Mitchell and Chadi), who each submitted more than 7,000 registrations, and the also-rans, who in total submitted fewer than 3,000 (see Table 4.2). The registration process was not, perhaps, "the greatest exercise in democracy ever seen in this province."[13] When asked why he had not turned in many registrations, one of the trailing candidates indicated that it was because he had played by the rules and did not enlist the support of big ethnic blocs![14]

The importance of determining the composition of the electorate is highlighted by two of the losing candidates, who admit to strategic errors in the nature of their campaigns. Germain suggested that instead of campaigning throughout the province, he would have been better served by staying in his home town and focusing solely on signing up supporters. Dickson indicated that he had planned on spreading his message through the media and the all-candidate forums. However, relatively few people attended these forums, and the media coverage was spotty at best (personal interviews). Therefore, basing his campaign on this strategy proved unsuccessful. The message of the Alberta tele-vote to future contestants is that in order to be competitive in attracting votes, you must be competitive in signing up voters.

Alberta's multicultural nature was demonstrated by the registrations submitted by the front-runners. One losing candidate attributed Mitchell's victory to the large number of Sikhs he was able to enrol, while the Chadi campaign, by its own admission, devoted a good deal of effort to registering the Native and Hutterite communities. The Chadi camp also reported solid support from the province's Arab community (personal interviews).

The submission of registrations to the party generated much controversy. Convention officials noted what they considered to be "substantial breaches" of the rules in the batches of registrations that were turned in. These breaches included the absence of witnesses, improper signatures on statutory declarations, and a large number of people claiming the same address. The Convention Committee decided to conduct an audit of the registrations. They conducted what they termed a random review, scrutinizing every tenth name and found significant errors in four of the five camps.[15] The audit raised a number of troubling issues. First, a sizable portion of the people contacted (estimated at 10% by one committee member) were unable to communicate in English. Second, many of the people contacted did not know they were "delegates."[16] Third, many of those telephoned admitted that they had not paid for their own registration.

Controversy surrounds the issue of the payment of registration fees. Membership in the Liberal Party of Alberta was free, but voters were required to pay a ten-dollar registration fee in order to obtain a PIN. Party officials anticipated that everyone would pay for his or her own registration.[17] When the audit suggested that this was not always the case, rumours circulated that thousands of registrations, mainly submitted by the Chadi campaign, would be invalidated (Arnold 1994a: A7).

In the end, after meeting with Chadi and a number of his lawyers, the election officials eliminated only a handful of registrations. It appears that Chadi held the Liberal Party to the letter of their own rules. Chadi emerged from this meeting jubilant, maintaining "I hope this clears it. We didn't sign up anybody who didn't exist – we signed up people, real people all across Alberta" (as quoted in Lunman 1994: A2). Of course, some of his opponents had hoped that the standard applied in invalidating registrations might be more that the actual existence of the individuals whose names were registered. One member of the Convention Committee suggests that the chief electoral officer (CEO) was bullied by the Chadi camp and that threats of lawsuits caused everyone to tread very carefully around this issue (confidential interview). Kevin Feehan, the chief electoral officer, indicates that the errors identified were good-faith errors, that there was no attempt at fraud, and that he approached the question with the goal of, as the Rules of Procedure (Section A6) put it, "enfranchising ... as many delegates as is properly possible" (personal interview).

Supporters of Dickson and Germain expected many of the registrations to be invalidated and were disappointed with the elimination of such a small number. A frustrated Brenda Schneider, Dickson's campaign manager, indicated that "there appears to be a number of abuses of the system. To me it calls into question the integrity of the process and the results, whatever they are" (as quoted in Arnold 1994b: A7). Terry Kirkland, one of the MLAs who supported Germain, was also disgruntled: "I think we should see a lot more disqualified" (as quoted in Crockatt and Gold 1994: A7).[18] In view of the decision to accept virtually all of the registrations submitted by the Chadi and Mitchell campaign organizations, the chances of either Dickson or Germain winning the leadership were essentially non-existent.

The treatment of registrations was critical because the cut-off point for submitting memberships and registrations was only one week before the opening of the convention. This provision placed the Alberta tele-vote in a different category from the previous tele-votes. In those processes, there were actually two cut-off points, one for membership in the party, and the other for acquisition of a PIN. In Alberta, the deadline for membership was the same as the deadline for PIN acquisition. In the earlier tele-votes, the party had a lengthy interlude in which to determine the validity of member-ships, and therefore, in order to process requests for PINs, they had only to determine whether the person making the request was on the membership list. In Alberta, the processing of these requests was more difficult.

This difficulty was compounded because some candidates were reluctant to submit their registration forms much in advance of the required dead-line, for fear that other candidates might poach their voters. It turned out to be difficult to distribute the PINs within the week, leaving many poten-tial voters enraged and disenfranchised (see Arnold 1994c: A7).

Proxy Voting

In an effort to enfranchise as many people as possible, the Rules of Proce-dure approved by the party permitted the use of proxy votes (Section A5). Proxy votes would be cast by the chief electoral officer. Initially, the belief was that these proxies would be used by those out of the province on elec-tion day or lacking access to a touch-tone telephone. Late in the campaign, it appeared that proxies would be more widely used, and the controversy surrounding the registrations submitted by Chadi ensured that proxies would be an important issue.

The treatment of the Chadi proxies emerged as critical to the outcome of the leadership race. There is no disputing the fact that if all of the proxy forms turned in by the Chadi camp had been counted, Chadi would have won.[19] The Chadi team turned in 3,567 proxies (see Table 4.2), a phenomenal number, and it appears that more votes for Chadi arrived in car trunks than were cast by telephone. Controversy erupted over the failure of some 2,100 of these proxies to be counted. Chadi supporters were incensed over this exclusion, and while Mitchell was delivering his victory address, Patricia Miksuta, Chadi's campaign manager, was explaining to reporters, "We won. Sine Chadi is the leader of the Liberal party."

The proxy issue raises two main questions for analysis. First, why were so many proxy forms submitted? Second, why were some of Chadi's proxies not counted? The answer to the second question is the simplest. The chief electoral officer explains that a deadline for the submission of proxies at 11:59 AM on 11 November was missed, and that the voting of proxies submitted after that could not be guaranteed.[20] The 1,407 proxies in his hands at the deadline were all cast. Attempts were made to cast a ballot for the remaining proxies, but each had to be verified against the voting list, have a PIN identified, and the vote then cast by deputy returning officers, who used the same phone system utilized by the other voters. Time constraints made it impossible to invalidate the PINs assigned to those voters, so dialing the vote was the only way in which the election officials could ensure that double voting did not take place.[21]

On the second ballot, 406 of the Chadi proxies were manually dialed in by election officials, which means that 2,034 of the 3,587 votes cast for Chadi came from proxies. The fact that 57% of the votes cast for Chadi came from proxies leads to questions concerning the commitment of these voters to the process, and raises concerns regarding the interest of such voters in the election.[22] Chadi offers a less invidious explanation for the large number of proxies and links the registration and proxy controversy (personal interview).

The deadline for submitting registrations to vote by telephone was 4 November, and Chadi's campaign submitted their registration forms close to that date. Many of these registration forms were challenged by election officials and, as discussed above, election officials initially maintained that these registrations reflected "substantial breaches" of the Rules of Procedure. This issue was not settled, and the party did not send out the PINs until the evening of 9 November.[23] Since Friday, 11 November was Remembrance Day, this left only one mailing day for the holders of these registration forms to receive their PINs. The estimated time for the delivery of PINs was two days in Calgary and Edmonton and seven to ten days in rural areas. Obviously, many voters were not going to receive PINs. Chadi workers were advised by Feehan that "they should have their delegates sign statutory declarations and proxy forms and he would 'do his best to vote them'" (Liberal Party 1994: 4). Thus, failure to receive PINs was accepted as a legitimate reason for voting by proxy. An airlift was organized by the well-financed Chadi organization to collect as many of these statutory declarations and proxy forms as possible from around the province and to deliver them to the chief electoral officer at the Calgary election centre. As mentioned above, only 1,407 of these requests had arrived by the deadline. Nonetheless, after Chadi's camp turned in all their forms, the candidate was extremely confident: "I knew I had won ... Proxies are guaranteed votes" (personal interview).

Counting the Votes

The guaranteed nature of the proxy votes was very much in question. On election day, the nature of all votes came very much into question. MT&T had assured the party that the tele-voting technology was capable of handling one thousand calls each minute, and that the overloading of the circuits that had occurred in Nova Scotia was a problem long since corrected. Unfortunately, this was not completely accurate. The circuits were overloaded, and many voters could not achieve a connection. The media reported stories of individuals attempting as many as 58 times to dial in their vote, with some giving up in frustration. Other voters claimed that they did not receive the message thanking them for their vote that the literature explaining tele-voting told them was necessary for their vote to be recorded. A few voters even suggested that when they tried to vote they were told that their PIN was invalid. These problems created some chaos. The party extended the hours for voting, and at one point announced that the process would be interrupted for a period of time to clear the circuits. The second vote went more smoothly, but even so, a number of complaints were subsequently voiced by voters who felt they might have hung up too early for their votes to be counted.[24]

Consequently, the Liberal party was left with a situation unique in the annals of leadership selection. Many individuals did not know whether they had voted or not.[25] The large number of people who were uncertain about casting their vote also calls into question the figures on turnout noted earlier. It may well be that more than 11,004 people attempted to cast their vote by telephone on the first ballot. The turnout rate is further boosted by the almost 2,500 proxy votes that were not counted.

The decline of voters on the second ballot might also be partially attributed to some voters disconnecting before their votes were recorded.[26] As well, people who were frustrated in their attempt to vote on the first ballot might not have tried again. It is also possible that some voters who turned on their television and saw a football game instead of coverage of the leadership election might have concluded that the election was over. Finally, the decline might be partially due to the nature of an immediate re-vote. A study of the BC tele-vote suggested that 7% of the first-ballot voters would not have been available to vote on a second ballot (Blake and Carty 1994). In Nova Scotia in 1992, the number voting on the second ballot was actually greater than the number who voted on the first. The differences among the three sets of tele-voters on this dimension suggests that the voters in Alberta had the least commitment to the process.

Technological problems provided an advantage to the candidates submitting substantial numbers of proxies. These voters could not grow annoyed or frustrated and give up. The difficulty in casting votes by telephone, the use of proxies, and the importance of candidate-generated registrations raised the possibility of the leadership being won by a candidate without widespread support from party regulars. Such an outcome could have disastrous results for the party. As Jewell asks in the American context, "what harm does it do to a minority party if relatively few voters participate in its primaries? The greatest risk may be that a small and unrepresentative group of minority party voters will choose a candidate who lacks an appeal to a broader group of voters" (1984: 284).

Leadership Selection as a Participatory Event

Party conventions as mechanisms of leadership selection serve multiple purposes. Parties use such events to recruit new members and to raise the party's profile. The latter is particularly the case when the party is in opposition. One of the measures of a party's perceived ability to govern is the degree to which it is able to organize a successful convention. In addition, the convention itself provides one of the rare opportunities for party activists from across the province (or country, as the case may be) to meet one another and discuss their views and preferences. Since parties often draw heavily on the party activists during election campaigns, conventions also provide opportunities for the activists to meet the candidates in person, an opportunity that can solidify one's attachment to the eventual winner.

Many of these social elements of involvement in leadership selections are lost in a tele-vote. The optimal strategy in tele-voting is to recruit as many new party members as possible and to delay registering these members until the last moments. This strategy will help ensure that opposing candidates have difficulty contacting the newer recruits. The consequence is that the party leader is chosen by a group that may have relatively strong ties to individual candidates, but weak or non-existent ties to the party as a whole. In addition, if one takes this a step further, as the Alberta Liberals did, and allow the use of proxy votes, the process can become leader-dominated to an even greater extent. The result is a highly atomized, and to a considerable extent, clientelist leadership selection process.

The fragmented character of the Alberta leadership selection process is illustrated in Table 4.3. The Mitchell campaign was the only one of the five that appeared to meet with considerable success in contacting potential voters. Either Mitchell or his supporters contacted about 7 in 10 voters in the leadership contest. In contrast, almost three-quarters of the respondents

Table 4.3

Engagement of voters in the 1994 Alberta Liberal leadership contest (percentage responses)

A. Approached by the candidate(s) for support

	Leadership candidate				
Who approached	Chadi N = 65	Dickson N = 68	Germain N = 139	Sindlinger N = 10	Mitchell N = 287
Candidate	5.7	4.9	5.6	2.4	8.7
Worker	14.7	11.8	22.6	2.6	41.7
Both	5.7	4.7	7.3	1.2	18.2
Not approached	73.9	78.6	64.6	93.8	31.4

B. Attended all-candidates forum (N = 586)

Yes	31.4
No	68.6

C. Attended a candidate event (N = 586)

Yes	32.2
No	67.8

D. Event for which candidate (N = 586)

Chadi	6.5
Dickson	7.0
Germain	8.9
Mitchell	20.3
Sindlinger	0.5

E. Knowledge of candidate

Candidate	Knew (met) before campaign N = 363	Met during campaign N = 274
Chadi	18.9	17.6
Dickson	20.5	17.6
Germain	21.7	20.1
Mitchell	44.4	29.7
Sindlinger	5.8	7.5

said they were not contacted either directly by the runner-up, Chadi, or by one of his campaign workers. Similarly, only about one-third of respondents or fewer were contacted by the Germain, Dickson, or Sindlinger campaign teams or by one of the candidates directly. The reasons for this are two-fold. First, so many registrations came in late in the contest that the candidates often simply did not know who would be eligible to vote. Thus, for logistical reasons, it was difficult for the candidates to contact all voters. Second, and perhaps more importantly, the tele-vote system with the use of proxies placed a higher premium on recruiting new members than on convincing long-time party members of the quality of one's characteristics. The leading candidates in particular understood that the contest would be won or lost on the basis of their recruiting efforts, rather than on their success in converting the supporters of other candidates.

A relative demobilization of the leadership voters can be seen in other respects in Table 4.3. Fewer than one in three voters attended one of the all-candidates forums, and a similarly small fraction attended an event sponsored by one of the candidates. Of the latter, slightly over one in five voters had attended an event sponsored by Mitchell, whereas fewer than one in ten had attended an event sponsored by one of the other candidates. Respondents were also asked if they knew, or had met, the candidates either prior to the campaign or during the leadership campaign. Once again, the data indicate that with the exception of Mitchell, many voters were choosing among people who were relative strangers to them. For example, about three in four respondents either knew Mitchell before the campaign or came to know him during the campaign. Although this might appear low in view of the fact that Mitchell had been a member of the legislature since 1986 and had contested the party leadership in 1989, it nonetheless dwarfs the percentages who admit to knowing the other candidates before, or as a result of, the campaign. For example, Chadi was known by only slightly more than one in three voters by the end of the leadership contest. Likewise, both Germain and Dickson were known by only about four in ten voters, and Sindlinger by about one in eight. Whatever strengths the tele-voting process brings to leadership selection, the informed engagement of voters in a rational and systematic selection among the candidates appears not to be among them.

Did the Best Candidate Win?
Theorizing on the effect of voting systems on election outcomes has suggested that the outcomes are often influenced by the voting process. In other words, different electoral systems applied to the same group of candidates and voters may produce significantly different election outcomes. Analyses of voter preferences in Canadian leadership contests have provided some empirical support for this theory. For example, Levesque (1983) argued that the 1993 federal Conservative leadership election erred in choosing Brian Mulroney as leader, because John Crosbie could have defeated Mulroney in a two-person ballot. Woolstencroft (1983) and Perlin (1983) argued that Levesque's conclusions were incorrect, but that the premises on which the conclusions were based had merit. That is, although Crosbie did not have sufficient first-preference support to upset either Joe Clark or

Table 4.4

**Preference ranking of Liberal candidates
(percentage responses and frequency distribution*)**

Preference ranking	Leadership candidate				
	Chadi	Dickson	Germain	Mitchell	Sindlinger
First	12.6 (67)	13.3 (69)	26.8 (140)	51.9 (287)	2.0 (10)
Second	8.6 (46)	32.0 (166)	31.4 (164)	19.3 (107)	8.7 (44)
Third	8.3 (44)	32.0 (166)	22.4 (117)	14.3 (79)	18.9 (95)
Fourth	14.7 (78)	17.0 (88)	13.4 (70)	6.3 (35)	43.9 (221)
Fifth	55.8 (297)	5.8 (30)	5.9 (31)	8.1 (45)	26.6 (133)
N	(532)	(519)	(522)	(553)	(503)

*   Frequency distribution is shown in parentheses.

Mulroney, he was the second preference of a significant number of delegates. Under a different voting system, he could have finished much closer to both Clark and Mulroney. Similarly, Archer (1991) demonstrated that at the 1989 NDP leadership election, Steven Langdon had more support than Dave Barrett, even though Barrett survived the third ballot and Langdon was eliminated. Although Barrett had greater first-preference support compared to Langdon, he also was much more likely than Langdon to be the least-favoured candidate, thereby reducing his overall preference ranking. And, as we saw in Chapter 3, the application of different rules in the 1992 Alberta PC election might have produced a different outcome.

The data on the Alberta Liberals indicate that some of these findings appear to apply to the 1994 Liberal candidates. We noted above that the party used a mixed electoral system – the first ballot used a simple majority method, and the second ballot used a preferential system with a transferable vote. Since no candidate won a majority on the first ballot, and Sindlinger won fewer votes than the other candidates, Sindlinger was dropped from the second ballot, and Dickson voluntarily withdrew, throwing his support behind Germain. Although the underrepresentation of Chadi supporters in the sample renders the analysis less accurate than one would hope, the findings are nonetheless sufficiently intriguing to merit some comment (see Table 4.4).

With the exception of Chadi, the overall preference rankings of candidates are similar to the voting results. Mitchell's first-preference support of approximately 50% is slightly higher than his vote total of 44%, whereas Germain's at 27% and Dickson's at 13% are higher than their vote totals of 15% and 7%, respectively. At 13% first-preference support, Chadi is significantly underrepresented in comparison to his first-ballot vote total of 34%. The underrepresentation of Chadi first-preference supporters in the sample accounts for his poor showing on the preference rankings in Table 4.4, but it does not, of course, explain the very high percentage of respondents (56%) who ranked Chadi fifth out of five candidates. Indeed, perhaps the most striking feature of the 1994 Alberta Liberal leadership contest is that the least-preferred candidate came within several hundred uncounted proxy votes from winning the contest. The use of a preferential ballot for the second round of voting helped to ensure that a candidate with little second-preference support, such as Chadi, would find it difficult, if not impossible, to win. However, the Chadi campaign strategy was premised on a first-ballot victory, and this strategy came remarkably close to being successful. The fact that the majority of those supporting other candidates ranked Chadi last would have been irrelevant, and these Liberals would have faced a party led by their least-preferred candidate.

Party Involvement and Socio-Demographic Characteristics: Support Patterns

Throughout the previous chapters, it has been emphasized that in a process aimed at selecting a party's leader, one of the most interesting questions is who supported which candidate. We continue our pursuit of this question by examining the party involvement and socio-demographic characteristics of the supporters of the four major Liberal candidates in 1994. We then probe for policy differences amongst these groups. As hinted above, the story of the Alberta Liberal leadership election is in many ways the story of the Chadi campaign, so we begin by discussing his supporters.

Chadi's supporters are very much underrepresented in our sample, an underrepresentation that raises some questions about the ability of standard mail surveys to generate an accurate portrait of future leadership voters. There are a number of possible reasons for this shortcoming. Media coverage suggested that a sizable number of the individuals who were registered by the Chadi camp might not be fluent in English. If this is true, then they would be unlikely to complete and return our survey. Media stories also suggested that some of the individuals registered by Chadi had no long-term commitment to the party and were just names on proxy voting sheets. Such individuals would also be unlikely to complete a survey. Finally, the survey was carried out with the cooperation of the provincial Liberal office. Many Chadi supporters were extremely bitter over the election and might well have refused to participate in any survey sanctioned by the party. Chadi concedes that many of his supporters were angry that he had not fully pursued his legal options in contesting the results of the vote (personal interview). Explanations aside, our sample does not accurately represent Chadi voters, and our description of his support must be interpreted in that light.

Cross-tabular analysis reveals a number of interesting features related to Chadi's support patterns (see Tables 4.5 and 4.6). As expected, Chadi supporters were much more likely to vote by proxy than were other voters.

Table 4.5

Liberal Party background by preferred candidate

	Chadi $N = 65$	Dickson $N = 68$	Germain $N = 139$	Mitchell $N = 287$
Joined only to vote	36	13	29	23
Member when vote scheduled	63	81	72	70
Proxy voter	35	4	7	8
Member before 1994	42	85	62	69
1993 election worker	30	61	48	46
1993 Liberal voter	76	90	85	88
1993 non-voter	14	8	4	5
1993 federal Liberal voter	70	81	63	73
1993 federal non-voter	15	6	5	4
Member of federal Liberals	30	52	28	39
Member of other federal party	9	11	18	8
Held party office	4	13	12	13

Note: For all variables, X^2 was significant at .05 or better.

Chadi's support from the Arab community is also noteworthy. Eighty-one percent of the voters who claimed an Arabic origin ranked Chadi first, and this group comprised more than a quarter of those who did so. Similarly, 63% of those who claimed to be Muslim supported Chadi. Chadi supporters were also much more likely to be immigrants than were supporters of the other candidates. Almost 40% of Chadi's backers said they were immigrants, while only about a fifth of the support for the other candidates fell into that category.

Chadi's support was concentrated in the northern parts of the province. Only 2% of his supporters resided in the central and southern regions of Alberta, and 60% were from the Edmonton area. Those who preferred Chadi were less affluent and less likely to hold a university degree than were supporters of other candidates. There was also a gender gap, with women comprising a much smaller proportion of the Chadi camp than they did of the other camps.

Additionally, there is evidence that Chadi voters were relatively new to the Liberal Party and to voting. Chadi's support coalition contained the highest proportion of voters who had not voted in either the 1993 federal election or the 1993 provincial election, and 43% of his supporters were not members of the party when the tele-vote was announced. Moreover, three-fifths of his supporters admitted to joining the party for the first time in 1994. Finally, his supporters were the least likely to report working for the provincial Liberals in the 1993 election, and less than a third of them were members of the federal Liberal Party.

Table 4.6

Socio-demographic characteristics by preferred Liberal candidate

	Chadi $N = 65$	Dickson $N = 68$	Germain $N = 139$	Mitchell $N = 287$
University graduate	31	62	41	50
Less than high school	21	3	10	8
Income over $75,000	22	36	44	39
Income under $35,000	36	14	20	23
Women	30	44	46	51
Age < 25	15	6	2	4
Age > 65	13	23	22	15
Immigrant	40	22	11	22
British	16	44	33	22
Other European	18	26	34	38
Canadian ethnicity	29	23	29	25
Indo-Canadian	7	0	0	3
Arabic	24	2	1	2
Catholic	10	16	27	34
Protestant	48	52	53	33
None	9	25	10	11
Muslim	18	1	0	3
Other	9	3	4	5
Calgary area	19	67	13	24
Edmonton area	61	16	27	50
Northern Alberta	15	7	47	12
Central Alberta	3	7	10	8
Southern Alberta	2	3	4	6
Population > 500,000	59	74	30	59
Population, 10,000 to 499,999	24	14	56	20
Population < 10,000	16	12	14	21

Note: For all variables, X^2 was significant at .05 or better.

The Chadi supporters were probably more diverse than our survey shows, since it does not include responses from two particular groups that by all accounts offered him significant levels of support. Most strikingly absent are voters of Aboriginal origin. The Chadi campaign directed substantial efforts to registering Aboriginal voters, and reports in the *Edmonton Journal* confirm the predisposition of many of these voters to support Chadi (Arnold 1994a: A7; Arnold 1994b: A7). Our sample provides no indication that Aboriginal peoples registered in substantial numbers nor that they voted for Chadi.[27] We are unable to provide a suitable explanation for their absence in our sample. Similarly, Hutterites do not appear in our sample. We are more confident that, in keeping with their religious traditions, people from these colonies may have been reluctant to participate in a survey. It may also be the case that, given the efforts directed at the Aboriginal communities and Hutterite colonies by the Chadi campaign, voters from these groups were more likely to heed the instruction to not participate in the survey. Finally, it is worth noting that media accounts and interviews indicate that the mobilization of support for Chadi was based partially on his campaign's ability to enlist community leaders who then convinced their followers to vote for Chadi. In such a case, the individual who actually voted might lack sufficient interest in the process to complete a somewhat lengthy survey.

In contrast, the supporters of Gary Dickson were extremely willing to complete the survey. His supporters provide an interesting comparison with those who supported Chadi on a number of other dimensions as well. Dickson supporters did not vote by proxy and came almost exclusively from British or European backgrounds, or described their ethnicity as "Canadian." More than 60% of them held university degrees, and only 14% reported family incomes below $35,000. There was also a clear regional tint to Dickson's candidacy, with two-thirds of his support concentrated in the Calgary region. Interestingly, Dickson supporters were also twice as likely as those of other candidates to claim no religious affiliation.

Dickson's supporters possessed the strongest Liberal ties. Eighty-one percent were members of the party before the tele-vote was announced, and 81% voted Liberal in the preceding federal election. Dickson backers were also most likely to report a Liberal vote in the 1993 provincial election. As well, only in the Dickson coalition did a majority report membership in the federal party and admit working for the party in the previous provincial election.

Germain's supporters could be distinguished from those of the other candidates mainly by their area of residence. His candidacy was quite strong in the northern part of the province, where he resided. More than half of the northern residents ranked him as their first preference. It appears that many of these people were from his hometown of Fort McMurray, since he also attracted a majority of first preferences from those who lived in communities of between 10,000 and 50,000. Germain also garnered disproportionately large support from federal Reform voters and members, and his supporters, similar to those of Dickson, reported only British, European, or Canadian ethnic origins. In terms of previous party involvement, those who preferred Germain fell between the extremes delineated by the Chadi and Dickson camps.

In almost any other contest, the key question would be who supported the winner, but given the dynamics of the 1994 Liberal vote, this is less important to our analysis. There are, however, some patterns in Mitchell's support. He was the only candidate who attracted substantial levels of support everywhere in the province. Perhaps because of this, his strongest support came from the southern part of the province, where the party is weakest, and where none of the candidates resided. Mitchell also did extremely well with Catholic voters, securing three-fifths of their first preferences. Only those who reported religious affiliations that were neither Christian nor Muslim came close to matching this level of support for Mitchell.

Our data do not substantiate the claim advanced by one of the other candidates that Mitchell owed his election to support from the Sikh community. However, we are unable to entirely reject this claim, since 88% of the Indo-Canadians who participated in the leadership election supported his candidacy. Like Chadi's, Mitchell's vote was somewhat underrepresented in our sample, which leaves open the possibility that the language difficulties were not exclusive to the Chadi camp. It may well be that Indo-Canadians were more likely to vote than they were to respond to our survey.[28] As was the case for Germain, those who ranked Mitchell first fell between the Chadi and Dickson camps on this dimension.

The Policy Division among Leadership Candidates

One of the perennial questions that emerges around leadership selection is whether the candidates present significant policy differences, or whether the differences centre more on matters of style over substance. Respondents to the Alberta Liberal survey were presented with a number of statements and asked to indicate whether they agreed or disagreed with each. As in Chapters 2 and 3, the questions have been grouped into categories pertaining to size of government, social policies and spending, populism, continentalism, moral issues, constitutional issues, class relations, and the status of women.

Before exploring the differences with respect to candidate support, we note that substantial disagreement existed among the Liberal voters. Using the consensus index (CI) described in Chapter 2, we find that the average CI for the Liberals was 14.9. There was actually less consensus among Liberals than we found among the Conservative voters.

Several consistent trends can be seen in Table 4.7. One of the more important trends is that on many questions of public policy, Liberals as a whole take rather centrist positions, which appear to balance the concerns of fiscal responsibility with the view that the state has an important role to play in providing services. For example, on the policy items dealing with size of government, approximately two-thirds believe that government should ensure a decent living standard, and a similar proportion believe that balanced budgets should be mandatory. Similarly, approximately 57% of Liberals feel that government should ensure everyone has adequate housing, while an almost identical percentage believe that debt reduction should be the government's top priority. Thus, to a certain extent, Alberta Liberals continue to support welfare liberalism, while also evincing considerable fiscal austerity.

Table 4.7

Issue positions by preferred Liberal candidate

		Chadi	Dickson	Germain	Mitchell	Overall
Individualism*	(0-4)	1.18	.82	1.33	1.12	1.14
Populism*	(0-4)	2.68	1.88	2.71	2.26	2.37
Continentalism*	(0-3)	1.08	.66	1.09	.83	.91
Moralism*	(0-2)	.45	.54	.65	.80	.70
Pro-government*	(0-3)	1.41	2.01	1.35	1.51	1.52
Feminism*	(0-2)	1.00	1.46	1.14	1.22	1.20

* The difference of means was significant at better than the .05 level.

When one examines the attitudes of Liberals according to their candidate preferences, a consistent pattern emerges (see Table 4.7). Mitchell's supporters are generally located very close to the mean party position. Furthermore, the remaining candidate support coalitions locate themselves across the range of issues in relatively predictable and consistent patterns. For example, Dickson supporters are usually placed somewhat to the left of the Mitchell supporters, whereas both the Chadi and the Germain supporters are generally placed somewhat to the right of Mitchell supporters.[29] It is important not to overstate the degree of variation among the support groups, for in most cases the groups were fairly close to one another. Nonetheless, the group means differed in a statistically significant manner on each of our scales, and it seems reasonable to conclude that those voting for Mitchell understood him to be somewhat to the left of Chadi and Germain, and somewhat to the right of Dickson, while maintaining a position near the party's ideological or policy centre. Many have observed, however, that Laurence Decore occupied a position somewhat to the right of Mitchell, thereby suggesting that a shift in policy emphasis had occurred under Mitchell. It is also instructive to bear in mind, though, that when Dickson left the leadership race, he threw his support behind Germain, despite the fact that Mitchell appeared to occupy a policy space closer to his own. Similarly, when Germain's votes were redistributed under the transferable vote mechanism following the second ballot, a disproportionate number went to Mitchell over Chadi, despite the finding here that on policy matters, Germain supporters were closer to Chadi than to Mitchell. It appears that, in the end, the impact of policy differences was moderated by the continuing impact of personality and leadership style among the candidates.

Table 4.8 includes a multivariate analysis of the determinants of support for Grant Mitchell across the first and second ballots. On first-ballot support, residence in Edmonton was the only demographic characteristic to predict support for Mitchell, and the impact was strongly positive. On the attitudinal measures, the "moralism" index had a strong positive impact,

Table 4.8

Multiple determinants of Liberal leadership choice

	Mitchell vs. others (2nd ballot)	Mitchell vs. others (1st ballot)
Rural	.15*	.13
Pro-welfare	-.07	.12
Moralism	.16*	.31†
Male	-.03	-.03
Populism	-.32†	-.23†
Rich	-.10	-.01
Edmonton	.12*	.20†
Individualism	-.03	.01
Feminism	-.02	-.10
University degree	-.02	.02
Pro-government	-.02	.06
Constant	.89	.46
R-squared	.09	.11

Notes: Table entries are regression coefficients. Dependent variables are dummy variables that scored 1 if vote for candidate listed first, and 0 for candidate(s) listed second. The attitudinal and participation variables are continuous variables. The other variables are dummy variables that scored 1 if respondent had characteristic , 0 otherwise. Rural refers to community size less than 10,000. Rich refers to family income over $75,000.
* Significance at .05 level.
† Statistically significant at .01 level.

whereas populism was strongly negative. These trends held for the second ballot, albeit with a general weakening of the impact of the predictors. It is interesting to compare determinants of support for Mitchell with those for Klein (from Table 3.7). Whereas "moralism" and residence in Edmonton were both positive factors for Mitchell, they were negative for Klein. Also, whereas populism was negative for Mitchell, it was strongly positive for Klein. Thus, it is apparent that when Klein eventually faced off against Mitchell in the provincial election of 1997, voters were given a choice between strikingly different leaders, with very different bases of support, and representing differences both of style and of substance.

Assessments of the Process of Tele-Voting

The final component of our analysis of the Alberta Liberal tele-vote reports the opinions of our respondents on tele-voting and the rules used to put it into practice in this instance: respondents were asked to assess various elements of the tele-voting mechanism that was used in the leadership contest (see Table 4.9). Overall, the data indicate a rather mixed assessment, exhibiting considerable support for tele-voting, mixed with some serious reservations. A strong majority of voters (57%) favoured the continued use of

Table 4.9

Assessments of the process of tele-voting

	Yes	No
1. Is tele-voting better than conventions?	56.5	43.5
2. Did the new system change the local constituency tradition?	77.2	22.8
3. Did you have enough information to make an informed choice?	84.5	15.5
4. Was the outcome of the contest different because of the tele-vote?	50.8	49.2
5. Was it OK for people to vote by proxy?	23.1	76.9

	Too High	Too Low	Just Right
6. Was the $10 fee too high?	18.8	2.6	76.9

	Yes	No
7. Should the government limit the money spent on leadership races?	81.6	18.4
8. Should the names of financial contributors be disclosed?	80.1	19.9

	No Effect	More Likely	Less Likely
9. Should the tele-vote process affect the likelihood of people working for the party in the next election?	72.6	8.3	19.2

	Yes	No
10. Did you know a help line existed?	64.9	35.1
11. (If yes to 10) Did you try to access the help line?	50.5	49.5
12. (If yes to 11) Did you receive help from someone on the help line?	65.1	34.9

tele-voting over a return to conventions. In view of the controversy surrounding the Liberal tele-vote, the persistence of majority support in favour of tele-voting is surprising. In addition, over three-quarters of the respondents felt that the new system changed the constituency tradition in their constituency, but apparently many thought this change was for the better. Furthermore, 85% felt they had enough information to make an informed choice. Again, this is a somewhat surprising result in view of our earlier finding that most did not attend the candidate speeches nor the candidate events, and that most were not contacted by the majority of the candidates.

The respondents were almost evenly split in their assessment of whether the outcome of the contest was altered by the use of the tele-vote. Since Mitchell was expected to win the contest, and to win more readily than he did, perhaps respondents were focusing more on the closeness of the contest or the relative position of the second-, third-, and fourth-place finishers, rather than on the winning candidacy of Mitchell. The harshest criticism of the tele-voting process, not surprisingly, concerns the use of proxies. Over three-quarters of respondents thought it was a mistake for the party to allow the use of proxies, a position subscribed to by most of the candidates as well. Although it would appear that the party chose to allow proxies so that those who would be out of the province during the contest could cast a ballot, in actuality this decision provided an important loophole that could be used to circumvent the more deliberative character that many have come to expect in elections.

On financial matters, most respondents considered the ten-dollar registration fee appropriate, although about one in six thought it was too high. Interestingly, there is very strong support in the party for tighter regulation of the financing of leadership contests. Over 80% felt the government should impose a spending limit on leadership contests, although we do not know if respondents felt the $250,000 limit set by the party was appropriate. Furthermore, 80% of respondents also believed that the names of financial contributors to leadership contests should be publicly disclosed. This latter perspective was one of the recommendations of the federal Royal Commission on Electoral Reform (1991), although to date it has not been implemented for leadership contests either federally or in Alberta. Indeed, the Liberal Party refused to publicly release data it required candidates to submit on their expenses and contributors.

Conclusions

There is little about the Alberta Liberal leadership selection process that merits recommendation. The vote raises questions about the viability of tele-voting as a means for electing leaders. The tele-voting process has had mixed results in its applications by provincial parties. While most of the votes have gone rather smoothly, there have been real disasters. The possibility of a disaster raises serious concerns for parties seeking a mechanism for choosing their leader. The technology involved in tele-voting has yet to become sufficiently advanced that parties can employ it without fear. Problems similar to those leading to the cancellation of the 6 June 1992 Nova Scotia Liberal tele-vote plagued the Alberta Liberals, and both of these processes were marred by rumours that losing candidates might launch lawsuits. Germain graphically describes the impact of tele-voting on the Liberal Party, claiming that "we were road kill on the technological highway" (personal interview).

While tele-voting has much to answer for, MT&T and the tele-voting process do not bear full responsibility for the Liberal difficulties in Alberta. The party itself must shoulder a portion of the blame. The controversy over registration, and the rumours that thousands of registrations would be invalidated, generated a good deal of negative publicity and ensured that the failure to carry through with a substantial number of invalidations would lead to questions about the integrity of the process. The rules for invalidating registrations were obviously unclear, and for that the party bears full responsibility.

The issue of registration raises issues concerning the security of tele-voting systems. It is obvious that not all of those who registered paid for their own registrations. That such an eventuality would result seems inevitable in retrospect and probably should have been predicted in advance.[30] Tele-voting affords no guarantee that the vote will be cast by the person requesting the PIN. The security measures that apparently alert those supervising when more than five calls come from a single phone seem inadequate.[31] If a candidate has a volunteer base of close to 1,000, those individuals could cast 5,000 votes without detection. Since the number of people voting for the two front-runners was significantly lower than the number of registrations they turned in, it seems that such a strategy might recommend itself to future candidates. If a candidate organization was successful in collecting PINs from the individuals it registers, concerns over turnout would evaporate. Candidates whose supporters are eager to participate themselves may thus be somewhat disadvantaged in terms of ensuring turnout.

Registering voters and turning out those you register were obviously critical to the outcome. The candidates who did not turn in many registrations were simply not competitive. The Alberta experience leads one to conclude that campaign strategies that focus on policy debate, or target long-time party members, are almost certainly less likely to lead to victory than is a strategy focusing solely on recruitment and turning out the vote. The tele-vote, with its proven ability to mobilize fewer voters than paper universal ballots, makes such a strategy even more attractive.[32]

The ten-dollar registration fee seems not to have served much of a purpose beyond helping the party defray the costs of the exercise. The fee probably discouraged many members of the party from registering and depressed the size of the electorate (see Stewart, Adamson, and Beaton 1994). Yet, the fee was sufficiently low to make it relatively painless for a campaign to ensure that the costs of registrations for interested voters were covered.[33] Indeed, this was not even prohibited by the rules and provides yet another means by which well-financed candidates were advantaged. The decision of the erstwhile Saskatchewan Conservatives later in 1994 to issue PINs to all members of the party seems to be a step forward. Not only does it permit fuller participation by individuals unwilling to pay a special fee for their participation, but it also provides more meaning to party membership.

Under the rules utilized by the party in 1994, membership possessed little cachet. Registration equalled membership, and both could be undertaken at the same time. The many thousands of Albertans who had perhaps been members of the party for years, but who did not purchase a PIN, were effectively removed from the selection of their party's leader. The failure of most Liberal members to register, despite a relatively low registration fee, suggests that there is little meaning inherent in a Liberal Party membership in Alberta.[34] The fact that the party gives its memberships away and does not necessarily cancel them provides another indication of the unimportance of membership. Indeed, unlike the previous Liberal tele-votes in Nova Scotia and British Columbia, prior membership did not even push Albertan members to the front of the queue for registration. At the very least, the ability to present tele-votes as examples of all-member votes is non-existent.

The participation of non-citizens and people who are not comfortable communicating in English raises serious questions about the nature of the Alberta Liberal leadership selection process. At the very least, it renders questionable any claim that the process is deliberative, as some candidates may find themselves unable to interact effectively with many registered voters. Since the selection of a party leader determines the short lists for premier, the ability of non-citizens to perhaps play an important role is also cause for concern. Providing a role for non-citizens in internal party elections is, however, a long-standing Liberal tradition, albeit one that cries for reconsideration in an era of universal ballots.

The Alberta Liberal election indicates that proxy voting is an idea whose time has not come. Proxy voting provisions were used in a way that the party had not anticipated, but perhaps should have. As Chadi indicated, proxy votes are guaranteed votes. Collecting proxies eliminates concerns over turnout, and the advantages of such votes to candidates is obvious. Phone problems do not affect proxies, and proxy voting may also make it easier for candidates to gain support from voters who have less interest in the process. They would not be required to turn out at a polling station or even to cast their vote by telephone. In fact, the existence of proxies may facilitate the registration of such voters. In the Alberta case, the use and treatment of proxies resulted in the defeat of the candidate for whom the most votes were "cast." Questions of legitimacy thus permeate the proxy issue.

A lack of transparency surrounded the process, and threats of lawsuits and requests for an investigation of the contest pushed the party to launch an inquiry. The one-person board of inquiry, Saskatchewan lawyer (and Liberal) Timothy Stodalka, was given full access to party documents and the freedom to interview whomever he wished. However, the report he issued was not released to the public. Liberal officials feared that the report would be misused by the Conservative government, but their failure to release the report raises serious questions about how effectively the party actually managed the process. At least some of the defeated candidates were unhappy with the inquiry, characterizing it as an attempt to make MT&T the "scapegoat," and as a "whitewash" (confidential interviews). The absence of transparency is also evident in the party's decision not to release publicly the reports candidates were forced to submit on their campaign expenditures and contributors (Section D). The requirement that such information be provided to the party seems to be one of the few ways in which the Liberal vote process appears superior to the Conservative universal ballot. The failure to disclose such information to the public vitiates much of this advantage.

Any evaluation of the Liberal leadership election must address the outcome. The impact of the process on the outcome in this case may, in the final analysis, have been limited. Grant Mitchell would probably have won the leadership regardless of how the leader was chosen. However, the process permitted Sine Chadi to come close to victory and see the door slammed in his face. Chadi's campaign recognized at an early point that the key to victory was registering voters. His campaign emphasis brought him within a whisper of victory. By the time the press became aware and critical of the mobilization strategies his campaign utilized, it was too late for other voters to register for the election. The electorate had already been determined. Chadi's failure to win stemmed not from his failure to register a sufficient number of voters, but rather from his failure to turn out sufficient numbers of those voters. If he had won, the party might have disintegrated. His near victory clearly reveals the ability of a well-financed "outsider" to mobilize support beyond traditional party lines. While this may be seen as bringing new constituencies to the party, it could also be considered as a movement of the party toward a looser coalition of supporters of the leader. The tele-vote seems somewhat more dangerous in this vein than a paper universal ballot. The campaign for the leadership devalued policy debate and placed a premium on organization. Such a campaign clearly favours candidates with either an established reputation or ample financial support.

Recall that in a discussion of the 1985 Alberta Conservative leadership convention, the conclusion was expressed that "Alberta Tories may provide important lessons for all Canadians on how not to select party leaders" (Archer and Hunziker 1992: 81). Our analysis of the Alberta Liberal leadership election suggests that on this dimension at least, the party, to its chagrin, has finally managed to eclipse its Tory competitors.

5
A Party of "Communities"? The 1994 NDP Leadership Convention

Innovations in choosing party leaders have not originated with the New Democratic Party. The Alberta NDP essentially chooses its leaders today in much the same manner as its Cooperative Commonwealth Federation (CCF) predecessor.[1] Thus, unlike the Alberta Liberals and Conservatives, Alberta's New Democrats, when faced with the need to choose a new leader in 1994, utilized the party's traditional convention method. Indeed, the Alberta wing of the party proved more resistant to increasing the role of ordinary members in the leadership selection process than even the federal party. In the 1995 federal leadership election, the party incorporated a series of advisory primaries allowing members in different regions and in the unions to express leadership preferences. In the end, the candidate who won the most votes in the primaries finished third at the convention. The New Democratic Party of Alberta has not been immune from the discussions of universal balloting that have affected its federal counterparts and the provincial Liberals and Conservatives. It has, however, explicitly rejected such a change. At its conventions in 1994 and 1995, the party debated and voted on measures that would have introduced some form of universal balloting. Indeed, at the 1994 convention, the Constitution and Party Affairs Committee presented proposals calling for a direct election of the leader. A two-thirds vote was required for modifying the provisions governing leadership elections, but in the end, not even a simple majority could be won.

The delegates voted to reject universal balloting and, in the debates on the subject, made much of the virtues of conventions. The virtues included their deliberative nature and the ability to involve youth and the labour wing of the party. No labour delegates spoke in favour of universal balloting, and it appeared that the imposition of such a system would be interpreted as a slap in the face for labour. A system of universal balloting could change the way the party operates and perceives itself, and such a change was not in the cards in 1994.

In this chapter, we examine the 1994 Alberta New Democratic leadership convention. Part of our focus is on identifying the party's core activists (the delegates) in terms of regional, demographic, and attitudinal characteristics. As well, an assessment of the background that delegates possessed in the party, and their involvement in the campaign, is presented. Attention is also given to an examination of the nature of voting divisions among the delegates. The analysis then focuses on some of the internal differences that are created or abetted by the convention process. In particular, we examine the background and beliefs of the delegates who directly represent labour at the convention. We also identify those delegates who participate in one or more of the party's caucuses and compare them to their counterparts who lack such a group opportunity. Finally, the chapter addresses the issue of universal balloting and identifies the groups at the convention who were hostile to the idea of the party moving in this direction. In so doing, it further discusses the role of the party's "communities."

Leadership Selection in the New Democratic Party

Leadership selection in the New Democratic Party has always been different from that of the other Alberta parties, and the portraits of leadership conventions that flow through much of the literature do not fully capture the reality of NDP selections (Whitehorn 1988). For the New Democrats, the election of the leader takes place as part of each convention. As such, there are no separate leadership conventions called only for that purpose, and even sitting leaders can be challenged at regular party conventions. Leadership conventions in the New Democratic Party have not traditionally involved the same sort of trench warfare that has marred recent Liberal and PC conventions, and NDP aspirants do not require access to the same level of financing. Moreover, the basis of representation at NDP conventions is different. Eschewing the equal representation of each constituency, which marks both federal and provincial Liberal and Conservative conventions, the New Democrats base convention representation on the size of constituency membership. Simply put, the more members a constituency association possesses, the more delegates it is entitled to send to a convention. Heated contests for these spaces are rare because constituencies often have problems filling their allotments. Additionally, unions affiliated with the party are entitled to delegate spaces, again tied to their membership size, as are central bodies of affiliated organizations. In addition, the New Democratic Youth, Women's caucus, and Aboriginal caucus are entitled to send delegates. Ex-officio representation is restricted to members of the NDP provincial council, members of the federal NDP executive who reside in Alberta, and elected members of caucus.[2] The New Democratic convention thus differs from Liberal and Conservative conventions in the presence of labour delegates, the unequal representation of constituencies, a relatively small number of youth delegates, a relatively small number of ex-officio delegates, and a relatively small number of delegates who had to win a contest in order to attend. As a result, the party's convention bears some similarity to systems of universal balloting. At NDP conventions, youth members are not present in sufficient numbers to have a significant impact, and the regional balance that is such a celebrated element in other conventions is absent.

The Campaign in Context

The leadership election in 1994, which was the first contested leadership vote since 1968, was held in discouraging circumstances. The party was devastated in the 1993 election, falling from official opposition status and sixteen MLAs to the status of "also-rans" with no elected members. Moreover, its share of the popular vote fell from 26% in 1989 to just 11% in 1993. Not surprisingly in the light of such a setback, the leader, Ray Martin, stepped down, and a convention was scheduled at which a new leader was to be chosen. Given the results of the provincial and federal elections in 1993, there were no elected New Democrats in Alberta to contest the leadership.

The 1994 leadership convention was destined to provide only temporary leadership to the party. At the party's next convention in 1995, the 1994 victor faced a leadership challenge, and although he was victorious, indications were clear that many in the party were unhappy over the party's inability to influence Alberta politics. By the time of the next convention in September 1996, the leader had read the handwriting on the wall and stepped down. Thus, the 1994 winner did not survive to contest even one election.

Of course, these events were unforeseen in February 1994. The party was disappointed by its electoral setback and was engaged in an internal review. Indeed, the 1994 convention opened with a resolution suggesting that the party not elect a leader, but rather focus on questions of organization and policy. This resolution was rejected, but the party did spend part of the convention in workshops that attempted to assess the future of the party. The leadership contest reflected the discussions of party renewal, as questions regarding the role of unions and caucuses in the party and the emphasis the party should place on education (versus electability) were debated.

Eventually, four candidates sought the leadership. The first entrant, and eventual winner, was Ross Harvey of Edmonton. Harvey had previously served as a researcher for the provincial caucus and emerged as a well-known public figure in 1988, when he became the first New Democrat in Alberta elected to the federal House of Commons. Harvey was supported by most prominent New Democrats, and his victory bears some similarities to the "Coronation" model outlined by Morley (1992: 132-3).[3] His three challengers had all contested the 1993 provincial election, but were, nonetheless, relative unknowns in Alberta politics. The challengers appeared to appeal to different segments of the party. Bruce Hinkley, from central Alberta's Wetaskiwin, was quite critical of the party and, in particular, raised questions about the role of unions and caucuses within the NDP. Lawrence Johnson, a young candidate from Stoney Plain (just outside of Edmonton), appealed to the youth wing and focused his campaign on the need to involve youth more directly in the party. The final candidate, Clancy Teslenko of Calgary, entered the contest only at the convention itself, and presented a strong defence of the role of unions within the party, while also stressing the need for the party to educate the public.

The contest took place in relative obscurity. Indeed, for much of the campaign there was no contest. It was not until the week before the convention that Hinkley and Johnson entered and, as mentioned above, Teslenko's candidacy was launched at the convention itself. The press paid virtually no attention to the party. In the two weeks preceding the convention, the *Edmonton Journal* published only four articles on the contest. By way of contrast, in the two weeks preceding the Conservative contest of 1992, there were forty articles, and the Liberal tele-vote of 1994 was preceded by sixteen articles. The lack of interest in the election was mirrored to a degree within the party itself. Only one of the eighty-three constituency associations sent its full complement of representatives to the convention, and labour sent less than half of its entitlement. Delegate spots were obviously available for the asking, as only 1% of the delegates admitted to facing a contest for their seat.

The absence of media attention and competition for delegate spots may have owed to a lack of suspense regarding the outcome. Ninety-four percent of the delegates indicated that they expected Harvey to win the leadership, and he did not disappoint. Harvey romped to an easy victory, securing 230 of the 422 votes cast (56%). The other candidates trailed well behind and were tightly bunched: Hinkley with 69 votes (17%), Johnson with 58 (14%), and Teslenko with 54 (13%).[4]

Identifying the Delegates

The 1994 convention demonstrated the peculiar nature of NDP conventions. Seventy-seven percent of the delegates represented constituency associations, 11% represented labour, and 6% represented the provincial executive, leaving only 6% from other categories, half of whom were life members of the party ("Convention 1993": 1). The small number of labour delegates somewhat masks the influence of labour in the party, as 30% of the delegates were members of a collective bargaining unit.

Delegates also demonstrated the degree to which the Alberta New Democrats are an urban party. In terms of regional representation, just over one-third of the delegates came from the Edmonton area, and just under one-third came from Calgary (see Table 5.1). Rural Alberta was poorly represented,

Table 5.1

_____

NDP delegate profile

	Total (%) N = 220	Union delegate (%) N = 19	Caucus goer (%) N = 107	Other (%) N = 94
Edmonton	34	42	33	25
Calgary	31	47	32	37
Hometown over 500,000	61	79	62	57
Hometown 1,000 or less	9	5	9	10
Women	49	21	57	45
Age > 65	11	0	8	17
Age < 25	9	0	11	7
Completed university	48	16	48	54
Less than high school	13	16	13	14
Family income < $30,000	29	22	30	31
Family income > $70,000	23	33	20	23
Businessperson	6	5	6	7
Farmer	2.5	0	1	5
Professional or white collar	38	33	40	37
Blue collar	12	58	7	6
Clerical/Sales	7	5	7	6
Employed in private sector	53	42	49	60
Retired	20	0	20	23
Student	9	0	11	7
Protestant	41	35	45	40
No religion	37	35	34	41
British origin	58	39	54	49
Other European	23	21	23	29
Non-European	8	11	7	11

with fewer than 10% of the delegates coming from areas with less than 1,000 residents.

The attendance of women at the 1994 New Democratic convention suggests that it is not conventions per se that account for the under-representation of women in Canada's parties. Women accounted for 49% of the delegate total, a figure unmatched in previous Liberal and Conservative conventions. There are obvious explanations for this equitable representation. First, the NDP has made a strong commitment to increasing the representation of women, and this may simply be one manifestation of that commitment. Second, Bashevkin's (1993) indication that the more competitive the position, the fewer women are involved, may have some bearing. The New Democrats were at a very low ebb in the party's fortunes, and the inability of most delegations to fill their entitlements might have increased the proportion of women. Recall that only 1% of the delegates said they had faced a contest to become a delegate. The second explanation carries more weight when one notes that federal party conventions have not displayed the same gender balance.[5]

Similarly, the New Democrats presented a distinctive face with respect to age. As the figures presented on delegate type reveal, only a handful of delegates directly represented youth. The proportion of youth was not increased substantially by their inclusion as part of other delegations, since only 9% of the delegates were under the age of twenty-five.[6] By way of contrast, almost one delegate in five claimed to be retired.

The New Democrat delegates presented a portrait familiar to those acquainted with the federal party in terms of education and income (see Archer 1991: 11). Almost three-quarters possessed some level of post-secondary education, and 47% held university degrees. Their income levels did not match their education, with 29% possessing family incomes of less than $30,000, and only 23% reporting incomes in excess of $70,000.

In terms of occupation, the New Democrat delegates revealed few connections to either the business or agricultural communities. Only 6% claimed to be owners, managers, or employees of a small business. An even smaller proportion were employed in farming (only 2.5%). Over a third of the delegates reported professional occupations, and 11% indicated that they held "blue collar" jobs. A relatively large proportion of the delegates were retired (20%), another 9% were students, and 5% of the delegates were unemployed.[7]

The party delegates resembled New Democratic delegates at the federal level and in other provinces with respect to their religious affiliations (see Blake, Carty, and Erickson 1991: 26). A plurality (37%) indicated that they had no religious affiliation, and only 15% were Catholic. This left the New Democratic assembly more representative of those with no religion than the province as a whole, and less representative of Catholics. Finally, the New Democrats were also somewhat more British than the province, with 58% of the delegates describing their ethnic origin as British.

Archer and Whitehorn have demonstrated the high degree of policy consensus among delegates to federal NDP conventions (1996: 164). A similar level of consensus existed among the Alberta NDP delegates in 1994. When we look at the twenty attitudinal questions asked in each of our surveys, we see a high degree of consensus among the New Democrats (see Appendix 2). Their average score on the Consensus Index was 31, almost twice as high as the scores recorded by the Liberals and Conservatives. On thirty-four of the forty attitudinal questions asked of New Democratic delegates, the percentage taking the same position was greater than 70%. The only area where substantial disagreement existed among the delegates related to populism (see Table 5.2).

Table 5.2

Opinion indices: Mean scores of New Democrats

	Total $N = 220$	Union delegate $N = 19$	Caucus goer $N = 107$	Other $N = 94$
Individualism	0.19	0.21	0.17	0.25
Populism	1.86	2.2	1.8	1.8
Continentalism	0.32	0.79	0.28	0.32
Social policy	2.71	2.5	2.5	2.3
Moral issues	1.87	1.8	1.8	1.8
Pro-union	1.9	3.4	2.2	1.5
Self-placement	2.2	1.7	2.2	2.4

As one would expect, the consensus expressed within the party appears somewhat left wing. The scales created to examine opinion within the party demonstrated a consensus that was hostile to continentalism (76%), non-individualistic (82%), heavily in favour of social spending (81%) and heavily liberal on moral issues (82%). Only on issues regarding populism was there substantial disagreement within the party, with 18% of the delegates giving no populist responses, and 32% of the party responding in a populist fashion to three of the four questions. In short, aside from questions regarding the participation of ordinary people directly in politics, there was widespread agreement among NDP delegates and, even in "conservative" Alberta, this consensus was rather left wing.[8]

The delegates to the 1994 convention demonstrated the basis for one of the arguments against the participation of all members in the leadership selection process, namely the desirability of leadership choices decided by a convention electorate possessing an extensive party pedigree. These delegates were very well-grounded in the party. Although this was the first convention for a fifth of the delegates, most delegates were not party neophytes. Only 1% reported joining the party in the last year, and 41% had been members for more than ten years (see Table 5.3). Sixty percent of the delegates had at some point served on a provincial constituency executive, 78% had raised funds for the party, and 92% of the delegates had worked for the party in a provincial election campaign. Indeed, one-fifth of the delegates had actually run in provincial elections as candidates. In short, this was a gathering of the party faithful, in a way that the Conservative and Liberal leadership elections were not.

Also reassuring to opponents of universal balloting (see Chapters 3 and 4) was the involvement of the delegates in the leadership campaign. Almost one delegate in three actually worked on the campaign of one of the candidates,

Table 5.3

NDP background

	Total (%) N = 220	Union delegate (%) N = 19	Caucus goer (%) N = 107	Other (%) N = 94
Member < 1 year	1	0	0	2
Member > 10 years	41	44	42	38
Constituency executive	60	37	60	64
Raised funds	78	58	83	75
Worked on campaign	92	74	96	90
Candidate	20	11	22	21

82% met a candidate during the campaign, and 69% felt they had enough information to make an informed decision. There were a number of events at the convention dealing with the leadership race, and 63% of the delegates pronounced themselves satisfied with these events. As earlier chapters have shown, this level of participation is absent in universal ballots.

One of the other striking differences between an NDP convention and universal ballots is the opportunity to participate as part of a group or caucus. In 1994, the meetings of the various party caucuses were not particularly well attended. The women's caucus turned out the largest proportion of delegates, with about 30% of the delegates attending. Almost one delegate in four attended the labour caucus, but no more than 7% of the delegates participated in the remaining caucuses. Nonetheless, 56% of the delegates attended at least one of the caucuses. It is thus possible to divide the New Democrats into the two separate categories of those who attend the caucuses and those who do not. As we will see, this division has some significance for both leadership choice and reform of the leadership selection process.

Delegates attending the 1994 Calgary convention were well aware that they and their party were not representative of the views of ordinary Alberta voters. On a seven-point ideological left/right scale, most delegates placed themselves well left of the midpoint, with an average self-placement of 2.2. These same delegates rated their fellow Albertans at 5.7. Interestingly, the delegates saw themselves as more leftist than the party as a whole, which they rated near the midpoint, at 3.3. Ideologically, the delegates placed themselves well to the left of most Albertans and well to the left of their own party.

Although the delegates recognized that their views did not necessarily reflect the views of most Albertans, they were reluctant to blame the party itself for the electoral debacle of 1993. When asked whether a number of factors were important to the party's 1993 results, the items upon which

Table 5.4

Delegate views on reform of NDP

	Total (%) N = 220	Union delegates (%) N = 19	Caucus goers (%) N = 107	Other (%) N = 94
Party caucuses have too much power*	40	33	32	51
All members should vote for the leader*	55	21	51	77
Revised policies attract voters	53	58	49	55
Party must not move too far left	38	33	35	43
Political education should be the party's focus	48	37	53	44
Electoral support from organized interests compromises the party*	41	22	41	43
Weaken the party's ties with labour*	28	11	29	32
Principle has precedence over electoral success	55	63	56	54
Change the name of the party	18	21	12	24
Close nominations before the convention opens*	52	26	52	58

* Values of X^2 significant at the .05 level.

the delegates expressed the most agreement were the appeal of Ralph Klein, strategic voting for the Liberals, and the media's coverage of the campaign. None of these factors were within the party's control. Thus, while the convention took place in the midst of disappointment, the need for significant change was not obvious to the delegates.

The absence of support for substantial change within the party is further evidenced by the views of delegates regarding a number of internal party issues. Delegates were overwhelmingly hostile to weakening the nature of the party's ties to labour, to the notion of revising policies in order to secure more popular support, and to changing the name of the party (see Table 5.4). In contrast to their views on politics more broadly, the delegates appear rather conservative with respect to changing the party itself, even in the context of an electoral setback of unprecedented proportions.

Voting Divisions among the Delegates

An examination of voting at the New Democratic leadership convention must begin with the acknowledgment of Harvey's overwhelming dominance (see Table 5.5). Most delegates voted for him, and most delegates ranked him as their first preference. There was, however, less than all-encompassing enthusiasm for him. After the convention, more than two-fifths of the delegates admitted that they would rather have seen someone other than Harvey

Table 5.5

Selected regional, demographic, and partisan factor by vote

	Harvey (%) N = 127	Hinkley (%) N = 39	Johnson (%) N = 21	Teslenko (%) N = 22
Edmonton*	68	13	14	6
Calgary*	61	6	11	20
Central Alberta*	33	53	7	7
Hometown over 500,000*	66	9	12	13
Hometown under 1,000*	47	37	11	5
Member of bargaining unit*	59	13	5	24
Union delegate*	68	5	0	26
Caucus goer*	65	12	13	11
Non-caucus goer*	55	30	9	7
Age > 65*	79	9	12	0
Age < 25*	29	29	41	0
Retired*	81	11	8	0
Student*	29	18	47	6
Businessperson*	33	42	25	0
Professional/White collar*	67	15	4	14
Blue collar*	59	9	5	27
Protestant*	73	15	5	7
No religion*	45	22	16	16
Catholic*	56	26	4	15

* Values of X^2 significant at the .05 level.

as party leader. This lack of enthusiasm undoubtedly contributed to the chain of events that saw Harvey challenged at the next convention and saw him step down before he had to face the delegates again in 1996. Those who did not support Harvey remained unconvinced at convention close that he would be a good leader.

As in so many leadership elections in Canada, regional differences in the candidates' support patterns were clear.[9] These divisions reflected a "friends and neighbours" dimension in the NDP vote. Hinkley was actually able to win a majority of the votes cast by the delegates from central Alberta, the region in which his hometown of Wetaskiwin is located. Similarly, Teslenko's best showing came from Calgary-area voters, while Harvey and Johnson both received their highest support levels from the Edmonton area. The weakness of rural Alberta is revealed in more than just the limited number of delegates – delegates from the smallest villages in the province offered the lowest levels of support to Harvey.

The division of delegates into union representatives, those who attended caucuses and those who did not, provides further insight into the nature of the 1994 New Democratic leadership vote (see Table 5.6). As one would expect, given the nature of Hinkley's campaign, the direct participation of delegates representing labour weakened Hinkley's candidacy. He polled his strongest support among the delegates representing constituency associations, whereas his support from local unions and central labour was non-existent. And he received more than twice as much support from the delegates who did not attend caucuses as he did from those who participated in such gatherings.

Delegates directly representing labour were crucial to Teslenko's candidacy. She was able to win more than a quarter of the votes cast by these delegates and almost a quarter of the votes cast by delegates who were members of bargaining units, but trailed all the other candidates among other delegates. Johnson received no support from union delegates, but fared relatively well with caucus goers, primarily because of the majority support he received from those attending the youth caucus. Harvey's highest support levels came from union delegates, while his lowest support levels came from the youth caucus and from those who did not participate in the caucuses. Only among delegates who attended the youth caucus was he unable to secure a majority.[10] In summary, Hinkley did particularly well among those New Democrats who did not participate in a caucus, garnering more than 30% of the vote. He was the only candidate who drew disproportionate support from voters in this category. Among those who attended a caucus, Harvey's vote share increased dramatically and Hinkley ranked last.[11]

Delegates who represented labour directly, or who were members of unions themselves, made Teslenko's candidacy credible, while at the same time ensuring that Hinkley's candidacy attracted only a handful more votes. In essence, the strong pro-labour element in the party was almost as numerous as the element wishing to rethink labour's involvement.

The social demographic variables appeared to exert a modest impact on voting. Age was an important dimension in support for Johnson, as he ac-

Table 5.6

Party caucuses: Attendance, support for universal balloting, and vote

	Attend $N = 220$	Support UB (%)	Harvey $N = 127$	Johnson $N = 22$	Teslenko $N = 21$	Hinkley $N = 39$
Women's	30	46	66	8	15	11
Labour	24	33	64	6	20	10
Green	14	38	72	7	3	17
Youth	7	71	21	57	7	14
Left	7	31	50	0	36	14
Regional	6	40	75	17	0	8
Municipal	4	29	75	13	0	13
None	43	55	55	9	7	7

tually received plurality support from the handful of delegates under twenty-five. Harvey's support was strongest among those over sixty-five. Social class further revealed the nature of Teslenko's support, with half of her support coming from the one-fifth of delegates who identified themselves as working or lower class (a relatively small group at party conventions, even NDP conventions). Occupational categories confirmed some of the age results, with Johnson winning a plurality from students, and Harvey's strongest results coming from those who were retired. Hinkley's best showings came from a group that was relatively small, those involved in business. He split their support with Harvey, but these individuals accounted for only 9% of the delegate total. Along with the retired, self-employed professionals were disproportionate Harvey supporters. Teslenko also polled well with this group, as she did with self-described blue-collar workers.

Additionally, religion was significantly associated with voting, with Harvey receiving disproportionate support from those who were Protestant or non-Christian. Somewhat interestingly, his weakest results were from those with no religious affiliation.

The background of delegates within the party had only a limited impact on voting. Harvey received similar levels of support regardless of whether delegates had worked for the party in the past, ran as a provincial candidate, or served on either constituency or provincial executives. There was, however, some indication that the fact that the convention was composed primarily of long-time party members was of some aid to Harvey. Delegates who had held membership in the party for less than two years proved less enthusiastic about Harvey, and he failed to secure a majority from delegates of this sort. In contrast, the delegates who had been members for more than ten years were his staunchest backers, with more than 70% voting for him. Support for Hinkley revealed the reverse pattern. His support peaked with short-term members and trailed off as the length of party membership increased. His message of changing the way the party operated was obviously unwelcome. A scale measuring involvement produced insignificant results; however, one should note that Hinkley's candidacy was strongest among the delegates possessing the most limited party background.

The convention process within the NDP appears not to provide extensive opportunities for new members to participate, and the absence of such a role may discourage citizens from taking out membership in the party. Also, notably, the presence of such a large proportion of party veterans weakened the candidacies of Hinkley and Johnson.

An analysis of voting within the party reveals that attitudinal disagreement did play a certain role. On the five scales outlined above, significant differences could be detected on three. Largely what one encounters here is the degree to which Hinkley and Johnson appealed to a small portion of the party. In each case, their highest level of support came from a minority

Table 5.7

Mean score of candidate's supporters on opinion indices

	Harvey $N = 127$	Hinkley $N = 39$	Teslenko $N = 22$	Johnson $N = 21$
Individualism	0.20	0.25	0.23	0.19
Populism	1.77	2.25	1.95	1.24
Continentalism*	0.26	0.30	0.50	0.30
Social policy*	1.83	1.55	1.95	1.76
Moral issues	1.83	1.83	1.77	1.81
Pro-union*	2.12	0.82	2.82	1.30
Self-placement*	2.2	2.8	1.4	2.4

* Values of X^2 significant at the .05 level.

disposition. For instance, they did best among those who held populist views, who were opposed to social spending, and who were more open to ties with the United States. Given the overall balance of opinion within the party, these were not positions that could lead to victory.

Supporters of the various candidates placed themselves somewhat differently on the seven point left/right scale (see Table 5.7). Teslenko voters were found exclusively in the two most left-wing placements and recorded a mean score of 1.4. Hinkley supporters anchored the right wing with almost one in four, placing themselves right of the midpoint. Nevertheless, their mean score was well to the left of the scale's midpoint (3.5) at 2.7. Supporters of Harvey and Johnson were clustered around the mean for the total delegate body (2.2) at 2.2 and 2.4 respectively. The self-placement of the voters lends further credence to the portrait of Harvey as a centrist candidate (within the NDP anyway) challenged by more left-wing and right-wing candidates. The degree to which delegates viewed Hinkley as right wing is striking. His mean placement by delegates on the seven-point scale was 4.8, well to the right of the midpoint.

There were also some significant differences with respect to opinion on matters internal to the New Democratic Party. Hinkley drew more than four-fifths of his support from those who felt that the caucuses had too much power within the party, that the party needed to revise its policies in order to attract voters, and that the party's support from organized interests compromises party operation. The peculiar tint of Hinkley's support with respect to the role of unions in the party can also be seen in the absence of support for him among those who were members of a bargaining unit or who attended the labour caucus. Moreover, he received strong support from those who felt that union ties were harmful to the party and those who wanted to weaken the ties between the NDP and unions. In short, it is evident that Hinkley's supporters were rather critical of the status quo within the New Democrats and wanted the party to change both its policies and its relationship with labour. These positions were rejected by an overwhelming majority of New Democratic delegates, and by the time the next election came in 1997, Hinkley was out of the party.[12]

A scale that attempts to measure the commitment of delegates to the involvement of labour within the party (Pro-Union) further illustrates this division. Delegates who attended the labour caucus believed that ties with unions were beneficial, that these ties should be strengthened, and that it was important that their candidate had the ability to strengthen ties with labour, scored a four. Delegates with none of these characteristics received a score of zero. Among the anti-union delegates, who comprised about a fifth of the delegate total, were half of Hinkley's supporters, and he actually tied Harvey among this group. Among the two-fifths of the voters scoring a three or four, Hinkley received the support of just 2%. In contrast, 73% of Teslenko's supporters were in this category.

Support for Johnson is harder to identify along attitudinal lines. In fact, it is abundantly clear that Johnson had an even weaker base within the party than Hinkley. Johnson was concerned with the role of youth in the party, and he received disproportionate support from those who attended the youth caucus or were under the age of twenty-five. Like those who supported Hinkley, Johnson's supporters tended to have less positive assessments of the role of labour within the party, and his support from union members and the labour caucus was extremely sparse.

The contrast with Teslenko's support was sharp. Teslenko's candidacy stands in polar opposition to Hinkley's. Her strong showing after declaring her candidacy only at the convention itself served as a warning that attempts to mollify Hinkley and his supporters might have undesirable consequences. Teslenko's support came disproportionately from those who were members of a bargaining unit, who believed that union ties were very beneficial to the party, and who wanted to strengthen the party's ties with labour. A quarter of her support came from the 10% of the delegates who represented organized labour, skewed toward those who represented local unions. It may well have been the case that her candidacy indicated a certain lack of faith in Harvey's ability or willingness to defend the role of labour in the party from detractors such as Hinkley. At any rate, her candidacy was an obvious signal to Harvey not to take labour for granted.

A multivariate analysis examining the determinants of support for Harvey revealed few significant factors.[13] The single significant attitudinal scale was feminism, which had a positive impact on support for Harvey. All other attitudinal variables, and all demographic variables, displayed no significant impact (see Table 5.8). These data suggest that, at least at the time of the convention, Ross Harvey was not the candidate of only a segment of the party. Instead, his support was drawn more broadly across the party's various groupings. However, as events following the convention would show,

Table 5.8

Multiple determinants of New Democrat leadership choice

	Harvey vs. others
Rural	-.07
Pro-welfare	.15
Male	.01
Populism	.01
Rich	-.03
Edmonton	.11
Individualism	.20
Feminism	.48*
University degree	.01
Pro-government	-.01
Constant	.01
R-squared	.07

Notes: Table entries are regression coefficients. Dependent variables are dummy variables that scored 1 if vote for candidate listed first and 0 for candidate(s) listed second. The attitudinal and participation variables are continuous variables. The other variables are dummy variables that scored 1 if respondent had characteristic, 0 otherwise. Rural refers to community size less than 10,000. Rich refers to family income over $75,000.
* Statistically significant at .05 level.

various groups within the party were less than enthusiastic in their support for Harvey, and eventually he relinquished the leadership without ever leading the party into a provincial election.

A Party of Communities?

Organizationally, and in terms of self-perception, the New Democratic Party differs from its traditional opponents. One of the major differences is the direct representation of affiliated organizations, particularly labour. Another difference is the opportunity to participate in recognized caucuses that represent areas of special concern or interest. Those representing labour and those participating in caucuses represent "communities" within the party. In this part of the chapter, we will explore these communities and investigate how their presence affects the party. The examination of voting reveals how differences on this dimension affected leadership choice.

The most notable community within the New Democratic Party is, of course, labour. The role and position of labour within the party is a matter of some internal debate. New Democrats are quick to point out that they are not a labour party, and they are correct. Delegates directly representing labour at the party's convention in 1994 were a distinct minority.[14] This, however, somewhat underestimates the role of organized labour within the party. The labour caucus at the convention was not a caucus of just those directly representing affiliated unions. Indeed, more than half of those in attendance represented constituency associations. Overall, almost one delegate in five was a member of a union executive, almost one delegate in three belonged to a collective bargaining unit, and more than 45% had a family member who was a union member. The New Democratic Party delegates, then, had a much greater involvement with the union movement than is true of Albertans in general.

The presence of delegates directly representing affiliated unions has some impact on the overall delegate profile. As Table 5.1 reveals, union delegates were overwhelmingly drawn from Alberta's two largest cities and were disproportionately male. These delegates, like delegates to national NDP conventions,[15] also stand out with respect to education and income. Union delegates were least likely to have completed a university degree and most likely to report family incomes of more than $70,000. As well, virtually all of the delegates who reported their occupation as blue collar represented unions, and the presence of these delegates somewhat reduced the level of representation of both the retired and of students. The union delegates were also less likely than other members to have served on a constituency executive, to have raised funds for the party, to have worked on a campaign, or to have contested an election (see Table 5.3).

What is also clear is that the presence of so many delegates with ties to the union movement exerts an impact on the operation and decisions of the party. As demonstrated above, delegates who belonged to collective-bargaining units accounted for two-thirds of Teslenko's support and were disproportionately unlikely to support either Hinkley or Johnson. Moreover, those who attended the labour caucus comprised almost half of Teslenko's supporters and were also somewhat more likely to support Harvey.

Finally, 50% of Teslenko's supporters were delegates who were at the convention to directly represent labour, while none of Johnson's supporters and only 3% of Hinkley's support came from this category. Harvey received his highest level of support from delegates representing central labour. Labour's role in the leadership election was two-fold. First, it accounted for Teslenko's candidacy and ensured that there was a candidate who wished to see labour's role within the party enhanced. Second, it limited Harvey's ability to reach out to delegates who had concerns about the nature of labour's involvement in the party.

Labour also had a substantial impact on the party's decision to preserve the convention as the mechanism for choosing the party's leader. Overwhelming opposition from the delegates selected to represent labour, and those who attended the labour caucus, combined with the support of a minority of constituency delegates to defeat any movement to universal balloting. Labour delegates, and their allies within the party, undoubtedly (and correctly) interpreted such a move as likely to diminish labour's role within the party.

As in the national party, the views of union delegates were largely similar to those of their non-union colleagues (Archer and Whitehorn 1993: 13). Although some within the party historically expressed the fear that the presence of labour delegates would move the party to the right (the "Waffle" movement for instance),[16] this was not the case in Alberta in 1994. The delegates directly representing organized labour were much more likely to place themselves as either a one or a two on a seven-point ideological scale than were other delegates. The mean placement for union delegates was 1.7, compared to 2.3 for the other delegates. Moreover, a comparison of self-placement between those who attended the labour caucus and those who did not revealed no differences.

In general, the delegates representing labour did not differ dramatically from other delegates with respect to attitudes toward public policy. Not surprisingly, they scored higher on the pro-union scale than other delegates. They were also more likely to give populist responses and were somewhat more continentalist than other delegates, but the basic portrait that emerges is one of attitudinal agreement. The general consistency between the views of union delegates and others may be strengthened by the participation of delegates supportive of labour in other caucuses within the party. It is worth noting that labour's influence goes beyond its own caucus. Fifty-seven percent of those who attended labour's caucus also participated in other caucuses.

Labour is, of course, not the only community within the party, and an examination of those who participated in caucuses provides further insight into the NDP. Overall, the delegates who participated in caucuses were difficult to differentiate from those who did not. The most striking differences were in the areas of gender, age, and sector of employment. Caucus goers were more likely to be women, and only half as likely to be over sixty-five. As well, while 51% of those who attended the caucuses were employed in the public sector, the same was true of only 40% of those who did not.

Given the high degree of attitudinal consensus within the party, it would be surprising to find much division between caucus participants and non-participants in the caucus process. However, a perusal of Table 5.2 suggests that caucus goers may be somewhat more leftist than their counterparts. Non-caucus goers generally appear to the right of their caucus-attending colleagues and, indeed, they place themselves somewhat more to the right in terms of ideology. Nonetheless, their views are scarcely right wing, and similarities outweigh differences.

One area where there is a difference between caucus participants and others is with respect to the possibility of changing the party (see Table 5.4).

Caucus goers were more contented with the status quo within the party, and consequently, they were less enthusiastic about universal balloting. They were also less willing to change the party's name, to revise party policies to attract votes, and to weaken the party's ties with unions.

Logically, one might expect that those who participate in a caucus would be more likely to involve themselves in party activities more generally, but this was not the case. The delegates who did not attend the caucuses proved to be equally involved in the party. Most of them reported lengthy party memberships, had served on a constituency executive, raised funds, and worked for the party in an election campaign. Unquestionably, they did not take a back seat to caucus goers in their actions on behalf of the Alberta New Democrats.

Universal Balloting

Data from our survey reveal a discrepancy between the general views of delegates regarding universal balloting, and the decision of the convention to reject resolutions moving the party in that direction. Unlike the vote at the 1994 convention, respondents to our survey indicated majority support for the implementation of a leadership selection process in which all party members would vote directly for their leader.

At the convention, this notion was debated heatedly. Those in favour of such a switch made much of the need to empower ordinary members and give the grassroots a more direct voice in the party. They also suggested that the costs of attending a convention disenfranchised members of the party who were poor. Those supportive of the status quo countered with the standard argument about the deliberative nature of the convention. They also raised some concerns specific to the NDP. These concerns revolved around the role of members with group affiliations and how they could be integrated into a universal ballot. The president of the party indicated that universal balloting focuses on the individual, and the NDP, unlike other parties, is a party of communities. Her fear was that the universal ballot would weaken the role of these communities within the party.

Positions with respect to universal balloting were related to the voting results. Those who voted for Teslenko were overwhelmingly opposed to a universal balloting system, with more than 70% of them rejecting such an idea. Supporters of Hinkley were even more united in their advocacy of this notion, as more than 90% of his backers approved such a movement. Harvey's supporters were split almost down the middle on this issue, with 52% supporting a direct vote for all members.

The attitudes of Teslenko supporters on all-member votes reflect the degree to which her candidacy was dependent on labour. When attitudes on universal balloting were compared by delegate type, a clear trend was evident. The rejection of universal balloting was most pronounced among labour delegates. Seventy percent of the delegates representing affiliated unions rejected this movement, as did 88% of the delegates from central labour. In contrast, 65% of the delegates from constituency associations were in favour.

An examination of the attitudes of those who attended the labour caucus further reveals the degree to which the party's rejection of universal ballot-ing is based in the labour movement. Almost one delegate in four attended this caucus, and of this group, 67% rejected an all-member vote. The pro-portion of other delegates endorsing the move was also 67%. Our scale measuring attitudes toward the role of unions within the parties illustrates this point dramatically. As one moves from one end of the scale to the other, the percentage of delegates favouring all-member votes changes by 74 percentage points, with 89% of the anti-union voters supporting it, as opposed to just 15% of the pro-union voters.

Labour was not alone in rejecting the all-member vote. With the excep-tion of those who attended the youth caucus, caucus attenders rejected universal balloting. The proportion varied from 54% of those who attended the women's caucus to 69% of those who attended the left caucus. Overall, more than three-quarters of the delegates who did not participate in a cau-cus favoured an all-member vote, compared to less than half of the caucus participants.[17]

As the overwhelming rejection of universal balloting by the left caucus suggests, universal balloting was favoured more by the delegates who placed themselves to the ideological right. Eighty percent of the delegates who placed themselves to the right of the ideological midpoint of the scale sup-ported universal balloting, compared to only 52% of those who adopted the most left-wing placements.

Conclusions

There is little doubt that the 1994 Alberta NDP convention enfranchised an electorate well-grounded in the party, actively involved in the party, gener-ally in agreement on policy matters, and distinctive from the other parties. There is also little doubt that the representation of labour at the convention affects the party's profile, operations, and decisions. Needless to say, it makes it more difficult for the party to mitigate its connections with labour. It also makes it more difficult for the party to adopt a system of universal ballot-ing, which would allow ordinary members more of a voice within the party.

The choice of the leader by the delegates assembled in Calgary in 1994 may well have ensured that the leader would be more left wing than one chosen by an all-member vote. The mean self-placement for the delegates came in at 2.2 on the seven-point scale, somewhat to the left of the placements of any of the candidates. Moreover, it appears that the delegates wanted to elect a leader farther to the left than the party itself. When asked to place the provincial party on the same scale, the average placement, at 3.3, was near the scale's midpoint. Harvey was placed more than half a point below this, at 2.6.

The post-1994 actions of the party reveal the machinations made possible by the selection and reselection of the leader at each convention. Despite the fact that the electorate was well grounded in the party and had extensive opportunities to interact with the candidates, the 1994 victor did not survive to contest a provincial election. Teslenko's candidacy symbolized a lack of full confidence in Harvey from union delegates. This want of confidence was further manifested in a challenge to Harvey at the 1995 convention, a challenge that saw him re-elected by a smaller margin than in 1994. As with some other NDP leaders who have faced a serious challenge for reelection, Harvey stepped down before the next convention. The requirement of convention selection and reselection at each convention undoubtedly aided his de-selection.

In the debate on universal balloting, the party president described the NDP as a collection of communities rather than individuals. Formally scheduled caucus meetings form part of the party's convention agenda, and with respect to leadership selection, delegates have been, at times, informed that they will have the chance to further interact with candidates within their caucus.

A substantial proportion of the 1994 delegates (44%) did not participate as part of a caucus community. In some ways, these delegates seem like second-class citizens. It was they who were most supportive of Bruce Hinkley, universal balloting, and changes to the party more broadly. These delegates are most likely to be unhappy with the way the party operates, but are unable to change it.

Although all delegates appeared rather leftist in terms of their political opinions, most were rather conservative with respect to changing the party. Most were likely to blame external factors for the 1993 electoral debacle, and were unwilling to see major changes in the way the party was structured with respect to caucuses and the role of unions. The preference for universal balloting was strongest among the delegates who did not participate in the caucuses. Their role in the party is somewhat limited by an absence of organization. Caucus participants have formal meetings to discuss leadership choice, strategy, and policy. As a result, they are in a much stronger position to influence the plenary convention. The leadership convention, which provides and entrenches such opportunities, unquestionably affects the party's evolution. A movement to universal balloting would almost certainly reduce such opportunities. The forces that support the status quo on internal party affairs within the NDP are unlikely to endorse such a movement. These forces are sufficiently numerous to block the constitutional amendments required for such a change.

6
Gender Differences among Party Activists

As previous chapters have indicated, the relative merits of utilizing a universal ballot system to choose party leaders has been the subject of controversy. Academic opinion seems both resigned and chagrined by the movement to such a system.

One of the more positive features attributed to a universal ballot is its potential for providing women with a more equitable role in what is likely the most important decision a political party makes (see Perlin 1991a: 87). Historically, the participation of women in political parties has not matched that of men (Bashevkin 1993). The selection of party leaders is one of the party activities dominated by men as, until recently, most Canadian parties chose their leaders at conventions in which women were guaranteed "some" representation but never achieved parity. The utilization of alternative means of selecting leaders, such as universal ballot systems, offers some potential for change. Research identifying gender gaps in voting and in public opinion indicates that an increased proportion of women is of more than just symbolic importance. In Canada, this attention has focused, for the most part, on the general population. One of the notable exceptions to this tendency is Brodie's work on the gender factor at national leadership conventions. Drawing on surveys of delegates to the 1983 PC and 1984 Liberal leadership conventions, Brodie (1988) found evidence of intra-party gender gaps in both voting and opinion. Another exception is the work by Archer and Whitehorn (1997) on the federal New Democrats, which also identifies gender differences in attitudes and candidate preferences.

This chapter builds on these studies by looking at gender in the context of leadership elections in Alberta. The distinctive elections held by the three major parties in Alberta affords an opportunity to investigate the degree to which gender differences affect each party and also to explore differences based on the method of selection. As noted in previous chapters, the Alberta PC leadership election permitted all members of the party to vote directly for the leader with rules governing participation that were far from stringent, the Alberta Liberals utilized a tele-vote allowing all members who registered in advance of a cut-off point to phone in their votes, and the New Democrats held a traditional convention.

Each of these leadership elections was marked by a high degree of participation by women. Indeed, the proportion of the electorate who were women far exceeded that recorded at previous conventions in Canada. Somewhat surprisingly, women were most equitably represented in the convention process utilized by the NDP (they accounted for 49% of the delegates). This stands in sharp contrast to federal NDP conventions, where women regularly accounted for only a third of the delegate total (see Archer and Whitehorn 1997: 16). Women were also well represented in the two universal ballots, as they accounted for 47% of the voters in both the Liberal tele-vote and the Conservative primary. At first glance, these participation figures suggest a limited impact for selection methods or party. However, as we suggested in Chapter 5, the surprisingly high proportion of women at the NDP convention tells us something about the party's weak competitive position. As well, a look at data from the 1985 Conservative convention in Alberta (Hunziker 1986) reveals that the Conservative universal ballot was associated with a significant increase in the proportion of women directly involved in choosing the leader, as the percentage increased to 47% from 30%. This lends support to Perlin's contention (1991a) regarding the participatory potential of universal ballots.

The participation of women was not limited to voting. Unlike previous Conservative leadership elections in Alberta, the 1992 race was contested by two women, one of whom, Nancy Betkowski, led after the first ballot and was thus one of the two finalists. Similarly, one of the four candidates for the NDP leadership was also a woman. This may be important in assessing the impact of gender since, as Brodie noted, "political constituencies rarely exist as independent factions in electoral contests. They are created and structured by the appeals of the candidates and the range of choices on the ballot" (1988: 186).

Media coverage of the nine-person PC race suggested that gender was highly relevant with women from outside the party getting involved to elect the first woman premier of Alberta (Cunningham 1992: A2). If that was their intention, they were unsuccessful as Ralph Klein overcame a first-ballot deficit to win easily the next week. The Liberal election with no female candidates and the NDP race with little media attention offered no hints of potential gender gaps in voting or preferences.

In this chapter, we seek to ascertain whether these processes were marked by some form of "gender gap." Did the men and women who participated in the leadership election support the same candidates, share the same attitudes and beliefs, possess similar backgrounds, and involve themselves in the same manner in the campaign? Moreover, did participation in this process have the same effect on both men and women with regard to future involvement in the party? To provide a preliminary answer for these questions, we examine voting behaviour, the attitudes of voters, their involvement in the process, the degree of previous involvement in the party, and considerations of future involvement.

The Gender Gap in Voting
The logical starting point for a study of voters in leadership elections is with their voting choices. Research has highlighted gender gaps in voting both internationally (for instance, in the US with women more supportive of Democratic candidates) and in Canada, where women were more supportive of the Liberal Party than were men (see, for instance, Wearing and Wearing 1991). The existence of such gaps within Canadian parties has rarely been addressed. There is some evidence that national conventions have been marked by gender divisions. Brodie's discovery (1988) of such gaps at the federal Conservative and Liberal conventions of 1983 and 1984 provides an indication that even within the same party men and women have different candidate preferences. Archer and Whitehorn's examination of the 1989 federal NDP leadership convention reveals the same pattern in that party (Archer and Whitehorn 1997: 223). Given the nature of the 1992 Conservative leadership campaign and the structure of the choice on the final ballot, one might expect a strong gender gap. As mentioned before, media reports suggested that women were involving themselves in the process in an attempt to make Nancy Betkowski premier. Perhaps in response to this, some of the caucus supporters of Ralph Klein seemed to suggest that Betkowski's gender would hinder her ability to serve as an effective premier (see Chapter 3).[1]

As we noted in Chapter 3, there was a gender gap among Albertan Tories in 1992 (see Table 6.1). Klein's support coalition contained proportionately more men than women and significantly fewer women than Betkowski's. More than half of the Betkowski voters were women, and she was supported by 45% of the women who voted but by just 35% of the men. The gender gap appeared even stronger on the first ballot, where Betkowski led Klein among women but trailed him with men. Betkowski and Elaine McCoy were the only candidates to get more than half of their votes from women.[2] The gender gap took the form of higher levels of support for women from women voters and higher support levels for male candidates from male voters. Male voters were considerably more reluctant than women to support Betkowski.[3]

The efforts of some Klein supporters to couch Betkowski's abilities in gender terms did not hurt his candidacy. Indeed, as suggested in Chapter 3, it appears that the women who voted only on the second ballot were, at least in part, motivated by a desire to prevent Betkowski from becoming the first

Table 6.1

Candidate choice or preference by gender and party

Vote by gender for Betkowski and Klein

Second-ballot vote*	Betkowski (%)	Klein (%)	Mean rank* Betkowski
Women (N = 413)	45	55	3.3
Men (N = 471)	35	65	3.8

First-ballot vote*	Betkowski (%) N = 268	Klein (%) N = 296	Other (%) N = 163
Women (N = 323)	46	33	21
Men (N = 397)	30	47	23

Ranking of Chadi and vote by gender

Preference*	Women (%) N = 269	Men (%) N = 305	Vote	Women (%) N = 269	Men (%) N = 305
First	8	17	Chadi	9	14
Second	7	11	Dickson	11	13
Third	9	8	Germain	25	22
Fourth	12	16	Mitchell	55	50
Last	64	49	Sindlinger	NA	NA

Ranking of Teslenko and vote by gender

Preference*	Women (%) N = 105	Men (%) N = 107	Vote	Women (%) N = 105	Men (%) N = 107
First	14	4	Harvey	60	62
Second	26	18	Hinkley	18	21
Third	36	40	Johnson	9	11
Last	24	37	Teslenko	14	7

* Differences between women and men produced values of X^2 significant at the .05 level.

woman to serve as premier of Alberta. Betkowski was able to attract slightly higher levels of support from the men who voted only on the final ballot. This antipathy to Betkowski was also evident in the candidate rankings.[4] Women who voted only on the second ballot ranked Betkowski almost two spots lower than those who voted on both ballots.

Betkowski's rankings raise some questions as to how women candidates were perceived within the party. Although she led after the initial ballot and attracted even more votes on the second, a surprisingly large number of the new voters ranked her dead last: 26% of the women and 22% of the men.[5] Betkowski's overall rankings were affected by the strong dislike of many Klein voters, as more than a quarter of them ranked her dead last. Thus not only did these voters prefer Klein to Betkowski, they preferred all of the other seven candidates to her as well. Betkowski supporters did not display the same antipathy toward Klein. While Klein voters did not indicate that gender was a factor in their support for Klein, the low rankings they gave Betkowski suggest that such considerations might have come into play.

A strong gender gap affected voting, but this gender gap was mitigated by the overwhelming opposition to Betkowski demonstrated by women who voted only on the second ballot. Klein's victory was based on voters who had not voted on the first ballot and among these voters he was every bit as popular with women as he was with men. It appears that the week between the two ballots allowed a backlash to develop against Betkowski, and this backlash inspired as many women as it did men. The increased proportion of women involved in the process undoubtedly helped Betkowski to her narrow one-vote first-ballot lead, but in the end it was not enough to elect her. Women in the party disproportionately supported Betkowski but they did not vote as a bloc. Indeed, fully a quarter of them were hostile to her candidacy.

Gender differences were not as stark in either the Liberal or NDP election. However, gender influenced assessments of candidates in each instance. Although gender was not significantly associated with voting among Liberals, it appears to have had some impact on support for Sine Chadi. Women were less likely to vote for Chadi than men and were significantly less likely to rank him as their preferred candidate. A similar pattern can be seen among New Democrats. Women were twice as likely to support Clancy Teslenko and were far more likely than men to rank her as their first choice.

Thus, in all of the elections, there is evidence that gender exerted an influence on candidate assessment. In the Liberal case, the absence of a female candidate suggests that the issue of candidate appeal is not solely a case of the gender of a candidate. The examination of the three elections indicates that gender differences were widest in the open ballot of the Conservative Party.

The Gender Gap in Political Attitudes

Research on gender and politics has pointed to a number of differences in the belief patterns of men and women. O'Neill (1992: 1, 2) points out a number of trends with respect to gender gaps in opinion in Canada. She notes, among other things, that women were more supportive of social welfare programs and the redistribution of power in the workplace, while they were less likely to favour privatization. These differences of opinion, however, were found in the general population. Research from the US suggests that differences

Table 6.2

Issue positions by party and gender (% agreeing)

Issue	NDP Women N = 105	NDP Men N = 107	Liberal Women N = 269	Liberal Men N = 305	PC Women N = 432	PC Men N = 469
Don't spend tax dollars on the sick	1	1	3	5	7	8
Need government to get things done without red tape	78	76	91	93	92	90
Rely on selves not government	15	25	39	29*	19	14*
Quebec separation inevitable	NA	NA	NA	NA	15	23*
Reduce government even if services cut	21	25	63	68	77	82
Abortion decisions between women and their doctors	93	94	77	73	76	74
Better to elect people who espouse strong Christian values	NA	NA	37	29	31	27*
Unions essential part of democracy	93	91	57	60	33	29
Grass roots can solve problems	49	58	69	64	67	70
Charlottetown Accord was a good deal	27	42*	38	40	34	31
Community should support seniors	81	85	38	45	32	35
Rural MLAs can't serve as many people	NA	NA	NA	NA	30	37*
Government should work to improve the status of women	92	92	59	47*	44	29*
Many welfare programs unnecessary	9	15	40	53*	61	66
Give Alberta companies preference for provincial contracts	NA	NA	NA	NA	43	33*
Trust down-to-earth thinking	49	58	55	61	60	65
Provinces should have more power	NA	NA	26	32	39	41
Foreign ownership threatens independence	94	91	69	58*	48	34*
Negotiate Native provincial land claims	86	87	77	70*	60	55*
Most unemployed people could find jobs	0	3	29	40*	40	45
Government should ensure living standard	97	92	77	66*	47	41
Social programs should remain universal	NA	NA	NA	NA	49	40*
Regulations stifle personal drive	8	4	19	30*	39	50*
Ensure independent Canada even if living standard lower	89	76	68	71	59	51*

What politicians do on their own time is their own business	NA	NA	48	59*	50	55
Referendums on all constitutional changes	35	33	53	49	50	47
Balanced budgets should be mandatory	NA	NA	69	72	97	94
Government shoud ensure adequate housing for all	97	96	72	56*	NA	NA
No hiring of replacement workers during strikes	96	99	52	45	NA	NA
Profits help create poverty	87	74*	28	22	NA	NA
Reducing debt and deficit should be top government priority	8	19*	52	68*	NA	NA
Kindergarten fees penalize poor	100	99	88	83	NA	NA
Tuition fees should cover more education costs	3	11*	47	47	NA	NA
Reduce health-care spending	7	13	18	35*	NA	NA
Lower taxes produce economic growth	19	18	64	73*	NA	NA
GST discriminates against poor	90	89	40	39	NA	NA
Roll back public sector wages	13	13	44	46	NA	NA
Contracting out services is OK	13	10	64	75	NA	NA
Ban discrimination on basis of sexual orientation	96	98	84	83	NA	NA
Environment takes precedence over jobs	89	93	72	69	NA	NA
User fees needed for health	0	6*	22	31*	NA	NA
Increase taxes to pay for programs	69	74	19	18	NA	NA
Reduce deficit through across-the-board cuts	3	4	27	33	NA	NA
Immigration helps economy	40	44	67	79*	NA	NA
Important to leave debt-free Alberta to children	27	48*	NA	NA	NA	NA
Unions decrease productivity	12	11	NA	NA	NA	NA
Government should legislate benefits for part-time workers	96	93	NA	NA	NA	NA
NDP should revise policies to attract voters	44	65*	NA	NA	NA	NA
NDP should not move too far to left	33	51*	NA	NA	NA	NA
Big corporations mean that we need big unions	77	84	NA	NA	NA	NA
Caucuses have too much power in NDP	50	47	NA	NA	NA	NA
The Free Trade Agreement has been good for Alberta	4	12*	45	59*	40	56*

Note: The percentages exclude voters who said they had no opinion.
* Attitudinal differences between men and women produced values of X^2 significant at the .05 level.

also exist within a single party. Kelley, Hulbary and Bowman, in a study of Florida precinct party activists, found "gender differences within each party" (1993: 70). In Canada, Brodie's study of federal convention delegates found similar differences between men and women on questions of social policy, business policy, and foreign policy and especially "on issues of special concern to women" (1988: 180, 181, 183). Men took more pro-business positions, were less supportive of women's issues, less progressive on social policy, and more hawkish and pro-American. Archer and Whitehorn have also found modest gender differences in attitudes among New Democratic delegates (1997: 101).

Using the attitudinal questions outlined in the previous chapters, we found evidence of differences in opinion between the genders in the elections of all three parties. The largest number of differences were found among the Conservative voters.

The 1992 Alberta PC survey asked twenty-seven attitudinal questions and statistically significant gender differences were evident (see Table 6.2) on thirteen of them.[6] Thus, on almost half of the attitudinal questions, men and women in the same political party displayed significant differences of opinion. One must be cautious in interpreting these differences since the mean difference between men and women was generally small; on just five of the questions did the difference reach ten percentage points.

Gender differences were also common among Liberal voters, as significant differences appeared in eleven of the thirty-six attitudinal questions. However, as was the case with the Conservatives, the gap exceeded ten percentage points on only a handful of occasions. Our analysis of the New Democratic delegates replicates Archer's earlier evidence of attitudinal cohesion among delegates, as significant differences were found in only six of

Table 6.3

Opinion indices mean score by party and gender

	NDP		Liberal		PC	
	Women N = 105	Men N = 107	Women N = 269	Men N = 305	Women N = 432	Men N = 496
Populism (4)	1.74	1.90	2.32	2.41	2.61	2.65
Issues of special concern to women (2)	1.78	1.75	1.30	1.12*	1.16	1.01*
Pro-government services (3)	2.50	2.35	1.67	1.37*	1.02	0.85*
Individualism (4)	0.19	0.23	1.03	1.22*	1.43	1.55
Continentalism (3)	0.18	0.41*	0.78	1.05*	1.00	1.47*

* The differences of means are significant at better than the .05 level.

forty-one questions. Thus, the number of gender differences decreases as the number of participants in the leadership election declined.

In order to simplify discussions of the opinion questions, we examined the same scales utilized in other chapters. These scales measured general support for government actions, individualism versus collectivism, populism, continentalism, and issues of special concern to women (see Table 6.3).[7]

As one would expect, given the relative lack of differentiation on specific attitudinal questions as well as earlier examinations of the party, the New Democratic delegates scored similarly on most of the scales. The sole exception was continentalism where women were significantly less likely to offer continentalist responses. Their continentalist score was a minuscule 0.18. One scale that we used exclusively in the chapter on the New Democrats focused on attitudes toward unions, and opinions on this scale did distinguish the party's men and women. The mean score for men was significantly higher on this scale (that is, more pro-union) than it was for women. Indeed, while almost a quarter of the men scored a four on this scale, the same was true for just 6% of the women.

Among Conservatives, the populism and individualism scales failed to distinguish women from men. Indeed, although populism was one of the most important factors differentiating support for the two final candidates (see Chapter 3), there were no significant differences between men and women in this issue area.

Like delegates to the 1983 and 1984 national leadership conventions, men and women in the Alberta Conservative Party had slightly different perspectives on the issues of special concern to women. Our index on these issues was constructed on the basis of the two questions deemed most relevant. This index summed responses to questions dealing with whether abortion was a matter between a woman and her doctor, and whether government should make a strong effort to improve the status of women. The resulting mean scores were 1.16 for women and 1.01 for men.

The remaining scales also differentiated opinion by gender. Women were more likely to support government activity rejecting the claim that a lot of welfare programs were unnecessary, and taking the positions that regulations are needed to protect citizens and that governments have a responsibility to intervene when "bad things happen." On balance, as one might expect of Conservative Party members, the support for government provision of services was rather low. However, women, with a mean score of 1.02, were somewhat more supportive of government than men, whose average was just 0.85.

The most striking differences between women and men were found with respect to continentalism. Women were substantially less enthusiastic than men on this issue. Conservative women were lukewarm in their enthusiasm for free trade and strongly nationalistic in considering foreign ownership a threat[8] and believing it essential to maintain an independent Canada regardless of the impact on the standard of living. On each of the latter two questions, the plurality of women gave a different response from that of the majority of men. Overall on this scale, the mean score for women was 1.00, while for men it was 1.47. Women were almost twice as likely to give no pro-continentalist responses. As with the New Democrats, a very clear difference between the sexes existed on this dimension.[9]

Gender differences with respect to continentalism were also evident among Liberal tele-voters. Indeed, on this scale the score for Liberal women at 0.78 was closer to that of Conservative women than it was to Liberal men (1.05). This result was replicated on a scale assessing issues of special concern to women. The mean score of Liberal men was 1.12, slightly lower than the 1.16 score recorded by Conservative women and even farther from the 1.30 of Liberal women.

Liberal men and women also differed significantly on the individualism and pro-government scales. Women were less individualistic and more supportive of government activity than their male counterparts. As with the Conservatives, the populism scale did not distinguish men from women.

Examining the scales by gender reveals relatively consistent differences among Conservative and Liberal men and women. We offer two reasons for this: first, the nature of the parties; and second, the nature of the leadership election. The Liberals and Conservatives are traditionally seen as more pragmatic parties and thus welcome a greater diversity of viewpoints. As well, the more open nature of their leadership elections seems likely to further broaden this diversity.

Our examination of the three parties suggests that party generally overwhelms gender in terms of opinion. New Democratic women are in each instance closer in their opinions to their fellow New Democratic men than they are to Liberal women. To put it another way, despite a general tendency for women to report opinions that were less individualistic, less populist, less continentalist, and more supportive of government, New Democratic men always surpassed Liberal women on these dimensions. With respect to Liberals and Conservatives this trend was not as universal. For instance, as we noted above, Liberal men were more continentalist than Conservative women, and Conservative women were more supportive of women's issues than Liberal men. On the other issues the ordering followed party lines. In each of the five scales, the polar positions were taken by New Democratic women and Conservative men, suggesting that both gender and party have an impact on attitudes. The New Democratic women, however, were clustered much closer to one pole than the Tory men were to the other. This suggests both the strength of ideology among New Democrats and the tendency of delegates to be more ideological than participants in universal ballots.

Gender differences were also apparent on variables not common to all three surveys and we will briefly discuss some of these. Among Liberal tele-voters, men were more likely to think that the deficit and debt should be the province's top priority, reductions in health care expenditures are ac-ceptable, user fees are needed for health, and higher taxes impede economic growth. As well, men were more inclined to believe that what politicians do on their own time is their own business and less willing to negotiate Native land claims. Among Conservative voters, men were less likely to think it important to elect people with strong Christian values, less willing to give Alberta companies preference for provincial contracts, and less likely to believe that social programs should be universal. In general, the differences on these issues support the general thesis that women are more supportive of government activities.

Although NDP delegates displayed a great deal of cohesion in terms of our scales, there were gender differences in a number of the specific ques-tions that are quite interesting. Men were twice as likely to support higher tuition for students, twice as likely to view the debt and deficit as the prov-ince's highest priority, more likely to accept user fees for health, and less likely to say that profits help create poverty. Moreover, while almost half the men felt it was important to leave a debt-free Alberta to our children, just over a quarter of the women shared this priority. And NDP men were much more likely to feel that the Charlottetown Accord was a good deal for Canada.[10]

There were also quite striking differences between men and women on some issues dealing with the party's future. For instance, while almost two-thirds of the men agreed that the party should revise policy in order to attract votes, a majority of the women took the opposite position. And, while a slim majority of the men felt that the party should not move too far to the left, only a third of the women agreed. The differences among the genders on these issues provides more support for the position that women are more supportive of government in general and are somewhat further to the left than men.[11] These results are consistent among the three parties.

Our analysis of opinion differences in the three processes suggests that gender disagreements were most common among Conservative voters, even though they were offered fewer occasions to voice their opinions. Disagree-ments were least common among New Democrats, who, conversely, were asked the most questions. This is consistent with Archer and Whitehorn's conclusions on the relative cohesion of views among New Democratic del-egates (1990). The relatively large number of gender differences among Con-servative voters replicates results reported by Archer and Gibbins in a general survey of Alberta voters (1997: 468, 469) and suggests that the more open process utilized by the party more accurately reflects the state of gender opinion differences in Alberta.

Gender Differences in Background

Study after study has noted the segregation of women into lower-paying and lower-status occupations (see, for instance, *Women in the Labour Force 1990-91*, Supply and Services Canada, 1990). Of course, these differences refer to the population in general and studies of party activists have not really addressed this issue. However, Brodie touched on the subject and her findings (1988: 179) suggest that "women and men convention delegates come from similar socio economic backgrounds." In understanding the changes that may flow from universal ballots, it is important to compare women and men voters in terms of their backgrounds (see Table 6.4).

Among Conservatives, gender differences in background were evident in a number of areas.[12] There were some differences in terms of education. Unlike convention delegates, the vast majority of universal ballot participants did not possess university degrees, but men were more likely to hold post-graduate degrees accounting for two-thirds of the voters in that category. Male Liberal tele-voters were also more likely to hold university degrees than were women. Slightly more than half of the men but just 40% of the women reported that they had completed university.

Occupational status distinguished Conservative men from women. A fairly large proportion of women (17%) said they were employed in the home, while not a single man placed himself in that category. Women were also three times more likely than men to be unemployed or employed on a part-time basis. Men made up the vast majority of the full-time employee category and were twice as likely to be self-employed. This pattern was also present among Liberals, with men almost three times as likely to be self-employed while women were five times as likely to report part-time involvement in the workforce.[13] And, while 10% of the Liberal women said they were homemakers, no man gave this response.

Gender differences were evident with respect to the specific occupation claimed as well. With the Conservative universal ballot, the proportion of voters who claimed a "professional occupation" was much smaller than at conventions. This may partially account for the increase in the proportion of women involved in the process since men were more likely to report professional occupations. Male voters were also far more likely to possess a business background, with fully 35% of the men, but just 14% of the women, claiming such an occupation. Once more a similar trend was evident among the Liberals: men were more likely to be involved in business or to claim a professional or white-collar occupation.

Conservative women dominated in what one could term the traditional female occupations (see *Women in the Labour Force 1990-91*, Supply and Services Canada, 1990: 4). Thirteen percent of women were health care employees, while only 3% of the men were employed in this field.[14] Women were more than twice as likely to be involved in education and were far more

Table 6.4

Socio-demographic characteristics by party and gender

	NDP		Liberal		PC	
Issue	Women $N = 105$	Men $N = 107$	Women $N = 269$	Men $N = 305$	Women $N = 432$	Men $N = 469$
University-educated	55	51	40	52*	10	17*
Not finished high school	12	15	8	11*	9	16*
Homemaker	1	0*	10	0*	17	0*
Part-time employee*	NA	NA	16	3*	11	3*
Unemployed*	4	7*	NA	NA	4	1*
Self-employed*	11	10	12	34*	17	37*
Businessperson*	6	7*	5	13*	13	35*
Professional occupation*	41	36*	32	49*	36	25
Health care*	NA	NA	13	2*	13	3*
Education*	NA	NA	17	9*	11	7*
Clerical or sales	12	1*	13	5*	18	7*
Public sector	51	44	51	35*	NA	NA
Farmer/rancher*	2	3*	3	4*	6	13*
Hourly employed or blue collar	3	19*	7	8*	4	10*
Married	45	68*	68	81*	NA	NA
Separated or divorced	28	6*	8	6*	NA	NA
High family income	21	25	35	41	55	63
Low family income	46	42	28	19	24	18

* Differences between women and men produced values of X^2 significant at the .05 level.

likely to be employed as clerical workers or as sales persons: 18% of women claimed clerical or sales occupations compared to just 7% of men. These results were largely replicated among Liberals, where women were six times as likely to be employed in health care and almost twice as likely to be teachers. Thirteen percent of Liberal women reported sales or clerical careers, while only 5% of the men claimed those fields as occupations. Finally, while 51% of the women were employed in the public sector, only 35% of the men were so employed.

Given these gender differences in occupational status, it was somewhat surprising to discover no significant gender differences in family income. Family income was the only measure of income utilized in the surveys and it probably presents a somewhat misleading picture. Given the proportion of women who worked in the home or part time, it seems likely that their family income is reflective of other sources of income. Perhaps, as O'Neill (1992) suggests, it may be more appropriate to use a personal income figure when investigating gender questions. The large proportion of women who were homemakers or part-time employees suggests stark differences between the genders with respect to personal income. This is without even considering the lower rates of remuneration women often receive for performing the same job as men.

To this point we have not discussed New Democratic delegates. This is largely because a somewhat different set of occupational questions was asked on their survey. However, even when similar questions were asked with respect to education, the significant gender differences found among Liberals and Conservatives were not present with the New Democrats. Indeed, although the differences were not significant, more women than men had completed university. As with the Liberals and Conservatives, no significant differences in family income were reported. New Democratic men and women did, however, differ somewhat with respect to occupation. Women were more likely to be employed in the public sector and were more likely to report careers in sales or clerical occupations. And, in contrast to the Liberals and Conservatives, New Democratic women were more likely to be found in professional or white-collar careers than men. As well, while almost one in five of the New Democratic men claimed a blue-collar job, the same was true of only 3% of the women. Another contrast between New Democratic women and women in the other two parties is found with respect to employment in the home. While 17% of Tory women said they were employed in the home and 10% of Liberal women claimed to be homemakers, only 1% of the NDP women described themselves this way. New Democratic women were also much less likely than Liberal women to report being married.[15] For both New Democrats and Liberals, men were far more likely to be married than were women. This was particularly striking among New Democrats, where 68% of the men but only 45% of the women were married.

The women who participated in the Conservative election and the Liberal tele-vote differed from their male counterparts in terms of occupation and education. Women were not as likely to possess graduate degrees or hold professional occupations. Women did not come from the same jobs as men and were far more likely to work only part time or not to participate in the paid work force at all. These universal ballots not only involved a higher proportion of women than traditional conventions, but the women it involved possessed backgrounds and were in occupational situations very different from the men. Examination of the Conservative election and the Liberal tele-vote suggests that these more universal ballots enfranchised an electorate that, like society in general, saw men and women employed in different occupations. This stands in contrast to Brodie's research on federal Liberal and Conservative conventions and provides further evidence that universal ballots are more representative of the wider population. This argument is buttressed by our look at the New Democratic convention, where there were no significant gender differences in education and where women were actually more likely to hold professional or white-collar jobs. The occupational patterns of the New Democratic Party appear to be affected by the rules that surround the convention, including the direct representation of union delegates. This explains the biggest gender difference among New Democrats, since the vast majority of the delegates who reported a blue-collar job were from a union background. Finally, we note that the background characteristics of New Democratic women reveal them to be least representative of Albertan women in a descriptive sense.

Gender Differences in Involvement in Party and Campaign

There has been much discussion in the past of women's involvement in politics, and in general, research has shown that women have been less involved than men. Walker in her study of women voters in Britain, France, and West Germany writes that "women are less likely than men to give money to a party or candidate and less likely to work for a political campaign" (1994: 63). She suggests that "gender differences also persist in expressions of interest in politics and campaigns" (1994: 64). In an article written for the Royal Commission on Electoral Reform and Party Financing, Brodie cites evidence from the 1984 and 1988 National Election Studies that indicate that Canadian women are also less interested in electoral politics than men (1991: 19,24).

The women who voted in the universal ballots were not as interested in politics as the men. In each case, more than half (54%) of the men claimed to be very interested in politics. In contrast, only 47% of Liberal women and just 37% of Conservative women made such a claim. This may again reflect the relative ease with which people could participate in the Conservative process.

Within the Conservative process, this relative lack of interest seems to have had little impact on campaign involvement. For some reason, women were less likely than men to attend an all-candidates meeting but on other dimensions of campaign participation, such as attending a candidate's campaign event, working for a candidate, or phoning a candidate's office for information, no significant gender differences could be identified. An involvement scale summing participation in the areas mentioned showed no significant differences between men and women. Thus, while women were in general less interested in politics and somewhat less likely to attend the candidate forums, they were as heavily, or actually in this case, as lightly involved in the campaign as men.

There was however a gender gap in terms of the focus of involvement. Women accounted for 48% of those who attended Betkowski campaign events but just a third at Klein gatherings.[16] Even more importantly, women made up more than half of the workers in Betkowski's campaign but just 33% of Klein's. Women were as involved in the campaign as men, but their involvement, as far as it can be measured, disproportionately placed them in the Betkowski camp. This gender gap in involvement exceeds the gender gap in voting and may account for media stories focusing on the attractiveness of Betkowski's campaign to Albertan women. Women were far more likely to vote for Klein than they were to attend his rallies or work for him. The greater likelihood of women working for and attending Betkowski rallies, together with Brodie's observation that political constituencies are structured by the range of choices (1988: 186), suggests that the universal ballot itself was not the only factor in raising the proportion of women voting. The universal ballot, in the absence of Betkowski's candidacy, might have involved fewer women.

Notable gender differences could be seen in past involvement in the Conservative party. The male voters possessed ties to the Conservative party that were rather more substantial than those possessed by the women. While the universal ballot virtually ensured that few of the voters would have held office previously in the party, this tendency was more pronounced among women. Only 7% of the men said they had held an office in the party, but this minuscule figure is still twice as high as the proportion of women who had held office (3%). Moreover, women were less likely than men to have been a member of the party when the campaign began: 35% versus 44%. The relative paucity of ties to the Conservative party can be seen in that fewer women reported memberships in a federal party. While 29% of them said they were also members of a federal party, 41% of the men made such a claim. Finally, women were less likely than men to have voted for the

Table 6.5

Liberal and Conservative Party background and process

Involvement by gender	Liberal		PC	
	Women (%) N = 269	Men (%) N = 305	Women (%) N = 432	Men (%) N = 496
Very interested in politics*	47	54	37	44
Attended forum*	29	33	17	24*
Worked for candidate	31	29	18	22*
Attended event	28	35	23	28
Phoned campaign office	NA	NA	27	22
Ever held party office*	10	12	3	7*
Member of federal party	46	54	29	41
Worked for party in past	47	46	16	19
Became member just for vote*	29	21*	62	48*
Plan to work for party in next election*	55	53	21	30*

* Differences between women and men produced values of X^2 significant at the .05 level or better.

Getty Conservatives in the 1989 provincial election. Seventy-six percent of the women and 82% of the men recalled voting Conservative (see Table 6.5).

Women were as involved in the leadership campaign as men, but they were not involved with the same candidate and they did not possess the same degree of past involvement in the party. Nor were they as likely to remain involved. More than three-fifths said their membership was taken out just to vote in the leadership election. Fewer than half of the men made such a claim. Similarly, women were less likely to say they planned to work for the party in the next provincial election. Thirty percent of the men and 21% of women said they planned to aid the party in this manner. This gap was not produced simply by the rancour of disappointed Betkowski voters. Men who backed Klein were more likely than women to say they would work in the next election, while women who voted for Klein were more likely to say they joined the party just to vote for the leader. Thus, these measures of "commitment" to the party reveal strong gender differences. They may also provide hints that the place for women in the Klein camp did not go much beyond voting.

Differences in involvement were not as common in the Liberal election. No significant differences were detected with respect to attending a forum, attending a campaign event, working for a candidate, holding office previously in the party, or intending to work for the party in the next election. A significant difference relates to the existence of the vote as a reason for

Table 6.6

Involvement in the NDP by gender

	Women (%) N = 105	Men (%) N = 107
Raised funds for provincial NDP	76	78
Raised funds for federal NDP	48	58
Worked in provincial campaign	90	94
Worked in federal campaign	71	81
Member more than 20 years	20	27
Member less than 5 years	47	30
Sought provincial nomination	18	26
Union delegate	4	14*
Attended labour caucus	15	34*
Attended women's caucus	54	5*
Attended green caucus	10	19*
Attended regional caucus	3	9*
Attended municipal caucus	8	1*
Worked for candidate	26	37

* Differences between women and men produced values of X^2 significant at the .05 level or better.

joining the party. Twenty-nine percent of women, compared to 21% of men, report joining the Liberal Party "just to vote." Men were also more likely than women to try and persuade other people to vote a particular way and were also more likely to have met a candidate during the campaign.

New Democratic delegates did not reveal many differences in general involvement and party background (see Table 6.6). However, the genders could be distinguished on a number of features unique to the party. Men were far more likely than women to represent unions (14% versus 4%), and participation in the party's various caucuses often differed by gender. Not surprisingly, more than half the women (54%) participated in the woman's caucus, while only a few men attended. Differences existed in other caucuses as well. More than a third of the men participated in the labour caucus, as opposed to just 15% of women. Men were also twice as likely to report attending the green caucus, three times as likely to participate in regional caucuses, and eight times as numerous at the municipal caucus. Thus, while New Democratic men and women did not differ in terms of their records of involvement in general party events and activities, there were still discernible differences in terms of delegate category and with respect to participation in the party's various caucuses.

Our evidence thus suggests that to the degree that differences in involvement existed, it was men who possessed records of greater involvement. We also conclude that particularly among Conservatives and New Democrats, the nature of involvement in campaign- or convention-related matters differed by gender. With the Conservatives, the difference related to participation in the Betkowski campaign, while among New Democrats it was caucus participation that was distinctive.

Conclusions

The leadership election processes of all three parties in Alberta demonstrate that internal party politics are marked by gender differences. These differences appeared most strikingly in the Conservative election, where some supporters of Klein attempted to mobilize support by raising gender questions. Less obviously, the men who voted differed significantly from women in their choice of candidate and in their attitudes, particularly with respect to the role of government and continentalism. Women also differed from men in terms of the candidate they worked for and the campaign events they attended. Finally, and partially explaining some of the differences in candidate preference and attitudes, the women who voted possessed fewer party roots and came from very different occupational situations.

The increased proportion of women involved in the process had an impact on the election as it strengthened Betkowski's candidacy. If women had been present in the same proportions as they were in the 1985 convention, she would not have led after the first ballot and Klein would have been close enough to victory to make the second ballot a mere formality. If this had been the case, the party would not have received the same publicity windfall and membership growth. However, Betkowski's support from women was mitigated by the turnout for the second ballot of a substantial number of women hostile to her candidacy.

Indeed, antipathy to Betkowski's candidacy appeared to strongly motivate a number of second-ballot Klein supporters. A large proportion of these voters, and more than a quarter of those who voted only on the second ballot, ranked her last out of the nine candidates. Betkowski was obviously not a fringe candidate nor was she an extreme candidate, so this antipathy is difficult to justify. Perhaps many Conservative voters, both men and women, simply did not want a woman as premier.[17]

The presence of such a large proportion of women affected the attitudinal profile of the party. It may have made the party appear less hostile to economic nationalism, less ruggedly individualistic, more sympathetic to issues of special concern to women, and less willing to slash government services. In short, it disguised or at least mitigated the neo-liberalism of the party. This might have made voters in the 1993 provincial election more willing to focus on the "He Listens, He Cares" aspect of the Klein campaign than on its harsh deficit reduction message.

Although the universal ballot increased the number of women voting for the leader, it was less successful in increasing the involvement of women in the party in general. As Randall noted, "the relationship of the vote to other

forms of political participation is also unclear. Voting is sometimes understood as the first step in a succession of increasingly demanding political
acts" (1982: 36). In the Alberta case, it does not appear to have been a first
step as much perhaps as it was the only step. Women who participated in
the process were significantly more likely than men to say they became
members just to vote for the leader, and were less likely to say that they
planned to work for the party in the next election. Klein's victory may partially explain this. Women were less likely to attend his rallies, vote for him,
or work for him. Most of the women voters who were active workers in the
campaign supported Betkowski. Her defeat and the hostility to her shown
by many Klein voters, combined with efforts on the part of some of Klein's
caucus supporters to organize opposition to Betkowski on the basis of her
sex, may have indicated to many women that the PCs were not eager for
their full participation.

The Liberal tele-vote also reveals gender differences. While there were no
female candidates and no significant voting differences, gender-based differences could be seen in the candidate rankings. And, Liberal tele-voters
displayed consistent gender differences in opinion. As with the Conservatives, women were consistently to the left of men in their opinions. Distinctive occupational and educational profiles were also evident contrary to
Brodie's data on federal Liberal delegates. We suggest that these differences
relate to the less exclusive nature of the tele-vote. Differences in involvement and background were not as common, but we think it significant that
women were more likely to report taking out memberships solely in order
to vote, further buttressing our argument with respect to the nature of the
election process.

Even the New Democratic convention displayed gender differences.
Women were disproportionately supportive of the lone female candidate
and involved themselves within the party in manners different from men.
The genders also differed significantly in their views on continentalism, the
role of labour within the party, and how the party should position itself in
the future. There were even a few differences with respect to background,
although these differences were less substantial than in the other parties
and at times ran in different directions.

Our analysis suggests that universal ballots appear to enhance opportunities for women to participate in party politics. They do not, however, necessarily ensure that women's involvement in their parties reach the same level
as those of men, and the involvement of women in the campaign itself may
be heavily dependent on the structure of the competition.[18]

With respect to broader electoral politics in Alberta, we believe that Premier Klein's relative weakness with women may expose the Achilles heel of
his government. Brodie's evidence from national conventions suggests that
gender gaps in opinion among delegates were narrower than those in the

general public. Indeed, differences in opinion and voting intention have become evident in Alberta (Archer and Gibbins 1997: 469-70). The actions of the government in reducing government services seems to foster a mentality that favours individualism over collectivism. The evidence from the 1992 leadership election indicates that such measures would be more popular with men than women. Women however account for more than half of the Alberta electorate and may yet, as they did in 1992, form the core of opposition to Klein.

In events that provide partial support for this hypothesis, the provincial New Democrats chose Pam Barrett as their leader before the 1997 provincial election, although she subsequently resigned. As well, in April 1998, the Liberals, in a move unprecedented in provincial electoral history, selected Nancy Betkowski[19] as their party's standard bearer. The next provincial election will provide a rematch between Klein and Betkowski.

7
Democracy, Representation, and the Selection of Party Leaders

In November 1992, the three parties represented in the Alberta legislature were led by political veterans well known to Albertans. Two years later, each of those parties had a new leader and was in a very different competitive situation. Leadership elections provide observers with a window into political parties as they perform what may well be their most important function (Carty 1988a: 84). The three windows into Alberta's main parties were particularly valuable, since each party used a different method to select its leader. We have used this opportunity not only to compare the three major Albertan parties at a similar point in time, but also to compare and analyze three different methods of choosing leaders. This comparison enriches our understanding of the individual parties, the various selection methods, and Albertan politics more broadly.

This chapter compares the participants in each of these processes. The participants are examined with respect to demographic and regional characteristics and attitudes. This comparison allows for an assessment of what each of the parties "represents" in terms of "descriptive representation" and political views. The analysis reveals that Alberta's three parties not only enfranchised a rather different mix of Albertans in terms of demographic and regional characteristics, but contrary to what one might expect in "one party dominant Alberta," the participants also provided a sharp contrast with respect to political opinions and values. We reflect on the degree to which these differences among party activists are based on the policy and ideological diversity of the parties and also question whether the differences may, instead, stem from the alternative methods of leadership selection.

The Partisan Backgrounds of Leadership Voters
The three leadership selection processes enfranchised very different electorates with respect to party background. In all three cases, however, the electorate was largely self-selected. Although the New Democrats utilized a

convention, there was no battle for convention spaces. Most constituency associations did not have enough interested bodies to fill all the positions open to them, and only 1% of the delegates said they faced a contest to attend the convention. Using more direct voting systems, the Liberals and Conservatives involved individuals who represented only themselves, as opposed to the NDP delegates, who represented their constituency or organization. Of course, candidate organizations were active in recruiting voters, and in this endeavour, the Liberal candidates proved much more successful.[1]

The NDP convention, as one might expect, was home to party regulars. Four-fifths of the delegates had previously attended a provincial convention, and one-fifth were actually former candidates in provincial elections. More than two-fifths possessed party memberships of longer than ten years, and only 1% were members for less than a year. In contrast, only a quarter of the Liberals had memberships of more than nine years, and 34% acquired their initial membership the year of the vote. Conservative voters displayed even less of a background in the party; only 10% were members for more than seven years, and 55% joined the year of the vote. As well, while 60% of the New Democratic delegates had held some sort of party office at some point in their lives, the same was true of only 11% of the Liberals, and just 5% of the Conservatives. The pattern was replicated with respect to previous work for the party. Every New Democratic delegate indicated having worked for the party in the past. The question asked of Conservative and Liberal voters focused only on work in the previous election and revealed less involvement: 46% of the Liberals said they worked in the previous election, as did 18% of the Tories. Finally, the leadership election process demonstrated the degrees of confederalism that exist in Canadian parties (see Dyck 1991: 129). By definition, all of the NDP delegates were also members of the federal party. Among Alberta Liberals, who formally severed their association with the federal Liberals in 1977, only 36% were members of the federal party, and only 20% of the Conservative voters were federal PCs (see Table 7.1).[2]

Vast differences exist in the patterns of party background, patterns produced mainly by the leadership selection process, but to a lesser extent also by the party. The New Democrats, with a unitary organization and a traditional convention, demonstrated the strongest partisan ties. The Liberal Party in Canada is both confederal and unitary in its organization (Dyck 1991: 138), and the Alberta Liberals, even though they have no formal links with the federal wing, fell between the New Democrats and the Conservatives on this dimension. The confederal Tories, with their highly inclusive ballot, produced a leadership electorate with very limited federal party roots. Indeed, as we saw in Chapter 2, a substantial minority of Conservatives possessed ties to other federal parties. It thus appears that between the tele-vote

Table 7.1

Partisan background comparison

	PC paper ballot (%) N = 943	Liberal tele-vote (%) N = 586	NDP convention (%) N = 220
Member < one year	55	34	1
Member > 7 years*	10	26	41
Held party office	5	11	60
Worked for party	18	46	100
Member of federal party	20	36	100

* For the Liberals, the percentage refers to those who were members for more than 9 years, while for the New Democrats it refers to those who were members for at least 10 years.

and the paper ballot, the tele-vote enfranchises an electorate with more of a partisan background.

Impressions of the Processes

Of the three electorates, the Conservative electorate was the most satisfied with the process it used to select the party leader. Almost all of the voters felt they had enough information to properly make their voting choice, and a similar proportion felt the direct vote to be an improvement over leadership conventions. They were also relatively content with the fee structure (a five-dollar membership fee). There was, however, some difference of opinion regarding the voting rules. Specifically, voters were split almost evenly in their viewpoint as to whether memberships should be available for purchase on voting days (see Table 7.2). As we saw in Chapter 3, that provision was critical in the process, as there were a significant number of voters who registered at the voting station during each of the two voting days.

Surprisingly, the Liberals, despite their election fiasco, were also relatively content with at least some aspects of the process. Eighty-four percent said they had enough information to make their decision, and almost four-fifths thought the process was an improvement over conventions. Most of the respondents, however, expressed a preference for utilizing some form of paper direct vote in the future. While 33% wanted to repeat the tele-voting exercise, 46% wanted actual paper ballots to be used the next time. As one would expect, there were significant internal divisions on the use of proxy votes. The vast majority of supporters of the second-place candidate favoured the use of the proxies, which were key to his candidacy.[3] Few of the supporters of the other candidates agreed, and thus the general opinion ran heavily against proxies. A great deal of uncertainty was expressed by respondents concerning the recording of their votes. Thirty percent said they were not certain their vote had been counted, and 45% experienced trouble

Table 7.2

Process evaluation comparison

	PC paper ballot (%) N = 943	Liberal tele-vote (%) N = 586	NDP convention (%) N = 220
Had enough information	94	84	70
Use all-member vote next time	NA	79	60
Close nominations before convention	NA	NA	52
Universal ballot improvement over convention	93	46	NA
Use convention next time	27	22	NA
OK to buy memberships voting day	49	NA	NA
Proxy voting OK	NA	23	NA
Fees too low	12	3	NA
Use tele-vote next time	NA	33	NA

in voting. This problem appears specific to tele-voting procedures but stemmed from more than technical problems. A number of those who were uncertain about the counting of their vote had filled out proxies whose fate was unclear.

New Democratic delegates, using the traditional leadership convention, were least satisfied with the process. Only 70% felt they had the necessary information for making a suitably knowledgeable voting decision, and a majority wanted the convention system of leadership selection to end. Sixty percent of the delegates favoured the use of a universal ballot system to choose future leaders. The proportion of New Democratic delegates favouring an all-member vote was actually deflated by the opinions of delegates from affiliated unions. Almost 80% of these delegates opposed the move to universal ballots. This level of opposition may make it difficult for the party to achieve the two-thirds convention approval it needs to move to such a system in the near future. More than half of the New Democrats were also opposed to a long-standing New Democratic tradition that allows aspirants to be nominated at the convention itself.

Support for the various processes appears inversely related to involvement. The New Democrat delegates experienced the most direct involvement with a candidate, as 82% of them actually met a candidate during the campaign. Only about half the Liberals and 30% of the Conservatives reported meeting even one of the candidates. Indeed, less than a third of the Liberals and Conservatives attended a candidate event, and even fewer attended an all-candidates forum (see Table 7.3). Nonetheless, the vast majority of respondents from these parties were satisfied with the forums and satisfied with their level of access to information on the candidates.

Table 7.3

Involvement in process comparison

	PC paper ballot N = 943	Liberal tele-vote N = 586	NDP convention N = 220
Number voting on final ballot	78,251	9,065	422
Attended all-candidates forum	20%	31%	NA
Attended candidate event	26%	32%	NA
Met a candidate	30%	47%	82%
Phoned for information	24%	NA	NA

Participants from all three parties and all three processes favoured the use of universal ballots. The Conservative voters were most satisfied with their procedure, while the Liberals, although preferring the tele-vote to a convention, wanted some sort of paper balloting in the future. Carty's suggestion that the Alberta Tory experiment seems most in keeping with the temper of the time (1994: 18) is borne out by the attitudes of the Alberta Liberals.[4]

Universal balloting appears to be the wave of the future. In Perlin's words, "Once one party uses this method, its more democratic aura will put pressure on other parties to use it as well" (Perlin 1991a: 86). The Alberta Liberals moved toward a universal ballot in part because they did not wish to appear less democratic than the Tories. Even the federal New Democrats have experimented with combining a primary system and a more traditional convention. New Democrats appear least likely to fully adopt the universal ballot, because of the opposition of labour delegates to such a process. Nonetheless, a majority of the Alberta New Democratic delegates in 1994 endorsed such a move. Although conventions have many advantages over universal ballots in terms of the experience of voters in the party and opportunities for evaluating candidates (Malcolmson 1992), the fact that convention delegates themselves favour universal balloting is a strong indication that parties will face increasing pressure to abandon traditional leadership conventions. It is thus important to evaluate the relative advantages of paper and tele-voting, and the Alberta examples afford such an opportunity.

The use of paper balloting, like that used by the Conservatives, appears to pose fewer risks than tele-voting, and in comparison with the provincial Liberals, it enfranchised more than four times as many voters. Neither of these observations appears unique to Alberta. The first tele-vote used by the Nova Scotia Liberals was almost as disastrous as the Alberta Liberal adventure, and in British Columbia, the paper balloting system used by the declining Social Credit Party involved more people than the tele-voting system used by the rising Liberal Party (Stewart, Adamson, and Beaton 1994; Blake and Carty 1994). Tele-voting, despite the convenience of voting from one's home, simply has not turned out as many people as paper balloting.

Allowing for time between ballots also appears to be an advantage of the system used by the Conservatives. The week between ballots saw the party garner much in the way of favourable publicity, and as we saw in Chapters 2 and 3, the influx of new voters was phenomenal.[5] In contrast, during the scant hours separating the two Liberal ballots, more than 2,000 of those who voted on the first failed to take part in the second. Such disappearances do not bode well for the ability of immediate re-votes to sustain interest.[6]

The Conservative Party moved from its 1985 provision of "important lessons for all Canadian parties on how not to select leaders" (Archer and Hunziker 1992: 81) to a hugely successful universal ballot, which the party's president described as "the greatest exercise in democracy ever seen in our province" (as quoted in Gunter 1992: 6). Liberal Party officials were not as enthusiastic in their evaluations of the tele-vote.[7]

Nevertheless, the tele-voting system did involve a higher proportion of people with previous experience within the party. As well, many of the problems the party experienced owed not to technical difficulties inherent in tele-voting, but to the party's decision to allow proxy votes. Although the chief electoral officer for the Liberal Party believed that the party would use tele-voting in the future, albeit without a proxy system, when the time came to choose a new leader in 1998, the party abandoned tele-voting. The fact that such a process left many participants uncertain as to whether their votes were counted is sufficiently problematic, but the potential for delivering enough votes as proxies in car trunks to win the leadership is a loophole that should be closed. In the Conservative process, participants had to attend polling stations to cast their votes, a requirement that ensures that individuals at least know a vote is taking place.[8]

The Alberta Liberals might also want to reconsider permitting individuals who are not Canadian citizens to participate in their leadership selection process. Media and party accounts noted language problems in communicating with a considerable number of the registrants.[9] The ability to attend meetings and assess candidates and even evaluate candidate literature is obviously inhibited by such a circumstance. The enfranchisement of non-citizens, who may or may not be able to communicate in English, may perpetuate one of the problems that came to beset conventions, namely the use of brutal machine politics to mobilize support in heavily "ethnic" areas (see Archer and Hunziker 1992: 86). This sort of mobilization proved more difficult in the Conservative process, since individuals had to attend polling stations, communicate with the election officials at those stations, and provide evidence of Canadian citizenship. The selling of memberships was less of a "problem" for the Conservatives, since candidates not only had to sell the memberships, they also had to turn the vote out across the entire province on a single day. Under the Liberal rules, it was technically possible for candidates to register voters and then either collect voter PINs or have the individuals sign proxy voting forms, thereby eliminating concerns about turn-out.

At this point in the evolution of universal balloting, the advantages of paper balloting appear to outweigh those of tele-voting. Technological advances and the closing of loopholes may narrow this advantage, but at the moment, parties considering universal ballots would do well to opt, as the Alberta Liberals did in 1998, for paper ballots and polling stations over tele-voting.

The Leadership Electorates: Demographic and Regional Background

The three parties and processes enfranchised somewhat different electorates with respect to demographic (Table 7.4) and regional (Table 7.5) backgrounds. Somewhat surprisingly, as Chapter 6 revealed, there was virtually no difference with respect to the proportion of women involved.

Table 7.4

Socio-demographic background comparison

	PC paper ballot (%) N = 943	Liberal tele-vote (%) N = 586	NDP convention (%) N = 220
Women	47	47	49
Age < 25	5	6	9
Age > 65	14	18	11
Mean age	48.5	49.0	47.3
Business	25	10	6
Professional	24	44	37
Farmer/rancher	10	4	3
Student	2	4	9
Retired	18	20	18
Income > $70,000	31	38	23
Income < $20,000	7	7	15
University degree	36	46	47
Less than high school	13	10	14
Canadian born	87	78	82
Protestant	54	35	34
Catholic	18	33	15
No religion	17	15	37
British	42	29	50
Other European	33	28	25
Other non-European	6	18	9

Table 7.5

Region and community size comparison

	PC paper ballot (%) N = 943	Liberal tele-vote (%) N = 586	NDP convention (%) N = 220
Calgary area	31	27	31
Edmonton area	26	41	35
Northern Alberta	14	20	11
Central Alberta	17	8	14
Southern Alberta	12	5	9
Hometown over 500,000	44	54	61
Hometown under 10,000	34	18	20

Conventions have traditionally badly underrepresented women, but the NDP convention indicates that this is not necessarily due to the convention system itself, since women accounted for over 49% of the NDP convention delegate total. Women accounted for 47% of the Conservative voting total, and female respondents comprised a similar proportion of the Liberal total. However, supporters of Sine Chadi, the runner-up in the Liberal contest, did not respond proportionately to the survey, but of those who did, men significantly outnumbered women. If this were true of Chadi supporters in general,[10] then the Liberal tele-vote resulted in the smallest proportion of women turning out to vote.

The two universal ballots enfranchised a different electorate with respect to age than that traditionally produced by Liberal or Conservative conventions. The proportion of participants under the age of twenty-five was relatively small, while those over sixty-five accounted for a substantial element. The proportion of participants over sixty-five was double that of the youth in each of the processes, and the mean age of participants was highest in the tele-voting exercise. The ease of voting from your own home is obviously a factor for older voters. The New Democratic convention reveals again the peculiar nature of that party's conventions. Unlike the Liberals and Tories, the New Democrats have not established rules to ensure that youth are overrepresented, and in fact, the convention produced an electorate close to that of the two universal ballots on this dimension. In all three processes, roughly a fifth of the participants were retired.

There were some deviations in terms of occupation, which seem to suggest as much about the parties as they do about the processes. Substantially more Conservatives had business occupations. More than a quarter of the Tory voters reported this sort of occupation, compared to 10% of the Liberals and 6% of the New Democrats. Similarly, the proportion of Conservatives who were farmers or ranchers was twice as high as that of the Liberals and New Democrats. Liberal and New Democratic participants were much more likely to be professionals, and students were also more numerous within those parties. The parties also differ when one combines professionals, business persons, and farmers. Individuals representing such occupations accounted for almost 70% of the Tory voters and over 60% of the Liberals. In contrast, less than half of the New Democrats came from these ranks.

Party appears to overwhelm process in terms of the income level of participants. Despite their delegate status, New Democratic participants were least likely to report household incomes in excess of $70,000, and most likely to indicate that their family income was less than $20,000. Liberal participants were the most affluent, with 38% claiming incomes of more than $75,000.

New Democratic delegates were, however, somewhat more likely to have completed a university degree than were participants in the two universal ballots. Forty-seven percent of the New Democrats, as compared to 46% of the Liberals and 36% of the Tories, possessed university degrees.[11] The New Democratic edge was even more striking with respect to postgraduate education.

The universal ballot seems to move the leadership electorates in the Liberal and Conservative parties closer to the New Democrats. It appears that the universal ballots attracted a somewhat less affluent and educated body than did conventions. The openness of the New Democrats, at least at the provincial level, to individuals of lower incomes and persons who are not from professional or business backgrounds is noteworthy. Among the universal balloters, the individuals who participated in the Liberal tele-vote were better educated, came from higher-status occupations, and possessed higher incomes than those who voted in the Conservative process. Again, it appears that the direct paper ballot enfranchises both a larger and wider proportion of voters.

Data on ethnicity and religion confirm some of the traditional impressions of the three parties. The Protestant tint of the Conservative Party is striking. More than half of the Conservative voters claimed to be Protestant, compared to just 35% of the Liberals and 34% of the New Democrats. The Liberals, as elsewhere in the country, were disproportionately Catholic. One Liberal in three said they were Catholic, while less than a fifth of the Tories and New Democrats reported such affiliations. Finally, New Democrats were relatively non-religious, as 37% reported "none" as their religion. Only 17% of the PCs and 15% of the Liberals fell into this category.

The Liberal ranks contained the highest proportion of voters who were not born in Canada, and there were a number of other interesting "ethnic" patterns. People of British descent accounted for a higher proportion of the delegates at the New Democratic convention than they do in the Alberta population. Slightly over half of the delegates identified themselves as British, compared to 42% for the Tories and just 29% of the Liberals. While three-quarters of the Conservatives and New Democrats claimed a European origin, only 57% of the Liberals did the same. Non-British Europeans were much more common in the Liberal ranks, as were those who claimed an ethnicity other than European or Canadian. Once more, the underrepresentation of Chadi in our sample probably makes this tendency appear weaker. Among the Chadi supporters, the proportion who claim a non-European ethnic heritage is even higher. The traditional portrait of the Liberals as the party of recent waves of immigration seems to be authenticated by these figures, as is the British tint of the New Democratic Party. The Tory electorate provided the most accurate "descriptive" reflection of the province with respect to both ethnicity and religion.

Finally, the data indicate the differences in the regional support for the various parties. Each of the processes resulted in the overrepresentation of areas that supported the particular party. The Conservatives appear as the party with support from across the province and especially from the rural and southern parts. More than half of the Conservatives said they did not reside in areas of more than 500,000, while only 46% of the Liberals and 39% of the New Democrats made such a claim. Members of the opposition parties were more likely to live in major urban areas. More specifically, they tended to reside in Edmonton. The strength of the Liberal Party in the Edmonton area is noteworthy. Fully 41% of the registered Liberals resided in that portion of the province, compared to 35% of the NDP and 26% of the Tories. Only in Tory ranks did participants from Calgary outnumber those from the provincial capital.

The data on residence provide another indication of the distinctive nature of New Democratic conventions. The New Democrats base their delegate entitlements on membership size, so their delegates do not provide a geographic microcosm of the province. The universal ballot processes used by the Alberta Tories and Liberals provided a leadership electorate more reflective of the provincial population. The closer resemblance between the Conservative participants and the demographic distributions of the province might have resulted from their more open process. It might also have resulted from the system of one-party dominance in which they received substantial levels of support from throughout the province, or from the fact that they were choosing someone who would become premier. The narrower geographic bases of the other two parties indicate the difficult task facing these parties as they try to defeat the Tories.

Ideological Division and Cohesion among Albertan Political Parties
One of the conventional wisdoms of Canadian politics is that Albertans are, for the most part, homogeneously conservative in their political views. And, it would appear that a prima facie case could be made for the ideological

conformity of Albertans. In classical analyses of Alberta politics, C.B. Macpherson (1962), and John Richards and Larry Pratt (1979) have argued that the province's unique economy (based in the 1950s on export-oriented agriculture and in the 1970s and 1980s on export-oriented energy resources) has produced a political mindset in the province based on a division between "us" and "them," "them" referring to the other provinces.

A brief review of the electoral record in the province also supports the conformity view. Between 1935 and 1971, for example, Alberta experienced thirty-six years of uninterrupted rule by the Social Credit government. Since then, the province has had more than a quarter century of uninterrupted rule by the Conservatives. Furthermore, during most of this period, the government faced little opposition in the legislature. Similarly, at the federal level during the 1970s and 1980s, it was typical for the Progressive Conservatives to sweep the province's seats in the House of Commons. When political winds shifted in Alberta in the early 1990s, away from the Conservatives and toward the Reform Party, the extent of the changes once again appeared to affirm the case for ideological conformity, as Reform won twenty-two of the twenty-six Commons seats in the 1993 election and increased their seat count to twenty-four in 1997.

Recent analyses have indicated that the extent of political dominance in Alberta is, at least in part, an artifact of electoral system distortion (Archer 1992). Electoral landslides in the province have often been produced on the basis of as little as 45% of the popular vote, and rarely has a party's vote exceeded 60%. In addition, at the provincial level, there has been a systematic decline over the past decade in the electoral support for the government. Indeed, in 1993, the Klein government obtained 44% of the vote, compared to 40% for the Liberal opposition, a result that indicates a high level of political competitiveness. Thus, it would appear that the extent of political and ideological homogeneity in Alberta is often overstated.

Another explanation is that people in Alberta may not perceive substantial or consistent differences between the parties. To paraphrase Gerald Pomper, "lack of clarity among voters is produced by a lack of clarity among parties" (1972: 415-28). If parties do not provide voters with clear alternatives to the current government, then there is little reason to expect voters to give them support. Many analyses of Canadian political parties have described the major parties as "brokers," suggesting that the parties are relatively undifferentiated on policy grounds, and instead move freely and widely across the political spectrum in search of voters.

Recent research into the opinion structure of the federal parties has suggested that, at least when focusing on party activists, the parties display reasonably distinctive views, and occupy reasonably unique positions in policy space. For example, a comparison of New Democrats, Liberals, and Conservatives indicated that the NDP was clearly on the political left, the

Liberals were near the centre of the continuum, and the Conservatives were toward the right, although not as far right as the NDP were toward the left (Archer and Whitehorn 1990; Archer and Whitehorn 1997). A similar analysis of Reform Party activists found the party to be very far toward the political right on some issues (such as support for decreased government spending) but more toward the centre, and internally more divided, on issues such as Canada's relationship with the United States (Archer and Ellis 1994).

At the provincial level, a similar analysis was conducted on British Columbian New Democrat, Liberal, and Social Credit activists. The analysis found that the New Democrats and Socreds were often located on opposite poles of the ideological continuum, with the Liberals located in a more moderate right wing position and much closer to the centre than either of the alternatives (Blake, Carty, and Erickson 1991). Yet, politics in British Columbia are often described as being ideologically volatile. Would one expect to see the same level of ideological and policy distinctiveness in a province such as Alberta, which is more often characterized as exhibiting policy consensus?

To explore the nature and character of policy division and cohesion among Alberta's parties, respondents to our surveys were presented with a series of questions on a wide range of policy items. The results for each party were reported in earlier chapters. Table 7.6 provides a comparison of the parties in terms of attitudes toward individualism, populism, continentalism, social spending, moral issues, land claims, the size of government, and the environment. The table's cell entries are simply the percentage of respondents from each party who agree, have no opinion, or disagree with the statement. Respondents not answering were excluded from the analysis.

The data indicate that party activists in Alberta have substantially different views on three of the four items tapping attitudes toward individualism, with the New Democrats taking the most distinctive position (against individualism) in each instance. For example, over 90% of New Democrats agreed that the government ought to ensure that everyone has a decent standard of living, compared to 68% of Liberals and only 44% of Conservatives. Indeed, Conservatives were slightly more likely (49%) to disagree with the statement. When asked whether most unemployed people could find jobs if they really wanted to, fully 96% of New Democrats felt that they could not, compared to 61% of Liberals and 49% of Conservatives. Once again, Conservatives were almost evenly divided on the item. Respondents also were asked whether the community should support someone after that person has worked until age sixty-five. Somewhat surprisingly, only 74% of New Democrats agreed. It is possible on this item that some of the disagreement or lack of opinion is due to different interpretations of the question's preamble, causing a situation in which not all New Democrats would agree that everyone should need to work until age sixty-five before being entitled

Table 7.6

Issue positions of NDP, Liberal, and PC activists

	NDP N = 220			Liberal N = 586			PC N = 943		
	Agree	No opinion	Disagree	Agree	No opinion	Disagree	Agree	No opinion	Disagree
Individualism									
The government ought to make sure that everyone has a decent standard of living.	92.1	2.7	5.0	68.1	4.4	27.5	43.6	8.0	48.5
Let's face it, most unemployed people could find jobs if they really wanted to.	1.4	2.3	96.3	32.6	6.1	61.4	42.9	8.3	48.8
Why should the government spend my tax dollars on sick people; my family always put aside something for a rainy day.	0.9	0.9	98.2	4.2	4.3	91.5	7.4	4.9	87.8
After a person has worked until 65, it is proper for the community to support him or her.	74.4	11.1	14.5	36.9	11.3	51.9	33.5	10.7	55.8
Populism									
In the long run, I'll put my trust in the simple, down-to-earth thinking of ordinary people rather than the theories of experts and intellectuals.	43.5	19.5	37.0	52.7	9.5	37.8	62.7	9.1	28.3

Statement								
We could probably solve most of our big political problems if the government could actually be brought back to people at the grassroots.	58.0	10.6	31.4	59.4	29.6	11.0	68.7	10.2	21.1
What we need is a government that gets the job done without all this red tape.	63.0	18.0	19.0	85.0	7.9	7.2	90.5	5.0	4.5
There should be a referendum on all amendments to the Constitution.	28.8	14.4	56.7	45.9	11.0	43.1	48.1	10.1	41.7

Continentalism

Statement								
We must ensure an independent Canada even if that were to mean a lower standard of living for Canadians.	72.7	10.7	16.6	60.7	13.2	26.1	54.6	12.5	32.9
The Canada-US Free Trade Agreement has been good for Alberta.	7.4	7.4	85.1	36.0	31.6	32.5	48.3	28.0	23.8
Canada's independence is threatened by the large percentage of foreign ownership in key sectors of the economy.	89.0	3.7	7.3	55.4	13.4	31.2	41.0	13.2	45.7

Social Spending

Statement								
Social programs should remain universal.	**	**	**	71.6	8.3	20.1	43.8	8.7	47.6

Table 7.6

	NDP N = 220			Liberal N = 586			PC N = 943		
	Agree	No opinion	Disagree	Agree	No opinion	Disagree	Agree	No opinion	Disagree
The government should see that everyone has adequate housing.	94.9	1.8	3.2	56.8	10.8	32.3	**	**	**
A lot of welfare and social security programs we now have are unnecessary.	11.4	3.2	85.3	41.7	9.8	48.5	63.6	10.6	25.8
Moral									
Abortion is a matter that should be decided solely between a woman and her doctor.	92.1	1.9	6.1	70.9	4.3	24.7	74.6	3.6	21.9
Discrimination on the basis of sexual orientation should be prohibited.	93.9	2.8	3.3	76.6	7.6	15.7	**	**	**
Land claims									
The provincial government should negotiate with the province's Native population on land claims.	81.9	5.6	12.5	61.6	15.8	22.6	57.4	16.3	26.3

Size of governments

The size of government in Alberta should be reduced even if it means a lower level of public services.	20.9	**	10.9	68.2	61.5	7.3	31.2	**	**	**
Balanced budgets should be mandatory.	**	**	**	66.0	5.9	28.1	91.7	3.9	4.4	**

Environment

Tougher environmental standards should take precedence over employment opportunities.	78.6	**	12.6	8.7	60.9	12.7	26.4	**	**	**

Notes: Three two-party comparisons were undertaken for each relevant question. All comparisons between the NDP and the PC revealed differences that were statistically significant at the 99% confidence level. With the exception of the first two items under populism, all comparisons of the NDP and Liberals were statistically significant. The third item under individualism was statistically significant at the 95% confidence level. All other comparisons provided differences that were statistically significant at the 99% confidence level. With the following exceptions, the PC and Liberal comparisons revealed differences that were statistically significant at the 99% confidence level: the third item under populism and the third item under individualism were statistically significant at the 95% confidence level; the differences on fourth item under populism, the fourth item under individualism, and the abortion question were not statistically significant.

** Question not asked in survey.

to community support. In any event, a majority of Liberals and Conservatives, in roughly equal proportions, disagreed with this statement. The one "individualism" item that differs from the rest explores attitudes toward health care. When asked to respond to the statement "Why should the government spend my tax money on sick people; my family always put aside something for a rainy day," a strong majority in all parties disagreed, ranging from a high of 98% of New Democrats to a low of 88% of Conservatives, with Liberals assuming the middle position at 92%.

Regarding attitudes toward populism, the results differ in two ways. First, there are generally less pronounced differences among the activists in the different parties, and second, the Conservatives tend to occupy the most polar positions on the issues. For example, when asked whether they would "put their trust in the simple, down-to-earth thinking of ordinary people rather than the theories of experts and intellectuals," New Democrats were close to being evenly divided, Conservatives favoured "ordinary people" by a margin of more than two to one, and the Liberals again fell between the two other parties. The data indicate an interesting consensus on the usefulness of government decentralization. Majorities in each party agreed (by wide margins) that problems could be solved by bringing government back to the grassroots. Conservatives (91%) and Liberals (85%) were each nearly unanimous in their belief that government "red tape" should be cut. New Democrats were also likely to reach this conclusion, although with less unanimity (64%). Finally, on the matter of referendums for future constitutional amendments, roughly half of the Conservatives and Liberals agreed, compared to about one-quarter of the New Democrats.

Previous analysis of party differences at the national level indicated a high level of opposition toward continentalism among New Democrats, general support among Conservatives, and ambiguity among Liberals. This is also an issue upon which the Reform Party has lacked consensus. Responses to the items in our surveys demonstrate clearly some of the contrasting views on this complex item. On the one hand, all parties have a majority in support of the view that Canada's independence is important even if maintaining independence requires a lower standard of living. Support for this view is strongest among New Democrats and weakest among Conservatives. However, in assessing the impact of the Free Trade Agreement (FTA), significant differences emerge. New Democrats are nearly unanimous in assessing the FTA negatively, Conservatives feel it has been positive by a factor of about two to one, and Liberals are completely divided in their assessments. When asked if foreign ownership threatens Canada's independence, about nine in ten New Democrats express the belief that it does, as do 55% of Liberals. Thirty-one percent of Liberals see little threat in foreign ownership, and Conservative opinions are close to equally divided. Thus, the polar position is occupied by New Democrats on this issue.

On the social spending topic, there is some lack of comparability due to the fact that not all questions were asked in each of our three surveys. But, where the data are comparable, the results are clear – New Democrats are strongly supportive of social spending, Liberals are generally supportive, and Conservatives are either split or opposed. For example, Liberals strongly support universality of social programs, whereas Conservatives are about evenly divided. New Democrats are nearly unanimous in their belief that government should ensure adequate housing (95%), whereas support among Liberals is a more modest 57%. In response to the statement that "a lot of welfare and social security programs are unnecessary," 85% of New Democrats disagree, Liberals are about evenly split, and almost two-thirds of Conservatives agree.

In a scrutiny of moral issues, all parties have strong majorities in support of the view that abortion is a matter between a woman and her doctor, and both New Democrats and Liberals have strong majorities in favour of prohibitions against discrimination based on sexual orientation. The latter was not asked on the Conservative survey. A majority from each party supports governmental negotiation of land claims with the province's Natives, with the size of this majority ranging from 82% of New Democrats to 57% of Conservatives. On environmental matters, both New Democrats and Liberals have strong majorities in support of instituting tough environmental standards. The Progressive Conservatives were not given the opportunity to respond to questions pertaining to the environment.

Respondents were asked a number of questions about their views toward the size of government. As with the questions on individualism and social spending, a number of consistent party differences emerge. When asked whether the size of government should be reduced even if the reduction would result in a lower level of public services, only one New Democrat in five advocated reduction, compared to three in five Liberals and four out of five Conservatives. When asked whether balanced budgets should be mandatory, over nine in ten Conservatives, and two in three Liberals, felt that they should (New Democrats were not asked).

Responses used in the preceding analysis were compared in a series of two-party comparisons to determine the extent to which those involved in selecting leaders from the various parties held opinions that differ in a statistically significant manner from one another. The data reveal a high degree of differentiation across the parties, with the vast majority of bi-party comparisons revealing significant differences. In the eighteen issues for which data are available comparing New Democrats and Liberals, significant differences were found in sixteen, with the exception being two questions relating to populist sentiment. Populist sentiment was lower among activists in both parties than among Conservatives. On the fifteen issues for which data were available for a New Democrat-Conservative comparison,

Table 7.7

Attitudes toward the role of government among Alberta NDP, Liberal, and PC activists

		Agreeing with statement (%)		
		NDP $N = 220$	Liberal $N = 586$	PC $N = 943$
1. (a)	Government regulation stifles personal drive.	5.9	25.0	44.7
or				
(b)	Without government regulations, some people just take advantage of the rest of us.	94.1	75.0	53.3
2. (a)	If I do my best, it is only right that the government should help me when I get some bad breaks.	80.5	33.9	16.3
or				
(b)	Each individual should accept the consequences of their own actions.	19.5	66.1	83.7
3. (a)	Governments should make a strong effort to improve the social and economic position of women.	92.2	52.5	35.6
or				
(b)	Women should help themselves and should not expect governments to make special efforts on their behalf.	7.8	47.5	64.4

attitudes were significantly different on all fifteen, indicating a clear differentiation among those involved in these two parties. For the Liberal-Conservative comparison, statistically significant differences were evident in thirteen of the seventeen issues for which comparable data were available. The issues on which the parties were not differentiated included abortion, land claims, the use of referendums on constitutional issues, and community support for retirees. Overall, however, supporters of these two parties are more likely to hold attitudes that are statistically different than to be undifferentiated. Albertans are offered real alternatives among parties.

Analyses of party differences over the size and role of government are pursued further in Table 7.7, in which respondents were given pairs of alternative statements and asked to choose the one most closely resembling their own viewpoint. The first pair asks whether government regulation stifles personal drive, or whether government is needed so that more people do not take advantage of others. New Democrats are nearly unanimous (94%) in their positive assessment of government regulation, and Liberals

Table 7.8

Opinion indices: Mean score comparison

Issue index (range)	NDP N = 145		Liberal N = 453		PC N = 722	
	Mean	S	Mean	S	Mean	S
Individualism (0-4) (pro-individualism)	0.19	0.98	1.17	0.35	1.52	1.03
Populism (0-4) (pro-populism)	1.86	0.59	2.45	0.24	2.69	1.14
Continentalism (0-3) (pro-continentalism)	0.32	0.65	0.97	0.33	1.30	1.01
Social policy (0-3) (pro-social spending)	2.71	0.99	1.72	0.67	1.05	1.11
Moral issues (0-2) (moral liberalism)	1.87	0.38	1.49	0.01	1.50	0.87
Land claims (0-1) (government should negotiate)	0.79	0.18	0.61	0.14	0.57	0.50
Size of government (0-5) (reduce size of government)	0.64	2.04	2.68	0.84	3.52	1.24
Environment (0-1) (tough environmental standards)	0.79	0.41	0.60	0.49	**	**

** Question not asked in survey.
S = Standard deviation.

take a positive view of government regulation by a three-to-one margin, whereas Conservative opinions are nearly evenly split.

The second item asks whether government should help if a person suffers bad breaks, or whether one should bear the consequences of his or her own actions. On this, the parties are deeply divided. Only one in five New Democrats feel that individuals must bear the consequences of their own actions, compared to two in three Liberals, and four in five Conservatives who feel this way. This is a general view that has an important bearing on people's attitudes toward a host of potential policy initiatives. On the specific issues of the government's role in supporting women, less than one in ten New Democrats fail to see a useful role for government, compared to one in two Liberals and two in three Conservatives.

Throughout the book, we have used a number of scales to elaborate and summarize attitudes across the issue areas in order to develop a more parsimonious understanding of the parties' positions on policy and ideological issues.[12] The mean and standard deviations for the three parties across these scales are presented in Table 7.8.

Table 7.8 indicates that the configuration of parties in Alberta varies across the issue areas. Although their alignment relative to one another is generally quite consistent with the New Democrats furthest to the left, the Conservatives furthest to the right, and the Liberals at the centre, their alignment relative to specific issue areas is highly variable. For example, on some items, the NDP holds a position near the pole on an issue, whereas the Liberals and Conservatives are near the centre position, with no party claiming the other pole. The scales measuring attitudes toward individualism and continentalism follow this pattern. If the opposite of the individualism index is collectivism, the NDP is firmly collectivist with a mean of 0.19. Note, however, that the Conservative position is 1.52, near the midpoint of this four-point index. In a relative context, the Conservatives are far more individualist than New Democrats. However, even the Conservatives accept a considerable degree of collectivism in their conception of society. Similarly, when perusing levels of continentalism, we see that New Democrats take a near-polar position of 0.32, whereas the Conservatives, at 1.30, are near the midpoint of this three-point scale. Although Conservatives are not as opposed as New Democrats to Canadian links with the United States, neither do the PCs fully embrace such links. A second type of opinion distribution reveals the Conservatives on one side of the continuum, with the New Democrats and Liberals nearer the centre, an opinion structure characteristic of the populism index. On this item, the Conservatives assume a relatively populist position of 2.69 on a four-point scale. It is important to note, however, that none of the parties can be considered anti-populist. The NDP, at 1.86, and the Liberals, at 2.45, indicate that populist sentiment forms part of the arsenal of all parties in Alberta.

On a number of survey items, the positions of the parties can best be described as consensual. For example, on moral items and on land claims issues, the prevailing sentiment for each of the parties is located in the same direction on the scale's continuum, with the parties differentiated more by the degree of concurrence with the position rather than by its direction. The data indicate that this may also be the case with environmental policies, although the absence of relevant data for the Conservatives leaves some ambiguity on the matter.

The last type of opinion distribution is exhibited by those areas on which the parties demonstrate a clear ideological division, with New Democrats toward one end of the continuum, Conservatives toward the other end, and Liberals somewhere in between. This latter distribution can be seen in attitudes toward social policy and toward the size of government. For example, on the three-point scale measuring attitudes in favour of government spending in social welfare policy areas, New Democrats occupy one pole (2.71), whereas the Conservatives are on the other side, albeit taking a less polar position (1.05). Similarly, examining attitudes in favour of reducing the size of government, New Democrats are opposed to such reductions (0.64), whereas Conservatives are in favour (3.52). Liberals are near the midpoint of the five-point scale (2.68). The degree of ideological division on these last two items is especially important in contemporary Alberta, because they are core features of the public policy changes that have become known as the "Klein revolution." In particular, a commitment to balance the budget without tax increases, to reduce the size and scope of government, and to cut spending across-the-board, including in areas of social policy, have been hallmarks of the Klein revolution. It is pertaining to these items that the largest and most consistent ideological division exists.

To provide a fuller portrait of the range of policy alternatives facing Alberta voters, activists from the New Democrat and Liberal parties were asked their opinions about some of the specific features of the Conservative government's policy, the results of which are presented in Table 7.9. The data illustrate some interesting differences between New Democrats and Liberals in Alberta. One should also bear in mind the electoral context of the two parties in the 1993 election – the Liberal Party improved its standing in the legislature from eight seats to thirty-one. The New Democrats, in contrast, fell from sixteen seats and official opposition status to no seats.

Whereas only one in eight New Democrats agree that the debt and deficit should be the top priority of government, fully six in ten Liberals categorize the debt and deficit as the province's top priority. Thus, a clear majority of Liberals were "on-side" with the Conservatives over the importance of deficit reduction, and an overwhelming majority of New Democrats opposed the government's prioritization of the deficit. Furthermore, New Democrats offered stark opposition to the major thrusts of the government; they disagreed with across-the-board cuts, they overwhelmingly opposed cutting funding for kindergarten programs, and they opposed tuition increases for post-secondary education, cuts to public health care spending, and the use of user fees for health care. In view of their overwhelming opposition to cutting social expenditures, New Democrats can be said to offer the alternative of increased taxes to pay for government programs, a position supported by 67% of New Democrats.

In contrast, with the exception of their attitudes toward increased taxes, in which they are even more strongly opposed (75%) than New Democrats are in favour, Liberals were more nuanced in their assessment of the government's initiatives. For example, almost one in three Liberals supported across-the-board cuts, compared to two in three opposed. Although Liberals believed that fees for kindergarten penalize children from lower-income families (83%), they were almost evenly divided in their assessment of whether post-secondary students should pay higher tuition. And, while Liberals were generally opposed to health care cuts and to user fees, fully one-quarter of Liberals supported even these policies. In addition, almost four in ten Liberals supported a rollback in public sector wages.

Table 7.9

New Democratic and Liberal attitudes toward deficit reduction and the Klein agenda

	New Democrat N = 220			Liberal N = 586		
	Agree	No Opinion	Disagree	Agree	No Opinion	Disagree
Reducing the provincial debt and deficit should be the top priority of the Alberta government.	13	4	83	58	4	38
The best way to reduce the deficit is through across-the-board cuts.	3	3	94	29	5	66
User fees for kindergarten penalize children from lower income families.	100	0	0	83	3	14
More of the costs of post-secondary education should be paid by tuition.	7	3	90	45	6	49
The provincial government should reduce its spending on health care.	10	3	87	26	4	70
User fees for medicare and hospitalization are necessary for fairness and efficiency.	3	1	96	25	5	70
The Alberta government should increase taxes to pay for government programs.	67	6	27	17	7	76
Public sector wages should be rolled back.	12	7	81	39	14	47

Conclusion

The selection of a party leader provides a rare opportunity for a political party to make a collective decision. It provides an opportunity for a party to decide not only who will lead the party, and therefore who can speak for the party, but also who can speak within a party – to whom does the party appeal, and how is their voice given effect in party deliberations. Thus, in the final analysis, leadership selection concerns defining the voice of and within the party.

Alberta's recent experience in the definition of voice provides, in many respects, a study in contrasts. Each of the parties used a different method of leadership selection, each had a different cut-off date for participation, and each had vastly different numbers of people directly involved in the selection process. Despite these differences, or perhaps because of them, we found that the people involved in selecting leaders for the three parties in Alberta were less of a socioeconomic elite than has traditionally been the case when leadership conventions were used by the parties. In addition, it is noteworthy that the relatively open process used by the Conservatives, and to a lesser extent, even the controversial tele-vote adopted by the Liberals, were viewed as preferable to the convention method of leadership selection.

Our examination of leadership selection in the three Alberta parties makes clear that intra-party democracy can best be described as "quasi-democracy." The New Democratic convention enfranchised the fewest voters and made it impossible for members who were not delegates to express a clear opinion as to who they wished to see become leader. The nominations for leader did not close until after the convention opened and, indeed, one of the candidates filed notice of her candidacy only at that convention. The campaign was thus very limited and other party members were effectively precluded from full discussion of the candidates and their merits. Conventions have been celebrated for the guarantees they provide for regional representation. With the New Democrats, there were no such guarantees and the delegates provided the least accurate regional portrait of Alberta. Celebrations of the regional representation provided by conventions obviously apply only to Liberal and Conservative conventions, they are not inherent to the convention process. It is also worth noting the different levels of participation available to different delegates. Those delegates who did not take part in any of the caucuses did not have the same opportunity to interact with candidates as other delegates. Finally, despite the preference expressed by a majority of the delegates for some form of universal balloting, pockets of opposition to this change within the party, particularly among union delegates, may make this impossible.

It is equally clear that while opening up the leadership selection process to ordinary members has been described as party "democraticization," the universal ballots used by the Liberals and Conservatives do not represent the full triumph of "democracy." Admittedly, both parties allowed essentially for universal suffrage. However, for both parties, voters who would not be eligible to vote in general elections could play a role in choosing the leader. Both parties permitted those under eighteen to vote, and the Liberals also permitted those who were not Canadian citizens to vote. It was thus possible for the party leader to be chosen by an electorate that would not be enfranchised in a provincial election. Given the critical role of parties in providing the pool from which ordinary voters must choose their premier, this issue merits debate.

It is also useful to keep in mind that many Liberal members were not given the opportunity to vote for their leader. Only those members who were willing to pay an additional $10 were given the right to vote. This meant that most Liberal members were not eligible to vote for their leader. The Liberal election was also marred by the proxy fiasco, the technological problems, and the possibility that votes were cast by someone other than the person registered.

The Conservatives escaped many of the problems associated with the Liberal tele-vote. The party provided a closer approximation of universal suffrage than any other party had previously or has since. Memberships could be purchased at the polling stations on the day of each ballot. In practice, this meant that the Tory leadership was heavily influenced by "tourists" and "party crashers." Tourists were voters who had little in the way of an ongoing commitment to the party. More than one-fifth of the electorate had not even voted Conservative in the previous provincial election, and more than one-quarter were not sure they would support the party in the next election. We defined "gate crashers" as those who joined the party after the first ballot was over. These people added a great deal of excitement to the process but ensured that the Tory election was unlike any held previously in Canada. If a candidate on the final ballot was not satisfied with the first-ballot results, it was possible to change the electorate. This permitted a large number of voters to join the party and many of these voters were animated by a desire to prevent someone from winning the leadership, rather than voting for more positive reasons. Their presence also made it more difficult to conceive of the election as a "deliberative" process.

The three elections also demonstrated the absence of internal agreement on the rules by which intra-party elections were conducted. Bruce Hinkley, the NDP runner-up, left the party shortly after the convention and in the 1997 election ran for another party. Two of the Liberal candidates contemplated lawsuits over the way their election was conducted, and the winner's tenure was marred by questions over the legitimacy of his victory. The aftermath of the Tory election saw the first-ballot leader, Nancy Betkowski, withdraw from politics for a time and when she returned, it was as a Liberal. Obviously, then, leadership elections dramatically affect the face the party is able to present, and there is no overarching party ethos that will keep losing candidates in the party. The British system has been described as reflecting "a nation so fundamentally at one that we can safely afford to bicker" (Lord Balfour). Such a description could not be made of any of the Alberta parties.

Each of the internal party elections demonstrates the difficulty in achieving "intra-party" democracy. The best description of Alberta leadership processes is "quasi-democratic." This does not mean that the processes were non-democratic any more than C.B. Macpherson's classic depiction of the Alberta party system as a "quasi-party system" implied a "non-party system" (1962: 238). The fact that none of the parties were able to provide a textbook example of democracy does not mean that their elections were "undemocratic." Nor does it mean that each party election was equally problematic. Although both the New Democratic convention and the Conservative primary had some shortcomings, it is indisputable that the Liberals were the "Gold Medallists" in this category. While many prefer the convention used by the New Democrats to the open primary used by the Conservatives, it is important to remember that the New Democrats themselves favour a universal ballot, and the NDP convention enfranchised fewer than 500 Albertans, while the Tory primary permitted all Albertans who wished to vote directly for a premier (for the first time in provincial history) to do so. Given the general dissatisfaction Canadians express with parties and parliamentary democracy more broadly (see the report of the Royal Commission on Electoral Reform and Party Financing 1991), a leadership election that affords citizens the opportunity to involve themselves directly in selecting their first minister may well be a positive development.

The data on attitudes of respondents to our three party surveys indicate that opinion structures within Albertan parties are complex, but also that the parties provide significant and systematic differences for Alberta voters, presenting them with a full complement of political choices. For example, although there are some issue areas where there appears to be a consensus on policy preferences, such as on moral issues and in relation to land claims, on most other issue areas the parties provide a range of political alternatives. On the individualism and continentalism items, the NDP takes a position on one side of the issue, whereas the Liberals and Conservatives are near the centre. On populism, the Conservatives are farther to one side, with the New Democrats, and to a lesser extent the Liberals, closer to the centre. However, the largest differences between parties emerged on the social policy and size of government items, where the New Democrats and Conservatives are located in polar positions.

It should be noted, of course, that the ongoing political debate in Alberta tends not to be between the New Democrats and Conservatives, but rather between the Liberals and Conservatives. Following the 1993 election, the

NDP was left with no seats in the legislature and a popular vote share that had fallen to only 11%. In 1997, their share of the popular vote suffered a further decline to 8%, but the vagaries of the single-member-plurality electoral system rewarded them with two legislative seats. The Liberals remained the dominant opposition party. A comparison of Conservatives and Liberals is less a study in contrasts, than a study in contrasting emphases. Similar to the Conservatives, Liberals generally agree that the deficit and debt should be the province's top priority and that increased taxes are not the best solution to achieve that goal. Significant minorities of Liberals are prepared to support the reduction of spending on social programs. Thus, the effective range of political choices in the province today is somewhat more limited than it would be were the NDP better able to express their alternative voice within the legislature. What remains, of course, is an examination of the linkage between party opinion, and the opinion of the mass public in Alberta. That examination will have to await subsequent analyses.

8
Quasi-Democracy?
Lessons from Alberta

Political leaders have a profound impact on party politics in Canada. The notion that a Canadian prime minister or provincial premier is "first among equals" is without question a constitutional fiction. Canadian political leaders often have a base of support that derives largely outside of parliament and of the cabinet, and this provides a considerable measure of independence from the caucus and from the party. When one couples the independence of political leaders with a party system that has weak and easily changeable partisan loyalties among the electorate, the result is a party system that is highly volatile, and subject to wide variations in support for the parties over relatively short periods of time (see, for example, Pammett 1994). The Canadian party system has witnessed such shifts in the 1990s. Paradoxically, the stability seen in the Alberta party system following the election of Ralph Klein as Conservative Party leader in 1992 also affirms the short-term character of party loyalties and the importance of leaders in establishing and maintaining voters' political allegiances, a point to which we shall return.

Our interest in political leaders and leadership, and in Alberta politics, led to the decision to focus this study on leadership selection in Alberta. It was fortuitous that each of the three parties with representation in the Alberta legislature at the time the study began held a leadership selection process within a period of about twenty-three months. Each party chose their new leader under challenging circumstances, and each used a different method of leadership selection. This provided a unique opportunity to compare directly the impact of different forms of leadership selection, recognizing, of course, that some of the differences between the experiences of the parties owed to their differing issue and/or ideological orientation rather than simply to differences in the manner the leaders were selected. Nonetheless, there are very strong currents in Canadian politics at both the federal and provincial levels toward the selection of party leaders by direct methods of selection, and the Alberta experience allows us to identify some of the implications of using direct election methods.

The Conservative Party chose Ralph Klein as leader in December 1992, using a direct election method in which the balloting was conducted in person at polling stations set up by the party across the province. Because the Conservatives were the government party at the time, although a government with dwindling support under leader Don Getty, their election drew considerable interest and attention because the victor would become premier of the province. The party used a majority electoral rule with a run-off ballot. This meant that if no candidate received a majority of votes in the first election, a second ballot would be held a week later between the top two candidates. With nine candidates in the race, including relative newcomer Ralph Klein, who had jumped from municipal to provincial politics three years earlier, no candidate was able to secure a majority on the first ballot, and a run-off election was held between Klein and then-Education Minister Nancy Betkowski. The run-off election required the party once again to orchestrate and manage an election across the province of almost 80,000 voters, no mean feat for a Canadian political party, given the amorphous character and weak organizational structure with which they are typically characterized.[1] The party's success in holding these two ballots on consecutive weekends was aided by its relatively strong financial position, which was at least in part a function of its forming the government of the day. Although in 1992 the opposition Liberals raised almost as much money in Alberta as the Tories, their fundraising has been less successful since, and it is now unlikely that they, much less any other party in Alberta, could muster the financial and organizational wherewithal to hold such a province-wide ballot involving nearly 100,000 voters even once, let alone twice.

If the Conservatives went into their leadership selection with serious challenges (given Don Getty's lacklustre leadership), the New Democrats were in a state of crisis in choosing a leader. The party lost all sixteen of its seats in the legislature in the 1993 election, as well as its designation as the official opposition. Similarly, its federal counterpart was reduced from forty-three to nine seats in the September 1993 federal election, and thus lost official party status in the House of Commons. To say that the New Democrats were demoralized is understating the state of dejection within the party. The Alberta New Democrats opted for a traditional convention in choosing their new leader. This was not entirely due to the party's resistance to change, although this is certainly partially the case. It also was due to financial and organizational reasons, and due to the party's relationship with organized labour. Since affiliated unions have guaranteed representation at party conventions (both federally and provincially), it is more difficult for the party to move to a system of direct election of party leader, since such a move would necessitate developing a mechanism to represent labour in the process. This by necessity would lead to a discussion of the appropriate role for organized labour in the party, and such discussions often are avoided in the NDP, partly because they can be quite divisive, as demonstrated by the experience with the "Waffle" in the late 1960s and 1970s. In addition, a province-wide vote of all party members in the NDP would have both strained the party's resources and revealed the small number of Albertans who continued to hold NDP memberships. Although the party could have used a mail ballot, given the state of disarray of the party in 1994, it was perhaps simply beyond the capacity of the party to hold any other kind of direct election involving all members. Thus, the convention of slightly more than 400 activists elected Ross Harvey as leader, the only candidate with parliamentary experience. Leading a party with no legislative seats is no easy task, and Harvey resigned from the leadership even before taking the party into the next provincial election.

Like the New Democrats, the Liberals chose their new leader in a state of disappointment. The party had led in provincial polls throughout 1992 and expected to win the 1993 election. The Conservatives' selection of Ralph Klein effectively ended those hopes. Decore had worked hard to position the Liberals as a party of safe change and fiscal responsibility. In essence, under his leadership, "the Liberals had attempted to outflank the Conservatives on the right and fight an election on the government's fiscal record" (Stewart 1995: 44). Many Liberal activists were unhappy when this strategy proved unsuccessful and it did not take long for Decore to announce that he would be stepping down. Although Decore's leadership saw the Liberals catapult from six seats and "also-ran" status, to thirty-two seats in the legislature (the largest opposition party in Alberta in recent memory), his failure to defeat the Conservatives sealed his fate. His move to the right had left many Liberal activists unhappy, and while this unhappiness might have been masked in government, in opposition it was destined to surface.

The party thus moved toward a new leadership election, and since the Tories had used a universal ballot, the Liberals felt that they could not show themselves to be any less eager to embrace "democracy" (confidential interview). Anxious to show its willingness to change, to be inclusive, and to take risks, the party opted to use a tele-vote direct election system in choosing its new leader. It also would use a majority election system, but since the ballot was via telephone, its run-off between the top candidates would occur on the same day as the first ballot. Unfortunately for the Liberals, the party organizers seemed unusually naïve in the manner in which "proxy" ballots could be used. In fact, proxy ballots were both used and abused to a far greater extent than anticipated. This issue, coupled with some technical difficulties with the tele-voting system, resulted in the Liberals' leadership selection being an unmitigated disaster. Instead of demonstrating the party's preparation for governance, it revealed a party with

serious organizational weaknesses. The victor, Grant Mitchell, partially attributed his unsuccessful tenure as leader to the damage done to his leadership and to the party by this leadership selection fiasco.[2]

In comparing the experiences of the Alberta political parties with these
alternative methods of leadership selection, a number of lessons can be
drawn. Perhaps the most obvious is the perception, and the reality, that
direct election of party leaders is a more open and inclusive process. Interestingly, this does not necessarily mean that more people are involved in
the leadership selection process when a direct election method is used. Canadian federal and provincial experience is rife with examples of parties
involving large numbers of their existing members, and recruiting a substantial number of new members, to select delegates to a party convention.
The number of people who cast votes in the direct election of party leader
for the Conservatives and the Liberals in Alberta in 1992 and 1994, respectively, did not necessarily mark an increase in overall rates of citizen participation. However, delegate selection meetings in Alberta, and in many other
parts of the country, were often controversial, with enterprising candidates
often attempting to recruit new party members by mobilizing members of
ethnic communities. The spectre of candidates "winning by a busload" became almost cliché in delegate selection meetings associated with leadership selection in Alberta. Thus, when parties use direct election methods,
the chances of the process being open to charges of manipulation are significantly reduced.

As evidenced by the Liberal Party's experience with direct election, though,
perceptions that the process was manipulated may persist with this method.
At issue in this instance is the need to anticipate and to control for compet-
ing principles and processes. For example, when there are legitimate reasons to expect that an eligible voter is unable to attend the polling station
on election day, it may be necessary to establish alternative voting arrange-
ments, such as the use of advance polling stations. However, with tele-voting,
there would appear to be a limited number of reasons for a voter to be
unable to call during voting hours, and such reasons could be expected to
apply to a small number of eligible voters. Allowing widespread "proxy voting" appears to be inconsistent with the direct election of a party leader
using tele-voting. Since the use of proxies had significant unintended consequences for the Liberal Party, other parties are now able to learn from this
obvious mistake. However, the more general injunction applies – namely,
for parties to be mindful and vigilant in anticipating difficulties with various voting systems that are being used.

This is often easier said than done. Political parties in Canada tend to be
underdeveloped organizationally and rely heavily on the labour of volunteer activists (see Carty 1991). Furthermore, parties are by their very character highly partisan, and party volunteers often are involved not only in

support of the party as an entity, but also of particular candidates. Since the rules of leadership selection can have different impacts for various candidates, activists may be more or less supportive of particular rules because of their perceived impact on a favoured candidate. Attempts to professionalize the operation of political parties could prove beneficial, but also run counter to the trend of increased personalization of political parties as they become more closely attached to the party leader.

A striking finding of the survey data was the high level of support that citizens gave to the direct election of leaders. Conservatives, Liberals, and New Democrats alike all indicated high levels of support for a process of selecting leaders that was viewed as more open and inclusive. The symbolic importance of a system viewed as more democratic provides a compelling prima facie case for supporting the move to direct election. The experience of the Liberal Party with direct election, though, provides a sobering example of the need to ensure that the system adopted by the party is consistent with the party's capacity to administer it with appropriate levels of professionalism.

In addition, evidence from the survey data also indicates the trade-offs that parties make when switching to a direct election system. For example, data from the survey of New Democrat convention delegates indicate that such delegates are considerably more deeply rooted in the party. Convention delegates often have participated in previous party conventions, including previous leadership selection processes, and have a higher level of involvement overall in party activities. They are, as a group, more intensely committed partisans, and more informed and knowledgeable both about party affairs and about policy discussions in Canadian politics more generally. In addition, convention delegates are much more likely to have had personal contact with the leadership candidates, some of which occurs either during the period of delegate selection or at the convention itself. Delegates interact not only with the leadership candidates at the convention, but also with one another. Consequently, the convention facilitates a leadership selection process that occurs amongst more informed observers, and with greater personal knowledge of, and interaction with, the leadership candidates. It also enables a more complex web of interpersonal relationships to develop within the party, and thereby strengthens its organizational coherence. Despite these qualities associated with party conventions, even New Democrats were in favour of abandoning this process for a more direct system of leadership selection. Such is the widespread appeal of direct election.

As we showed in Chapter 1, many worry that the trend toward the direct election of party leaders is further reinforcing tendencies in the Canadian political system toward weakening the strength, impact, and organizational clout of political parties (see Courtney 1995). As leadership candidates are forced to appeal to a much broader array of voters at the time of the election, the costs of being a serious contender are likely to increase, and with this, there will also be a lessening in the importance of the party. For example, in a traditional convention process, candidates are required to appeal in the first instance to a broad electorate that will select convention delegates. However, following the delegate selection process, the number of eligible voters is reduced, often to several thousand delegates. The party is responsible for maintaining and distributing the list of delegates, and these delegates are then drawn into lines of communication within the party, for example, through constituency associations. The period between the selection of delegates to a convention and the actual convention vote is characterized by intensive communication both between the party and the delegates and between the candidates and the delegates. The leadership selection process is thereby used to further strengthen the party as an organization.

With a direct election system, in contrast, candidates must communicate with the entire electorate until the cut-off point for acquiring a party membership, which in the case of the Alberta Conservatives was election day, for both the first and second ballots. With a very late closing date for acquiring a party membership, the party becomes largely redundant in the period leading up to the election. Individual leadership candidates put in place their personal election machinery, maintain their own lists of potential voters, and cultivate an allegiance in the first instance to themselves and only secondarily to the party. The campaign of David Orchard for the federal PC leadership in 1998 demonstrates this. Mr. Orchard, who had vociferously opposed the major policies of the Mulroney government, was able to make a very credible showing. Other candidates, however, expressed concerns about the lack of commitment his supporters had to the party.

The need to appeal to a broader electorate makes necessary a number of adjustments to the style of campaigning for leadership. Campaigns become based to a greater extent on mechanisms of mass marketing and less on direct personal contact; they become focused on recruitment of new party members, including many who may have an ephemeral connection to the party, rather than on the conversion of existing party members to one of the candidates. Indeed, there was evidence that certain of the candidates for the Liberal Party leadership did not fully appreciate the implications of the system of leadership election that the party had adopted, focusing more of their efforts on conversion rather than on recruitment. Candidates who fail to appreciate the implications of the system of leadership selection under which they operate are bound to suffer from their miscalculations.

A comparative assessment of tele-voting and paper balloting must acknowledge that a paper ballot has shortcomings with respect to access, which, theoretically, could be mitigated by a tele-vote. Some members who had children may not have been able to access the polls in the time available, and it is likely that some elderly members could not access them at all – although access for older members was also an issue in the tele-vote process, as many had difficulties using the telephone technology. Moreover, voters in some constituencies had to travel some distance in order to find a polling station.

In spite of this advantage, the number of people voting in the paper ballot was much greater than the number who participated in the tele-vote. Certainly, the difference in the competitive positions of the parties played a role, but it is impossible to maintain that the inconvenience of leaving one's home to vote discouraged participation in the 1992 Tory election. Moreover, the Tory voters appeared more engaged by the process. Although voting required taking time out of the day to travel to a polling station and stand in line, the Tory turnout was substantially higher than the 58% Liberal turnout in 1994. And, as we saw in Chapter 4, even that modest turnout was bolstered by the fact that almost 2,000 of the votes cast were proxies, which meant that these voters did not have to brave the telephone lines.

There is also no evidence that the convenience of voting from home by phone enfranchised a more representative electorate. Liberal tele-voters were virtually indistinguishable from Tory voters. And when differences could be observed, it was the paper ballot that appeared more inclusive, as it attracted a higher proportion of voters without university degrees and from non-professional occupations. There is, therefore, no evidence to indicate that the tele-vote is more inclusive than a paper ballot.

One other obvious advantage of the Tory election is that it generated nowhere near the same degree of controversy as the 1994 tele-vote. The desire to enfranchise as many members as possible influenced the party's decision to allow people to register at polling stations and after the first ballot was completed, but these issues paled in comparison to the registration and proxy controversies of 1994.

The technically regressive paper ballot has many advantages over tele-voting. Admittedly, the proxy problems of 1994 cannot be attributed solely to tele-voting. Nonetheless, a consideration of the logic behind proxies identifies one of the pitfalls of tele-voting. A major advantage of proxies is that they eliminate concerns of voter turnout. Candidates who manage to collect large numbers of proxies knew that these voters would not forget to vote on election day. A well-organized campaign could achieve the same result without proxies, simply by collecting PINs and allowing workers to vote on election day. As Carty concedes, "the technology cannot guarantee that only qualified electors cast ballots" (1996: 20).

Paper balloting, with its requirement of attendance at a polling station and presentation of identification, is less susceptible to abuses of this sort. Moreover, paper balloting offers a level of scrutiny absent from tele-voting.

A system of paper balloting provides transparency, as voters are able to see their ballots deposited in balloting boxes and know that when these boxes are opened each candidate is entitled to have a scrutineer present. Tele-voting offers no such certainty, and in 1994 only 59% of Liberal voters were sure their vote had been recorded. As for the vote count itself, with a paper ballot, candidate scrutineers are again present, while with a tele-vote, the absence of human hands and eyes requires faith in the integrity of the technology used. Few voters have sufficient knowledge to make this faith rational.[3] Voting at polling stations alleviates concerns of this sort, while the absence of scrutiny that accompanies tele-voting provides fertile soil for conspiracy theories. The electoral process in Canada has benefited from sustained efforts to eliminate voting irregularities, and these efforts are of use to parties utilizing a paper ballot but have little relevance for tele-votes.

The last advantage of the paper ballot is perhaps the most obvious. A paper ballot is unlikely to be delayed or derailed by technological difficulties. Problems such as voting suspension and voting extension beset the two largest tele-votes held in Canada. Admittedly, other tele-votes have been successful, but this mixed record does not inspire confidence in the process.

In spite of its many shortcomings, there is something seductive about tele-voting with its image of "cutting edge" technology and its promises of inclusion. As Carty notes in his discussion of tele-voting, "it is difficult to believe that tele-voting will not be on the agenda as more Canadians have some experience of the technology at their workplace or the market. The evidence of the leadership televotes ... suggests that Canadians can easily embrace the technology and when they do so their experience is generally very positive" (1996: 20).

The experiences of the Alberta Liberal Party demonstrate that many of the supposed advantages of tele-voting are equally associated with paper balloting. A leadership selection process in which the mechanisms for casting, recording, and counting votes are not only outside the direct control of the party, but are not easily understood by ordinary voters, needs to be reconsidered and, at present, the paper ballot appears vastly superior.

This analysis of the changing character of leadership selection leads to a number of expectations with respect to potential directions of the party system in Alberta. The move to direct election of party leaders will contribute both to an increased importance of leaders, as they become less dependent upon their caucus colleagues for support, and also to increased instability of party loyalties. Canadians' flexibility of partisanship will become even further magnified, leading to even more labile party ties. The aggregate stability in voting patterns in Alberta is therefore misleading, and should not be taken as an indication of strong and stable attachments to parties. Alberta has experienced almost thirty years of uninterrupted Conservative governance despite, rather than because of, the character of party loyalties.

This feature of Canadian and Alberta party politics is manifested in Albertans' greater allegiance to the premier than to the Conservative party. When he ran for the leadership of the party in 1992, Klein styled himself as a Conservative "outsider," running against the establishment candidate Nancy Betkowski. Klein proceeded to transform the Conservative Party into his own image, so much so that his leadership of the party is unquestioned. He saved the Conservatives from almost certain electoral defeat in 1993 and won by an even larger margin in 1997. The former Conservative establishment candidate, Nancy Betkowski, has re-emerged to challenge Klein, not within the party, but rather as leader of the provincial Liberal Party, under her new name Nancy MacBeth. Her decision not to challenge Klein within the Conservative Party, where he is almost completely unassailable, but rather as leader of the rival Liberals, is another indication of the almost total conflation of a party with its current leader.

While Ralph Klein remains the leader of the Conservative Party, it appears that the party will remain as popular as the premier. This is an optimistic assessment of the Conservative Party's prospects for two reasons. The first is that Klein's appeal has more to do with his populist image and persona than it does with any particular policy initiative. Klein has unquestionably benefited enormously from his success in eliminating the provincial deficit almost overnight and from being well along the road to eliminating the provincial debt as well. Yet, a study of his approach to governance either as Calgary mayor or as premier reveals that he is anything but an ideologue. Klein was determined to balance the budget not because of an ideological commitment to fiscal restraint, but because of a commitment to heed the advice of the electorate and to deliver on election promises. A leader with strong populist appeal can often weather fluctuations in the changing issue agenda.

The second reason for the Conservatives to be optimistic with Ralph Klein as leader is a function of electoral geography in Alberta, and Klein's base of support. The province can be thought of as having three distinct electoral regions – Edmonton, Calgary, and the rest. A party's electoral success is assured by winning two of these three regions. With Klein, the Tories have a stranglehold on Calgary and "the rest," with Edmonton being largely Liberal terrain. It is difficult to imagine any Liberal leader, especially one from Edmonton, wresting one of the two strongholds away from the Tories under a Klein government.

In view of the strong linkage between the premier's personal image and that of the party, the obvious question then becomes, what is the Conservative Party without Klein? The answer to this is far from certain. Voters in the Conservative leadership selection demonstrated a greater commitment to populist beliefs than to fiscal or social conservatism, and thus the latter attitudes may not provide sufficient glue to cohere current Conservative supporters to the party. Instead, as is typically the case in Canadian party politics, the new leader will need to remake the party once again in his or her image. The party's ability to do so, and to do so while retaining the reins of government, will depend both on the abilities of the new leader and on the competitive environment with respect to the alternative parties.

The Liberal Party remains well poised to form a credible opposition party during the Klein years, and possibly to mount a challenge for governance in the post-Klein era. Liberal support, like that for the Conservatives, is closely tied to the personal character of the leader. Laurence Decore built a solid foundation for the Liberals among Edmontonians, although he did so without challenging the fiscal conservatism of the Tories. Indeed, if anything, the Liberals and Conservatives became less differentiated fiscally under Decore's leadership. When Grant Mitchell replaced Decore, an effort was made to shift the focus slightly away from a rigid application of fiscal conservatism. This effort may have ensured that the Liberals retained their support in Edmonton, but led to no growth elsewhere. Now, under the leadership of Nancy MacBeth, the Liberals have a former Conservative cabinet minister, albeit one who is less fiscally or socially Conservative than the Tories have been of late. Klein's non-ideological base, however, provides him with great latitude to adjust his policies should there be signs of Liberal incursions into his support. In the first eighteen months or so of MacBeth's leadership, there are few signs of such changes. In the short-term, MacBeth appears poised to retain and possibly strengthen the Liberal Party's hold on Edmonton, but growth beyond that core may need to await the departure of Klein from the Conservative leadership.

The New Democrats continue to struggle to find their place on the electoral landscape in Alberta. To a certain extent, the NDP demonstrates the limits of an explanation of party politics that focuses exclusively on leadership. The party at both the federal and provincial levels often performs much worse than one would expect given the assessments of leaders of the party. This was certainly the case during the Broadbent era at the federal level and the era of Grant Notley provincially. However, the ideology of the NDP appears to be somewhat antithetical to the political culture of Alberta, with its greater emphasis on individualism. Where this is the case, even popular party leaders may find limited electoral success. From this perspective, the prospects for the Alberta New Democrats continue to look bleak.

Thus, for the Liberals and Conservatives, and to a much lesser extent the NDP, the political future remains uncertain. Current trends point toward a continual increase in the importance of party leaders, and party leaders are highly changeable. Despite the apparent stability of party politics in Alberta, the opportunities for substantial changes in party support are ever-present and never far below the surface. Alberta politics is leadership politics, encouraging direct, populist links between the leader and the public. Parties in this environment become vehicles of convenience for the successful leadership candidates, rather than instruments of political consistency and stability. This produces in Alberta, politics with remarkable variability within a party system of almost impervious stability. Paradoxically, the end result is a party and political system that is able to accommodate profound change.

Appendices

Appendix 1: Attitudinal Scales

The populism, individualism, continentalism, feminism, and pro-government scales were constructed from responses to the following statements.

Populism

1 In the long run, I'll put my trust in the simple down-to-earth thinking of ordinary people rather than the theories of experts and intellectuals. (Agree)
2 We would probably solve most of our big national problems if government could actually be brought back to the people at the grass roots. (Agree)
3 What we need is a government that gets the job done without all this red tape. (Agree)
4 There should be a referendum on all amendments to the constitution. (Agree)

Individualism

1 The government ought to make sure that everyone has a decent standard of living. (Agree)
2 Let's face it, most unemployed people could find a job if they really wanted to. (Agree)
3 Why should the government spend my tax money on sick people; my family always put something aside for a rainy day. (Agree)
4 After a person has worked until sixty-five, it is proper for the community to support him or her. (Disagree)

Continentalism

1 We must ensure an independent Canada even if that were to mean a lower standard of living for Canadians. (Disagree)

2 The Canada-US Free Trade Agreement has been good for Alberta. (Agree)
3 Canada's independence is threatened by the large-scale ownership in key sectors of the economy. (Disagree)

Feminism

1 Abortion is a matter which should be decided solely between a woman and her doctor. (Agree)
2 Governments should make a strong effort to improve the social and economic position of women. (Selected this item over "Women should help themselves and should not expect governments to make special efforts on their behalf.")

Pro-government

1 A lot of welfare and social security programs we have now are unnecessary. (Disagree)
2 Without government regulations, some people just take advantage of the rest of us. (Selected this item over "Government regulation stifles personal initiative.")
3 If I do my best, it is only right that the government should help me when I get some bad breaks. (Selected this item over "Each individual should accept the consequences of their own actions.")

The remaining scales were not used for all three parties.

Moralism

1 What politicians do on their own time is their own business. (Disagree)
2 The country would be better off if we elected people who espoused strong Christian values. (Agree)

Pro-welfare

1 A lot of welfare and social security programs we have now are unnecessary. (Disagree)
2 The size of government in Alberta should be reduced even if this means a lower level of public services. (Disagree)
3 Social programs should remain universal. (Agree)

Participation

1 phoned a candidate's office for information (Yes)
2 met a candidate during the campaign (Yes)
3 attended a candidate's campaign event (Yes)
4 attended an all-candidate forum. (Yes)

Moral Issues

1 Abortion is a matter which should be decided solely between a woman and her doctor. (Agree)
2 Discrimination on the basis of sexual orientation should be prohibited. (Agree)

The following scale was used only for the New Democrats.

Pro-union

1 attend labour caucus (Yes)
2 importance of ability to strengthening labour ties to party in your choice of candidate (Very Important)
3 union links with the NDP (Very Beneficial or Beneficial)
4 ties between unions and the NDP should be strengthened. (Yes)

Appendix 2: Consensus Index Comparison

	CI NDP $N = 220$	CI Liberal $N = 586$	CI PC $N = 943$
Government ought to ensure living standard	42	18	6
Most unemployed could find work	49	17	7
Don't spend tax money on sick	49	46	43
Community support for seniors	24	13	16
Trust ordinary people over experts	7	3	13
Grass roots could solve problems	8	9	19
Reduce government red tape	14	35	41
Referendums on all constitutional amendments	21	4	2
Ensure independent Canada at all costs	23	11	5
FTA good for Alberta	42	14	2
Foreign ownership a threat	39	5	19
A lot of welfare unnecessary	38	8	14
Reduce government size	29	12	30
Need government regulations	44	25	5
Individuals accept consequences	30	16	34
Government should help women	43	3	14
Abortion matter for woman and doctor	42	21	25
Charlottetown Accord good deal	22	22	18
Negotiate land claims with Natives	32	12	7
Unions essential for democracy	38	3	19
Mean consensus index	**32**	**15**	**16**

Notes

Chapter 1: Party Democracy in Alberta?

1 A closed primary is one in which potential voters must register in advance in order to participate.

2 It is difficult to define "conservatism" with precision. We use it in the general sense as a reference to views that are predominantly right wing or individualistic. "Nineteenth-century liberalism" and "neo-liberalism" are also terms that capture the set of views to which we are referring.

3 The reported first-ballot votes were distributed as follows: Klein, 40.7%; Betkowski, 36.9%; Orman, 6.5%; Main, 5.6%; Oldring, 3.9%; Quantz, 2.2%; Nelson, 1.9%; McCoy, 1.5%; and King, 0.7%. The actual first-ballot results were Betkowski, 31.1%; Klein, 31.1%; Orman, 14.5%; Main, 9.6%; Oldring, 5.2%; Quantz, 2.8%; Nelson, 2.4%; McCoy, 2.1%; and King, 1.1%. Although there is a clear underrepresentation of supporters of the minor candidates, the overall order was accurate.

4 This invitation caused us some difficulty since it is essential that the entire population be available for sampling. We were able to hire a polling firm that worked for the Liberal Party to draw our sample. Thus, the names of the voters were not released to us. We were nonetheless able to obtain a full list of the people who registered for the tele-vote. However, in light of the fact that a number of voters requested that their names be withheld, we did not consider it appropriate to use this list to draw our own sample.

Chapter 2: The "United Right"?

1 It is important to stress that this comparison is based solely on those members of the federal Conservative and Reform parties who deigned to participate in the universal ballot. It is impossible to determine whether they are a representative sample of all federal members of those parties in Alberta. The comparisons must be interpreted with this caveat in mind.

2 This rule distinguishes the Alberta Conservative process from virtually every other universal ballot held in Canada. Most of them possessed some sort of cut-off point after which one was not eligible to vote for the leader. In some cases, the cut-off points were at about the midway point of the contest. For a discussion of three universal ballots that utilized some form of cut-off, see Latouche (1992), Woolstencroft (1992), and Preyra (1994).

3 For a discussion of the 1985 convention, see Archer and Hunziker (1992).

4 The candidates were, in order of first-ballot finish: Health Minister Nancy Betkowski, Environment Minister Ralph Klein, Energy Minister Rick Orman, Culture Minister Doug Main, Social Services Minister John Oldring, Lloyd Quantz, Reuben Nelson, Labour Minister Elaine McCoy, and former Education Minister David King.

5 However, the candidates did not hesitate to distance themselves from the Getty government. As the *Calgary Herald* explained, "candidates have charged the party fell out of touch with Albertans during Getty's leadership"(Geddes 1992: B6). The *Edmonton Journal* indicated that Getty did not seem to mind this: "Getty said he isn't holding any grudges de-

spite Betkowski's promise of a new politics and Klein's railing against the status quo" (Helm 1992b: A7).

6 The only candidate not to formally endorse Betkowski was David King, who finished last.

7 Main's comments during the campaign probably helped persuade Klein not to include Main in his cabinet, in spite of the fact that Main was the only MLA, other than Betkowski, from the city of Edmonton. Klein included none of his opponents in his cabinet, although he made extensive efforts to convince Betkowski to accept a position.

8 Klein supporters, however, did focus on policy in the sense that they claimed Betkowski might introduce a sales tax and close hospitals in rural Alberta.

9 It appears that Liberals did indeed like Betkowski because in April 1998 she was elected as that party's Alberta leader.

10 For a description of the data collection method used for this chapter, as well as a more elaborate explanation of the results, see Chapter 1.

11 The data on 1985 delegates presented in the tables is taken either from Hunziker (1986: Chapter 4) or Archer and Hunziker (1992: 85-92). The actual phrasing of questions and response categories are available from the authors.

12 Given the focus of this chapter, these voters were excluded from the analysis.

13 It is possible that the level of Reform participation in the leadership process is underestimated by this study. As will be shown later, second-ballot Reform voters were quite likely to have voted for one of the minor candidates on the first ballot. The reported first-ballot votes of respondents underestimates support for these candidates, suggesting that many of their first-ballot backers did not participate on the second ballot. It seems likely that a significant number of federal Reformers might have decided not to vote on the second ballot, when their preferred options were no longer available.

14 The 1992 Nova Scotia Liberal tele-vote proceedings provided such an example. The provincial CBC convened a panel representing the three main Nova Scotian parties. The Conservative representative on the panel made much of the fact that he was going to cast a vote for the new Liberal leader, thus attempting to ridicule the integrity of the process.

15 This lends support to McCormick's contention that Reform is "reaching out into groups not previously politically mobilized" (1991: 347).

16 The high proportion referring to speeches may be somewhat misleading given that most of the voters must have heard or seen the speeches through the media.

17 There was one interesting (and statistically significant) difference among the three groups in relation to the print media they most often utilized. Federal Tories were least likely, not only in proportionate terms but also in absolute numbers, to claim a small city paper as the daily they most often read. Only 4.5% claimed such a newspaper as their major daily. In contrast, almost one-fifth of Reformers cited a Red Deer or Lethbridge daily as their regular newspaper. Another 20% of Reformers mentioned one of the provincial *Suns* as their major newspaper. Tories were particularly unlikely to mention the *Sun*, with barely 8% making such selections. Federal independents were less likely to read the *Sun* than Reformers, but much more likely to do so than Tories. Reformers appear quite different from Tories in their newspaper reading, with almost 40% reading either the *Sun* or a small city paper. Tory newspaper readers also stood out for their selections of "out of province" papers as their major daily: more than 16% did so. Notwithstanding these variations – which suggest that the print information going to Reformers and Tories is somewhat different and that independents resemble Reformers more than Tories in their reading habits – the majority of voters in all federal partisan groups read either the *Edmonton Journal* or the *Calgary Herald*.

18 The high proportion of Reformers who were farmers or ranchers stands in sharp contrast to McCormick's report. On the basis of a 1989 internal Reform membership survey, McCormick drew attention to the striking absence of employment in the agricultural sector (1991: 347). Reform may well have developed a broader base in rural Alberta since that survey.

19 The degree of Catholic underrepresentation may be exaggerated, since 6% of the respondents claimed "Christian" as their religious affiliation. This also complicates treatments of Protestant denominations. Intra-Protestant comparisons are further complicated by the percentage of respondents claiming to be "Protestant" (14%) or "Evangelical" (2%).

20 For instance, in 1985 Edmonton provided 27% of the delegates, Calgary 27%, southern Alberta 15%, northern Alberta 15%, and the central region 16% (Hunziker 1986: 67). In

1992, Edmontonians accounted for 26% of the second-ballot voters, Calgarians for 31%, the south 12%, the north 14%, and central Alberta 17%. In essence, there were no major changes in the regional composition of the electorates.

21 Reformers were proportionately more likely to live in Lethbridge and Red Deer (the third and fourth largest cities in Alberta) than other participants. Lethbridge is in southern Alberta, while Red Deer is in the central region.

22 The attitudinal questions asked in the survey were adapted from a survey of delegates to the 1986 BC Social Credit Leadership Convention. These questions were used to facilitate inter-provincial comparisons as well as to generate similar scales. The authors wish to express their gratitude to Ken Carty for making the survey and data available. For an examination of that convention, see Blake, Carty, and Erickson (1991).

23 A consensus index was used to chart the level of agreement. The consensus index was used in the same manner as it was in Blake, Carty, and Erickson's "Social Credit Leadership Selection in B.C." (1988: 519-20). It helps provide a graphic indication of the level of disagreement within the party. Basically, a score is determined by subtracting the absolute value of 50 from the percentage who agree with a particular statement. If 100% or 0% agree with the statement, the score is 50 – perfect consensus. If 50% agree, the score is zero, indicating an even division of opinion, or no consensus. The higher the score, the closer the opinions are to perfect consensus.

24 For the purposes of comparison with the Liberals and New Democrats, the Consensus Index was also calculated using only the 20 variables common to all three surveys. The mean score for the Conservatives on this scale was 16. As will be shown in Chapter 7, the corresponding scores for the Liberals and New Democrats were 15 and 32 respectively.

25 See Appendix 1 for a list of the items in each index.

26 See Christian and Campbell (1990: 101-4) for a discussion of business liberalism.

27 The individual versus collective responsibility scale was also adopted from Blake, Carty, and Erickson. For this scale, scored in an individualist direction, voters who did not believe that government should ensure a decent standard of living, who thought most unemployed could find work, that tax money should not be spent on the sick, and that the community should not support people over the age of sixty-five, scored a four on the scale. Those who took none of those positions received a zero. As the mean scores suggest, the leadership election participants were not overwhelmingly individualistic in their views.

28 In the "Pro-Welfare" scale, voters who disagree with the statement "A lot of welfare and social programs are unnecessary," who did not believe that government should be reduced even if this means lower levels of public service, and who thought that social programs should be universal, scored a three. Those who took none of these positions received a zero. The "Pro-Government" scale was also constructed on the basis that those who did not find many social programs to be unnecessary, who believed that we need regulations to protect us and that government should help us if we suffer bad breaks scored a three, and those who took none of these positions received a zero. The mean scores suggest that Tory voters were somewhat hostile to government as none of the group means were even at the midpoint of the scales.

29 The third question used in constructing the scale asked about ensuring an independent Canada even if it would entail a lower standard of living.

30 Recall from Chapter 1 that the correspondence between reported and actual first-ballot votes was not as close as the match for the second ballot. Of course, there was no reason to expect it to be. The survey targeted only those individuals who either voted on both ballots or just on the second. Individuals who voted only on the first ballot were not surveyed. The reported first-ballot votes suggest that a substantial proportion of those who voted for a minor candidate on the first did not come out to vote on the second ballot. The vote totals also indicate that the Betkowski camp suffered more defections than Klein, either through vote switches or second-ballot abstentions.

Chapter 3: Electing the Premier

1 According to *Alberta Report* (28 June 1993: 6), the Conservatives were at 18% in the polls in the fall before the election. The "miracle" might also refer to one of the eccentricities of

Alberta politics, namely the collapse of each dynasty when their third leader sought endorsement at the polls. Klein was the first "to beat the curse of the three's."

2   The only Calgary riding not to deliver a second-ballot majority to Klein was actually the
riding he represented in the legislature.

3   The federal rules mirror those used by the PC Party of Ontario. See Woolstencroft (1992)
for a discussion of the Ontario system.

4   This factor may also illustrate the pitfalls of the equal-representation-per-riding notion.
Questions of legitimacy would have undoubtedly marred any lead Klein might have taken
into the second ballot.

5   See, for example, Johnston (1988).

6   An *Edmonton Journal* editorial indicated that "there is evidence that women were rushing
to the party to elect Betkowski." ("New Tory Politics with a Bit of the Old," 1 December
1992: A6). See also a 3 December 1992 *Edmonton Journal* story (A7) about women networking to place Betkowski into the premier's office ("Women from Outside Politics Flocking to
Help Put Betkowski over the Top").

7   Most of the youth delegates at leadership conventions may well have been students. Students were actually more supportive of Betkowski than the electorate as a whole. However,
the youth who were not students obviously did not share that affinity.

8   See also Kornberg et al. (1982).

9   In order to generate a category large enough for systematic analysis, the candidates other
than Betkowski and Klein were examined as a group for the purposes of analysis. Unfortunately, this makes it impossible to identify differences among them.

10 The attitudinal questions used here are identical to those discussed in Chapter 2.

11 The variables used to construct each of these scales are outlined in Chapter 1.

12 Betkowski also did better with voters who agreed with the thrust of the Charlottetown
Accord. For instance, more than half of her first-ballot voters agreed that the Charlottetown
Accord was a good deal for Canada, while only about a third of the other voters took that
position. On the second ballot, her supporters split almost evenly on this question, while
69% of Klein voters did not think it was a good deal for the country.

13 It is important to keep in mind that supporters of all candidates on both the first and second
ballot received mean scores that placed them below the midpoint on each of the scales.
The Conservative voters were not exactly enthusiastic about government or its actions.

14 In understanding the support coalitions of the minor candidates, it is interesting to note
that a significantly higher proportion of their support came from voters who were regular
attenders of religious services. When this is combined with the data on "moralism," it
appears that the minor candidates drew much higher proportional levels of support from
the more traditional elements within the party than did either Betkowski or Klein. Of
course, combining the minor candidates into one group disguises differences that likely
existed among them.

15 Once again, it is important to keep in mind that the data do not provide an accurate
picture of all first-ballot voters. Those who chose not to participate in the second round are
missing. It may well be that those who chose to vote again were those who had been most
involved in the campaign, and therefore most prepared to make a second choice.

16 As Chapter 2 showed, the voters did express some familiarity with the campaign. Seventy-
seven percent saw one of the candidate's television commercials, 74% heard candidates speak
on the radio, 87% read candidate newspaper advertisements, and 61% said they had seen
other forms of candidate advertising as well. An amazing 75% watched coverage of the
first-ballot voting results on local cable television, which provided them with an opportunity to hear brief speeches from the three candidates who would be on the second ballot.
There were no significant differences in candidate support with respect to this exposure.

17 Shumacher (1993: 9) suggests that as many as 30,000 memberships were sold after the first
ballot and that these sales enabled the party to show a profit for the process.

18 There were no significant differences of means associated with the other attitudinal scales.

19 The MLAs supporting Klein were certainly energized by the possibility of defeat. Many of
them worked long hours contacting supporters in their constituencies and urging them to
come out and vote for Klein on the second ballot. Betkowski, with less caucus support, had
no such network of resources in the local constituencies on which to rely.

20 See Stewart and Carty (1993).
21 However, Betkowski's support from women might have been more significant because of the all-member vote. If a traditional convention had been held, proportionately fewer women would, in all likelihood, have participated, and Betkowski's overall showing might have been lower. Similarly, one should also keep in mind Betkowski's support from "tourists."

Chapter 4: Electronic Fiasco
1 The Nova Scotia Conservatives pioneered a system of telephone voting utilizing operators who recorded votes given orally. The Nova Scotia Liberals later followed their lead.
2 For a discussion of some of the dangers universal ballots present for parties, see Preyra (1994) and Malcolmson (1992).
3 As noted in a press release issued by the Liberal Party in March 1995. Despite the controversy that attended the tele-vote, the party decided not to release the full report. In April 1998, the party chose its next leader through a paper ballot, with polling stations located in each constituency.
4 This particular candidate, Sine Chadi, had been an active Conservative supporter in the Lougheed era. Chadi reported spending the $250,000 maximum allowed by the party on his campaign. This was more than four times the amount the other losing competitors reported. Preyra points out the opportunities universal ballots offer well-financed outsiders (1995: 215). Chadi's lone caucus supporter subsequently crossed the floor to join the Conservatives.
5 See Chapters 2 and 3 for details.
6 Confidential interview.
7 In his coverage of universal ballots, Courtney reports the Liberal membership as an estimated 56,000 (1995: 359). However, as Jim McCartney, campaign director for Grant Mitchell suggests, that data on party membership are notoriously soft, since there is no fee to join. The considerable expense involved in sending mail-outs to up to 60,000 party members led many of the candidates to focus their efforts more effectively. Interview with Jim McCartney, 15 May 1996.
8 In the end, Chadi did not file suit and Germain discontinued his appeal.
9 The turnout must be treated with caution, since it is not clear how many people tried to vote and gave up because of technical problems. Also, more than 2,000 of the proxy votes were not counted for reasons that will be explained below.
10 One example of this followed an all-candidate forum in Grande Prairie, and was hardly the kind of attention the party desired. The *Edmonton Journal* headlined its story on the forum as follows: "Identity Crisis for Liberal Candidates: Few Know Who's Running or Why."
11 This two-stage process was actually one stage shorter than that of the BC Liberals, who had a deadline for membership that arrived before the deadline for registering.
12 Confidential interview.
13 Those were the words the Conservative Party president used to describe his party's universal ballot in 1992 (Courtney 1995, 240).
14 Confidential interview.
15 Confidential interview.
16 The party may have created problems for itself with this terminology. The process was described as a "leadership convention" and the voters as "delegates." "Delegate" has had a different meaning in past leadership selection processes, so it is possible that some voters may have been confused by the term.
17 Interestingly, the party did not place such a restriction in their Rules of Procedure. Section 3(a) prohibits candidates from incurring leadership expenses "for the purchase of a membership in the ALP," but membership in the ALP is free, so this particular provision was of no effect. Party officials suggest that the intent of Section 3(a) was to prohibit leadership campaigns from paying for registrations. This is not, of course, specifically indicated by the provision.
18 Germain suggested, "One of the ways to get members is to do it the hard way by campaigning and encouraging people to support a candidate of their choice. That's how we got our

large numbers. Other people may have got by playing loose and fast with the rules. To my knowledge we are guilty of absolutely zero dirty tricks" (*Edmonton Journal*, 9 November 1994: A7).

19 There is a dispute as to whether all of the proxy votes submitted were valid. In a report on proxy voting issued 15 November 1994, the chief electoral officer indicated that "the ratio of submitted to validated Chadi proxies was approximately 66%, therefore, if one applies this ratio to unvoted proxies" Chadi would still have lost (Liberal Party 1994: 9).

20 The Chadi campaign had a different understanding of the deadline. They believed that a provision allowing proxies to be handed to the CEO up to five minutes before the close of voting ensured that the votes would be recorded. Three thousand five hundred and thirty-five of their 3,567 proxies were turned in before the close of voting on the first ballot. They interpreted a proxy vote as the equivalent of being present in a polling station when the hours allotted for voting expired. Everyone on the premises would, nonetheless, be allowed to vote. This was not the interpretation of the CEO (personal interview).

21 Feehan indicates that this consideration was brought to his attention by MT&T officials who were concerned that adding proxy votes to votes cast by telephone would make double voting possible. In other words, someone who filled out a proxy form might subsequently receive a PIN and decide, either naïvely or unethically, to cast their vote by telephone, as well.

22 Candidate Dickson, when asked why he had not submitted many proxies, indicated that the people who were supporting him wanted to participate personally and would have been insulted by a request to sign a proxy form (personal interview).

23 The party maintains that the PINs were sent earlier.

24 The extension of the balloting cost the Liberals the live coverage CBC television was providing, because the extension took the party into a time period that had been allotted to the CFL western semi-final. CBC cut away from the Liberals to the football game and came back only after the game was over. The results of the second ballot were in the hands of the chief electoral officer shortly before the end of the game, and he decided not to announce them until CBC was able to again provide live coverage.

25 Indeed, 29% of the voters who responded to our survey said that they were not sure their vote was recorded. Since Chadi supporters were least likely to reply to the survey, this problem cannot be attributed to the proxy situation.

26 Apparently voters were required to press the "pound" button three times in order to record their vote. On the first ballot, only one entry was necessary. Some voters subsequently felt that perhaps they had not pushed the "pound" key enough times to record their vote.

27 Only two respondents described their "ethnic" origin as "Aboriginal." One of them reported voting for Chadi.

28 Circumstantial evidence of this contention is provided by the list of registered voters. One of the most common names on the voters list was "Singh," which was found 183 times. In contrast, the name "Smith" was listed only 48 times. In the Edmonton telephone book, there are 48 columns of "Smith's" and only 83 "Singh's."

29 The positions on the "Moralism" scale are rather different. Obviously, Chadi supporters were not likely to suggest that it would be better to elect candidates with strong "Christian" values.

30 See Stewart, Adamson, and Beaton (1994: Chapter 10) and Schumacher (1993). In that round table, Len Simms, a former PC leader in Newfoundland states, "Let us be frank. If you are a half decent candidate you will make sure that people will be out buying PIN numbers for your delegates" (1993: 10).

31 Indeed, an election official and one of the candidates report that they learned the technology was not as effective in identifying multiple vote phones as had been claimed.

32 Germain compared the process to the method used for selecting winter carnival queens in Fort McMurray. The contestant who sells the most buttons becomes queen.

33 That registrations were not always paid by the person registering is conceded by a number of candidates or their campaigns.

34 The Liberal Party of Alberta implicitly acknowledged this prior to the 1998 leadership election by beginning to sell its memberships.

Chapter 5: A Party of "Communities"?

1 Like the other federal parties, the NDP has a form of universal balloting. See Archer and Whitehorn (1997) for a full description of that process.

2 See Archer (1991: 4-8) for a discussion of the representational basis of federal NDP conventions and convention procedures.

3 In this model, Morley suggests that there must be a widespread consensus among key activists as to which of the candidates should be leader and a willingness by other likely prospects to endorse this candidate. These elements seem to have been in place in Alberta in 1994 (1992: 132-3).

4 The reported votes of our respondents were Harvey, 61%; Hinkley, 19%; Johnson, 10%; and Teslenko, 10%.

5 Archer's examination of the 1989 federal NDP convention found that 51% of the delegates faced a contest for their selection (1991: 15). This provides further evidence that in 1994, the Alberta New Democrats were at a very low point in their history. In his analysis of the 1989 federal convention, Archer (1991: 11) found that women only accounted for 37% of the delegate spots, while Blake, Carty, and Erickson have shown that women comprised only 34% of the delegate total at the 1987 BC NDP convention (1991: 26).

6 The small proportion of young delegates is somewhat ironic given that some delegates who opposed a universal ballot referred to the ability of conventions to involve youth in the party. In fact, the party's conventions have historically enfranchised a very small proportion of young delegates. For further explanation, see Archer (1991: 11).

7 In marked contrast to the Liberal and PC voters, only one respondent reported her occupation as "homemaker."

8 The fact that the party's core activists hold rather leftist views reveals something of the party's nature. It appears that the views of New Democrats do not vary much according to province. Even in what is widely regarded as the most conservative province in the country, the party's attitudinal consensus is well to the left. The party appears to overwhelm provincial political culture in this regard.

9 For further elaboration of the importance of regionalism to convention voting, see Carty, Erickson, and Blake (1992: 11).

10 It should be noted that Harvey, in fact, only managed to split the vote of those who attended the left caucus. These delegates were disproportionately likely to back Teslenko.

11 This is not an artifact of the labour caucus. Even when those who attended only the labour caucus are excluded from the analysis of caucus goers, the same pattern is evident.

12 In the 1997 provincial election, Hinkley ran as a candidate for the Forum Party – an NDP fragment in Alberta.

13 We limited our multivariate examination to variables used in the earlier Conservative or Liberal analysis. Thus it does not include participation in caucuses or attitudes toward the role of unions within the NDP.

14 This is an even greater minority than they constitute at federal NDP conventions, where they generally hold more than a fifth of the delegate spots (Archer and Whitehorn 1993: 7).

15 See Archer and Whitehorn (1993: 8,9).

16 The "Waffle" movement was a movement within the NDP that challenged the party to move to the left and charged that unions were a conservative force within the party. The high point of the movement came in 1974, when a candidate from this faction finished second at a federal leadership convention. Shortly thereafter, the leaders of the faction were expelled from the party on the grounds that they constituted a "party" within the party (see Brodie 1985).

17 Opposition to universal ballots among caucus goers surpasses the 50% level when the union delegates who attended a caucus are added to other caucus goers.

Chapter 6: Gender Differences among Party Activists

1 As mentioned in Chapter 3, one of the MLAs supporting Klein indicated that women were moody and, in an attempt to respond to the negative publicity his comments received, issued a clarification maintaining that he was only joking. In his clarification he explained, "you know what the female race is like. Some days aren't as good for them as others – same as men" (as quoted in Laghi 1992: A7).

2 Statements about the first ballot are more speculative. The sample on which this paper was based was of second-ballot voters. Many of those who voted on the first ballot did not vote again.

3 The relative disdain men had for Betkowski's candidacy could also be seen in the candidate rankings, as men ranked her a half place lower than women.

4 The survey asked respondents to rank order the candidates from 1 to 9, with 1 referring to the candidate they liked most and 9 to the one they liked least.

5 "New voters" refers to those who did not vote on the first ballot.

6 It should be kept in mind that the questions included were not put in for the primary purpose of identifying gender differences. The purpose of the attitudinal comparison is simply to discover whether men and women hold different views. No attempt is made to use men as a standard for evaluating women. (For a discussion of the potential dangers of simple comparisons, see Sapiro [1983: 59]).

7 Obviously these scales are limited by the questions asked and must be interpreted with that in mind. The scales that were created were restricted to the variables common to all three surveys. Differences on questions asked only on one or two surveys will be discussed later.

8 In this, they differed from women who were delegates to the 1983 PC national convention. These delegates were heavily in favour of freer trade with the US and were not concerned about foreign ownership (see Brodie 1988: 180).

9 Since previous examinations of this data demonstrated significant attitudinal differences between Betkowski and Klein supporters (see Chapter 3), an attempt was made to discover the degree to which the gender differences noted above were related to the fact that women were more likely to support Betkowski while men preferred Klein. Looking, in turn, at Klein and Betkowski supporters reduced the magnitude of the gender differences. Nonetheless, significant differences between men and women could be found among Klein voters on issues of special concern to women, individualism, and economic nationalism. Among Betkowski supporters, significant differences were evident with respect to economic nationalism and government provision of services, while the individualism scale just missed the standard .05. (See Table 6.4). Thus, gender differences in opinion could be noted even among voters who supported the same candidate. Even within the same party, and even among those who support the same candidate, gender gaps in opinion are visible. While these gaps, with the exception of economic nationalism, are far from wide, differences persist. The increased proportion of women in the selection process brought more voting power to a constituency with a somewhat different mix of political attitudes and values.

10 This is the one item asked of all parties on which the New Democrats display a gender gap not evident in the other parties. We speculate that this may be due in part to the opposition to the accord on the part of the National Action Committee on the Status of Women.

11 This in spite of the fact that there were no significant gender differences in the ideological self-placement of NDP delegates.

12 Questions regarding marital status and the number of children living at home would have been of value in comparing the situations of men and women. Unfortunately, such questions were not included in the survey.

13 We are unable to compare New Democrats on this dimension as the same question was not asked.

14 This excludes medical doctors.

15 This question was not asked of Conservative voters.

16 Of course, these references are limited to second-ballot voters.

17 It seems that women in politics are judged by a different standard. For instance Robinson and Saint-Jean show that women are covered and evaluated differently by the media (1991: 151,152).

18 It is possible that this might also be the case for men and this indicates again the danger Sapiro noted of using men as a standard for evaluating women in politics. Men in Canada are rarely faced with a partisan situation in which the structure of competition is such that

there is no man involved. It would be interesting to study their behaviour in such a situation. The voting behaviour of women in Britain in the Thatcher years makes clear that gender gaps in terms of support from women do not necessarily work to the advantage of women candidates (see Brodie 1991: 20; Wearing and Wearing 1991: 344).

19 Ms. Betkowski now goes by the name of MacBeth.

Chapter 7: Democracy, Representation, and the Selection of Party Leaders

1 All but a few hundred of the Liberals who registered used the auspices of one of the candidates. In contrast, thousands of Tories actually purchased their memberships at the polling stations on voting day.

2 In 1991, the provincial Tories removed from their constitution sections committing provincial members to supporting the federal party.

3 More than 40% of his first-ballot support came from proxies (Liberal Party 1994).

4 As we noted in Chapter 4, the Liberals acted on this preference and in 1998 used a constituency-based system of universal balloting to choose their leader.

5 The number of people voting increased by almost 26,000.

6 Interestingly, one of the reasons the Liberals used an immediate re-vote was because they felt the week between the Conservative ballots allowed party elites too much time to mobilize support. In 1998, the federal Tories allowed two weeks to elapse between their first and second ballot. The number of people declined. This was likely due to the huge lead Joe Clark had on the first ballot and the fact that two of the three candidates eligible for inclusion on the second ballot declined to participate.

7 In fact, "party officials acknowledged the telephone vote ... was a disaster." (*Calgary Herald*, 19 November 1994, A3).

8 One of the respondents to our survey of Liberals confessed that he thought he had completed registration and proxy forms one night in an Edmonton bar, but if he had, that was the extent of his involvement with the Liberal Party. It seems difficult to see the advantage of a system that permits such "participation."

9 Party officials privately indicate that an audit conducted of all registered voters revealed many difficulties in communicating in English.

10 A conversation with a prominent Chadi organizer suggests that this was the case in terms of the people that registered.

11 Chadi supporters were least likely to report completing a degree, so the actual proportion of Liberal voters without such educational attainments is likely higher.

12 The way in which the scales were constructed is somewhat different from the descriptions in the appendix. The variables in each scale can be seen by examining Table 7.6 and Table 7.7. The three items in Table 7.7 are included in the size of government scale. If a question was not asked in a particular survey, a mid-range score was provided in order to assist in scale construction. Further details can be obtained from the authors.

Chapter 8: Quasi-Democracy?

1 Even the 1998 federal Conservative leadership election did not deal with as many voters.

2 In the 1997 Alberta election, under Mitchell's leadership, the Liberals suffered a decline in their popular vote and the loss of most of their legislative seats.

3 One of the candidates for the leadership in 1994 reported that he had been advised that it was possible to tie up the phone lines using computer-generated phone calls in such a way that his vote would be maximized and that voters supporting other candidates would have greater difficulty making a connection. He maintained that he did not utilize such a strategy and did not know if the claims were accurate. Neither do we, nor, we suspect, would most voters!

References

Aikenhead, S., and J. Crockatt. 1992. "Betkowski Camp 'Devastated' by Loss." *Edmonton Journal*, 6 December: A1.

Alberts, S., and M. Zurowski. 1992. "Getty Era Ends Today." *Calgary Herald*, 5 December: A1.

Archer, Keith. 1991. "Leadership Selection in the New Democratic Party." In *Canadian Political Parties: Leaders, Candidates and Organization*, ed. Herman Bakvis. Toronto: Dundurn Press.

– . 1992. "Voting Behaviour and Political Dominance in Alberta, 1971-1991." In *Government and Politics in Alberta*, ed. Allan Tupper and Roger Gibbins. Edmonton: University of Alberta Press.

– , and Faron Ellis. 1994. "Opinion Structure of Party Activists: The Case of the Reform Party." *Canadian Journal of Political Science* 27 (2): 277-309.

– , and Roger Gibbins. 1997. "What Do Albertans Think?" In *A Government Reinvented*, ed. Christopher J. Bruce, Ronald D. Kneebone, and Kenneth J. McKenzie. Toronto: Oxford University Press.

– , and Margaret Hunziker. 1992. "Leadership Selection in Alberta: The 1985 Progressive Conservative Leadership Convention." In *Leaders and Parties in Canadian Politics*, ed. R.K. Carty, Lynda Erickson, and Donald Blake. Toronto: Harcourt Brace Jovanovich.

– , and Alan Whitehorn. 1990. "Opinion Structure among New Democratic Activists: A Comparison with Liberals and Conservatives." *Canadian Journal of Political Science* 23 (1): 101-13.

– , and Alan Whitehorn. 1993. *Canadian Trade Unions and the New Democratic Party*. Kingston, ON: Industrial Relations Centre, Queen's University.

– , and Alan Whitehorn. 1996. "Opinion Structure Among Party Activists." In *Party Politics in Canada*, ed. Hugh Thorburn. Scarborough: Prentice-Hall.

– , and Alan Whitehorn. 1997. *Political Activists: The New Democrats in Convention*. Toronto: Oxford University Press.

Arnold, T. 1994a. "Close to 4,000 Voters Could Be Turfed from Liberal Race." *Edmonton Journal*, 9 November: A7.

– . 1994b. "Questions Raised about Liberal Registration Process." *Edmonton Journal*, 11 November: A7.

– . 1994c. "Some Liberal Delegates Stuck with No PIN." *Edmonton Journal*, 11 November: A7.

Bashevkin, Sylvia. 1993. *Toeing the Lines: Women and Party Politics in English Canada*. Toronto: University of Toronto Press.

Bell, Edward. 1993. *Social Classes and Social Credit in Alberta*. Montreal and Kingston: McGill-Queen's University Press.

Bibby, Reginald W. 1987. *Fragmented Gods*. Toronto: Irwin.

Blais, André, and Elizabeth Gidengil. 1991. *Making Representative Democracy Work: The Views of Canadians*. Toronto: Dundurn.

Blake, Donald, and R.K. Carty. 1994. "Televoting for the Leader of the British Columbia Liberal Party." Paper presented to the annual meeting of the Canadian Political Science Association, Calgary.

– , R.K. Carty, and Lynda Erickson. 1988. "Ratification or Repudiation: Social Credit Leadership Selection in British Columbia." *Canadian Journal of Political Science* 21 (3): 513-37.

– , R.K. Carty, and Lynda Erickson. 1991. *Grassroots Politicians*. Vancouver: UBC Press.

Brady, Henry, and Richard Johnston. 1988. "Conventions versus Primaries: A Canadian American Comparison." In *Party Democracy in Canada*, ed. George Perlin. Scarborough: Prentice-Hall.

Braid, D. 1992a. "The Perfect Voter Is Old, and Can't Speak English." *Calgary Herald*, 2 December: B6.

– . 1992b. "He's Still a Master Campaigner." *Calgary Herald*, 6 December: A1.

Brodie, Janine. 1985. "From Waffles to Grits: A Decade in the Life of the New Democratic Party." In *Party Politics in Canada*, ed. Hugh Thorburn. Scarborough: Prentice-Hall.

– . 1988. "The Gender Factor and National Leaderships in Canada." In *Party Democracy in Canada*, ed. George Perlin. Scarborough: Prentice-Hall.

– . 1991. "Women and the Electoral Process in Canada." In *Women in Canadian Politics: Toward Equity in Representation*, ed. Kathy Megyery. Toronto: Dundurn Press.

Carty, R.K. 1988a. "Campaigning in the Trenches: The Transformation of Constituency Politics." In *Party Democracy in Canada*, ed. George Perlin. Scarborough: Prentice-Hall.

– . 1988b. "Choosing New Party Leaders: The Progressive Conservatives in 1983, the Liberals in 1984." In *Canada at the Polls, 1984*, ed. Howard Penniman. Washington, DC: American Enterprise Institute for Public Policy Research.

– . 1991. *Canadian Parties in the Constituency*. Toronto: Dundurn.

– . 1994. "Transforming the Politics of Party Leadership." Paper presented to the annual meeting of the Atlantic Provinces Political Studies Association, St. Mary's University.

– . 1996. "Televoting for Canadians." *Canadian Parliamentary Review* 19 (3): 17-21.

– , and Donald E. Blake. 1999. "The Adoption of Membership Votes for Choosing Party Leaders." *Party Politics* 5 (2): 211-24.

– , Lynda Erickson, and Donald E. Blake. 1992. "Parties and Leaders: The Experiences of the Provinces." In *Leaders and Parties in Canadian Politics*, ed. R.K Carty, Lynda Erickson, and Donald E. Blake. Toronto: Harcourt Brace Jovanovich.

Christian, W., and C. Campbell. 1990. *Political Parties and Ideologies in Canada*. 3rd edition. Toronto: McGraw Hill Ryerson.

Clarke, Harold, Jane Jenson, Lawrence LeDuc, and Jon H. Pammett. 1979. *Political Choice in Canada*. Toronto: McGraw-Hill Ryerson.

Clokie, Hugh. 1945. *Canadian Government and Politics*. Toronto: Longmans.

"Convention 1993." 1994. New Democratic Party of Alberta report.

Courtney, John C. 1973. *The Selection of National Party Leaders*. Toronto: Macmillan.

– . 1986. "Leadership Conventions and the Development of the National Political Community in Canada." In *National Politics and Community in Canada*, ed. R.K. Carty and Peter Ward. Vancouver: UBC Press.

– . 1995. *Do Conventions Matter*. Montreal: McGill-Queens University Press.

– , and George Perlin. 1988. "The Role of Conventions in the Representation and Accommodation of Regional Cleavages." In *Party Democracy in Canada*, ed. George Perlin. Scarborough: Prentice-Hall.

Crockatt, J., and M. Gold. 1994. "Liberals Squirming over Confusion Tied to Leadership." *Edmonton Journal*, 11 November: A7.

Cross, William. 1996. "Direct Election of Provincial Party Leaders in Canada, 1985-1995." *Canadian Journal of Political Science* 29 (2): 295-317.

Cunningham, J. 1992. "Klein's Win Seen as Blow to New Politics." *Calgary Herald*, 6 December: A2.

Dacks, Gurston. 1986. "From Consensus to Competition: Social Democracy and Political Culture in Alberta." In *Socialism and Democracy in Alberta*, ed. Larry Pratt. Edmonton: NeWest.

Dobbin, Murray. 1992. *Preston Manning and the Reform Party*. Halifax: Formac.

Duverger, Maurice. 1978 [1954]. *Political Parties*. London: Methuen.

Dyck, Rand. 1991. "Links between Federal and Provincial Parties and Party Systems." In *Representation, Integration and Political Parties in Canada,* ed. Herman Bakvis. Toronto: Dundurn Press.

Elton, David, and Arthur Goddard. 1979. "The Conservative Takeover, 1971-." In *Society and Politics in Alberta,* ed. Carlo Caldarola. Toronto: Methuen.

Flanagan, Tom. 1992. "A Comparative Profile of the Reform Party of Canada." Paper presented to the annual meeting of the Canadian Political Science Association, Charlottetown.

Gallagher, Michael. 1988. *Candidate Selection in Comparative Perspective: The Secret Garden of Politics*. London: Sage.

Geddes, A. 1992. "Pot Shots Just Fine with Getty." *Calgary Herald*, 2 December: B6.

– , and S. Alberts. 1992. "Anti-Klein Forces Swell." *Calgary Herald*, 1 December: A1.

Gibbins, Roger. 1979. "Western Alienation and the Alberta Political Culture." In *Society and Politics in Alberta,* ed. Carlo Caldarola. Toronto: Methuen.

– . 1992. "Alberta and the National Community." In *Government and Politics in Alberta,* ed. Allan Tupper and Roger Gibbins. Edmonton: University of Alberta Press.

– , Keith Archer, and Stan Drabek. 1990. *Canadian Political Life: An Alberta Perspective*. Dubuque, Iowa: Kendall Hunt.

– , and Margaret Hunziker. 1986. "Issues and Leadership Conventions: The 1985 Progressive Conservative Leadership Convention." Paper presented to the annual meeting of the Canadian Political Science Association, Winnipeg.

Gunter, L. 1992. "How Premier Ralph Klein Fooled the Pundits." *Alberta Report*, 14 December.

Hanson, Lawrence. 1992. "Contesting the Leadership at the Grassroots: The Liberals in 1990." In *Canadian Political Party Systems,* ed. R.K. Carty. Toronto: Broadview.

Harrison, Trevor, and Gordon Laxer. 1995. "Introduction." In *The Trojan Horse: Alberta and the Future of Canada,* ed. Trevor Harrison and Gordon Laxer. Montreal: Black Rose.

Helm, R. 1992a. "Orman Quits, Will Back Betkowski." *Edmonton Journal*, 1 December: A5.

– . 1992b. "Getty Confident Either Candidate 'Could Mop Up' Opposition Leaders." *Edmonton Journal*, 2 December: A7.

Hunziker, Margaret. 1986. "Leadership Selection: The 1985 Alberta Progressive Conservative Leadership Convention." Unpublished MA thesis, University of Calgary.

Jewell, Malcolm E. 1984. *Parties and Primaries: Nominating State Governors*. New York: Praeger.

Johnston, Richard. 1988. "The Final Choice: Its Social, Organizational and Ideological Base." In *Party Democracy in Canada,* ed. George Perlin. Scarborough: Prentice Hall.

Kelley, Anne E., William E. Hulbary, and Lewis Bowman. 1993. "Gender, Partisanship and Background Explain Differences in Grass-Roots Party Activists' Political Attitudes." In *Women in Politics: Outsiders or Insiders,* ed. Lois Lovelace Duke. Englewood Cliffs: Prentice Hall.

Kornberg, Allan, William Mishler, and H.D. Clarke. 1982. *Representative Democracy in the Canadian Provinces*. Scarborough: Prentice-Hall.

Laghi, B. 1991. "Alberta PCs Break with Federal Party." *Edmonton Journal*, 8 April: A1.

– . 1992. "Moody Women Comment 'a Joke.'" *Edmonton Journal*, 4 December: A7.

Latouche, Daniel. 1992. "Universal Democracy the Experience of the PQ." In *Leaders and Parties in Canadian Politics,* ed. R.K. Carty, Lynda Erickson, and Donald E. Blake. Toronto: Harcourt Brace Jovanovich.

Levesque, Terrence J. 1983. "On the Outcome of the 1983 Conservative Leadership Convention: How They Shot Themselves in the Other Foot." *Canadian Journal of Political Science* 16 (4): 779-84.

Liberal Party. 1994. *Without Prejudice: Analysis of the Proxy Vote Rules and Process at the 1994 ALP Leadership Convention,* report. 15 November.

Lisac, M. 1994. "Leadership Derby Has Been a Disaster for Liberals." *Edmonton Journal*, 12 November: A8.

– . 1995. *The Klein Revolution*. Edmonton: NeWest Press.

Lunman, K. 1994. "Party Clears Chadi Camp of Campaign Dirty Tricks." *Calgary Herald*, 10 November: A2.

McCormick, Peter. 1980. "Voting Behaviour in Alberta: The Quasi Party System Revisited." *Journal of Canadian Studies* 15 (3): 85-98.
– . 1991. "The Reform Party of Canada: New Beginning or Dead End?" In *Party Politics in Canada*, ed. Hugh Thorburn. 6th edition. Scarborough: Prentice Hall.
MacIvor, Heather. 1994. "The Leadership Convention: An Institution under Stress." In *Leaders and Leadership in Canada*, ed. Maureen Mancuso, Richard G. Price, and Ronald Wagenberg. Toronto: Oxford University Press.
– . 1996/97. "Some Reflections on Technology." *Canadian Parliamentary Review* (winter).
Macpherson, C.B. 1962. *Democracy in Alberta: Social Credit and the Party System*. 2nd edition. Toronto: University of Toronto Press.
Malcolmson, Patrick. 1992. "Two Cheers for the Leadership Convention." *Policy Options* (December): 45.
Manning, Preston. 1992. *The New Canada*. Toronto: Macmillan.
Martin, D. 1992. "No-name Candidates in Surprisingly Tight Race." *Calgary Herald*, 12 November: B4.
– . 1994. "Horror Show." *Calgary Herald*, 13 November: D1.
Michels, Robert. 1962. *Political Parties*. New York: Collier.
Morley, Terry. 1992. "Leadership Change in the CCF/NDP." In *Leaders and Parties in Canadian Politics*, ed. R.K. Carty, Lynda Erickson, and Donald E. Blake. Toronto: Harcourt Brace Jovanovich.
O'Neill, Brenda. 1992. "Gender Gaps in Opinion: The Canadian Situation." Paper presented to the annual meeting of the Canadian Political Science Association, Charlottetown.
Ovenden, N. 1992. "Clark among Tory MPs Backing Betkowski." *Edmonton Journal*, 5 December: A5.
Pal, Leslie. 1992. "The Political Executive and Political Leadership in Alberta." In *Alberta Politics: Change and Continuity*, ed. Allan Tupper and Roger Gibbins. Edmonton: University of Alberta Press.
Pammett, Jon H. 1994. "Tracking the Votes." In *The Canadian General Election of 1993*, ed. Allan Frizzell, Jon H. Pammett, and Anthony Westell. Ottawa: Carleton University Press.
Panzeri, A. 1992. "Klein Lashes Out at Tory Establishment." *Edmonton Journal*, 1 December: A7.
Perlin, George. 1980. *The Tory Syndrome*. Montreal: McGill-Queen's University Press.
– . 1983. "Did the Best Candidate Win? A Comment on Lévesque's Analysis." *Canadian Journal of Political Science* 16 (4): 791-4.
– . 1988. "Conclusions." In *Party Democracy in Canada*, ed. George Perlin. Scarborough: Prentice-Hall.
– . 1991a. "Attitudes of Liberal Convention Delegates toward Proposals for Reform of the Process of Leadership Selection." In *Canadian Political Parties: Leaders, Candidates and Organization*, ed. Herman Bakvis. Toronto: Dundurn Press.
– . 1991b. "Leadership Selection in the P.C. and Liberal Parties: Assessing the Need for Reform." In *Party Politics in Canada*, ed. Hugh Thorburn. 6th edition. Scarborough: Prentice-Hall.
– , Allen Sutherland, and Marc Desjardins. 1988. "The Impact of Age Cleavage on Convention Politics." In *Party Democracy in Canada*, ed. George Perlin. Scarborough: Prentice-Hall.
Pomper, Gerald. 1972. "From Confusion to Clarity: Issues and American Voters, 1956-1968." *American Political Science Review* 66: 415-28.
Preyra, Leonard. 1994. "The 1992 Nova Scotia Liberal Leadership Convention." *Canadian Parliamentary Review* 16 (4): 2-12.
– . 1995. "Changing Conventions: Plebiscitarian Democracy and Party Selection in Canada." In *Party Politics in Canada*, ed. Hugh Thorburn. 6th edition. Scarborough: Prentice-Hall.
Randall, Vicky. 1982. *Women and Politics*. London: Macmillan Press.
Richards, John, and Larry Pratt. 1979. *Prairie Capitalism*, Toronto: McClelland and Stewart.
Robinson, Gertrude J., and Armande Saint-Jean. 1991. "Women Politicians and Their Media Coverage." In *Women in Canadian Politics: Toward Equity in Representation*, ed. Kathy Megyery. Toronto: Dundurn Press.

Royal Commission on Electoral Reform and Party Financing. 1991. *Reforming Electoral Democracy*, Volume 1, Ottawa: Supply and Services Canada.

Sapiro, Virginia. 1983. *The Political Integration of Women*. Chicago: University of Illinois Press.

Schumacher, Stan. 1993. "Reforming the Leadership Convention Process, Roundtable Discussion on Leadership Selection." *Canadian Parliamentary Review* 16 (3): 7-9.

Simms, Len. 1993. "Reforming the Leadership Convention Process, Roundtable Discussion on Leadership Selection." *Canadian Parliamentary Review* 16 (3): 10.

Steward, Gillian. 1995. "Klein the Chameleon." In *The Trojan Horse: Alberta and the Future of Canada*, ed. Trevor Harrison and Gordon Laxer. Montreal: Black Rose.

Stewart, David K. 1992. "'Friends and Neighbours': Patterns of Delegate Support at Maritime Liberal and Conservative Conventions." In *Leaders and Parties in Canadian Politics*, ed. R.K. Carty, Lynda Erickson, and Donald E. Blake. Toronto: Harcourt Brace Jovanovich.

– . 1995. "Klein's Makeover of the Conservative Party." In *The Trojan Horse: Alberta and the Future of Canada*, ed. Trevor Harrison and Gordon Laxer. Montreal: Black Rose.

– . 1997. "The Changing Leadership Electorate." *Canadian Journal of Political Science* 30 (1): 107-28.

– , and R.K. Carty. 1993. "Does Changing the Party Leader Provide an Electoral Boost?" *Canadian Journal of Political Science* 25 (3): 313-30.

Stewart, Ian, Agar Adamson, and B. Beaton. 1994. "Tele-Voting for the Liberal Leader in Nova Scotia." In *Roasting Chestnuts*. Vancouver: UBC Press.

"Tele-Voting." 1994. Alberta Liberal Party press release.

Tupper, Allan. 1996. "Debt, Populism and Cutbacks: Alberta Politics in the 1990s." In *Party Politics in Canada*, ed. Hugh Thorburn. 7th Edition. Scarborough: Prentice-Hall.

– , and David Taras. 1994. "Politics and Deficits: Alberta's Challenge to the Canadian Political Agenda." In *Canada: The State of the Federation, 1994*, ed. D. Brown and J. Hiebert. Kingston: Institute of Intergovernmental Relations.

Walker, Nancy J. 1994. "What We Know about Women Voters in Britain, France and West Germany." In *Different Roles, Different Voices: Women and Politics in the United States and Europe*, ed. Marianne Githens, Pippa Norris, and Joni Lovenduski. New York: HarperCollins.

Wearing, Joseph, and Peter Wearing. 1991. "Does Gender Make a Difference in Voting Behaviour?" In *The Ballot and Its Message*, ed. Joseph Wearing. Mississauga: Copp Clark Pitman.

Whitehorn, Alan. 1988. "The CCF/NDP in Convention." In *Party Democracy in Canada*, ed. George Perlin. Scarborough: Prentice Hall.

Women in the Labour Force 1990-91 Edition. 1990. Ottawa: Minister of Labour, Supply and Services Canada.

Woolstencroft, Peter. 1983. "Social Choice Theory and the Reconstruction of Elections: A Comment on Lévesque's Analysis." *Canadian Journal of Political Science* 16 (4): 785-91.

– . 1992. "Tories Kick Machine to Bits." In *Leaders and Parties in Canadian Politics*, ed. R.K. Carty, Lynda Erickson, and Donald E. Blake. Toronto: Harcourt Brace Jovanovich.

Youngman, L., and R. Gibbins. 1995. "Gender and Neoconservatism: Public Policy Implications of the Alberta Experience." Paper presented to the annual meeting of the New Zealand Political Studies Association, Wellington, New Zealand.

Index